African oral literature, like other forms of popular culture, is not merely folksy, domestic entertainment but a domain in which individuals in a variety of social roles are free to comment on power relations in society. It can also be a significant agent of change capable of directing, provoking, preventing, overturning and recasting perceptions of social reality. This collection examines the way in which oral texts both reflect and affect contemporary social and political life in Africa. It addresses questions of power, gender, the dynamics of language use, the representation of social structures and the relation between culture and the state.

The contributors are linguists, anthropologists, folklorists, ethnomusicologists and historians, who present fresh material and ideas to paint a lively picture of current real life situations. The book is an important contribution to the study of African culture and literature, and to the anthropological study of oral literature in particular.

Power, marginality and
African oral literature

Power, marginality and African oral literature

edited by

Graham Furniss and Liz Gunner

School of Oriental and African Studies
University of London

CAMBRIDGE
UNIVERSITY PRESS

Published by the Press Syndicate of the University of Cambridge
The Pitt Building, Trumpington Street, Cambridge CB2 1RP
40 West 20th Street, New York, NY 10011-4211, USA
10 Stamford Road, Oakleigh, Melbourne 3166, Australia

First published 1995

Printed in Great Britain at the University Press, Cambridge

A catalogue record for this book is available from the British Library

Library of Congress cataloguing in publication data
Power, marginality and African oral literature
edited by Graham Furniss and Liz Gunner.
p.   cm.
Includes bibliographical references and index.
ISBN 0 521 48061 2
1. Oral tradition – Africa.   2. Folklore – Africa.   3. Narrative poetry, African.
4. Power (Social sciences) – Africa.   5. Social structure – Africa.   6. Marginality, Social – Africa.
7. Africa – Politics and government.   8. Africa – Social life and customs.
I. Furniss, Graham.   II. Gunner, Elizabeth.

GR350.P69   1995   94–38051
398.2'096 – dc20   CIP

ISBN 0 521 48061 2 hardback

Contents

vii

Contributors

KOFI ANYIDOHO is a well-known poet and Associate Professor, Institute of African Studies, University of Ghana, Legon.

CHUKWUMA AZUONYE was formerly Lecturer in Oral Literature in the Departments of Linguistics and African Languages at the Universities of Ibadan and Nsukka. Since 1992 he has been Head of the Department of Black Studies at the University of Massachusetts at Boston.

KOFI AGOVI is Associate Professor and Director of the Institute of African Studies, University of Ghana, Legon.

HERBERT CHIMHUNDU is Senior Lecturer in the Department of African Languages, University of Zimbabwe.

JEAN DERIVE is Professeur de littérature générale et comparée at the University of Savoie, and also teaches postgraduate studies at INALCO and at the University of Paris III.

LUCY DURÁN is Lecturer in African Music at the School of Oriental and African Studies, University of London.

PAULO FERNANDO DE MORAES FARIAS is Lecturer in African History, Centre of West African Studies, University of Birmingham.

GRAHAM FURNISS is Senior Lecturer in Hausa, School of Oriental and African Studies, University of London.

VERONIKA GÖRÖG-KARADY is a member of the French CNRS research team 'Language and Culture in West Africa', attached to INALCO, Paris.

LIZ GUNNER is Senior Lecturer in African and Commonwealth Literature, School of Oriental and African Studies, University of London.

ISABEL HOFMEYR is Professor of African Literature at the University of the Witwatersrand, South Africa.

JOHN WILLIAM JOHNSON is Associate Professor at the Folklore Institute, and African Studies Program of Indiana University.

PENINA MLAMA is Professor in the Department of Art, Music and Theatre at the University of Dar es Salaam.

JEFF OPLAND is Professorial Research Associate of the Centre of African Studies, University of London.

SABINE STEINBRICH is Wissenschaftliche Assistentin at the Department of Anthropology of the University of Münster.

KWESI YANKAH is Associate Professor, Institute of African Studies, University of Ghana, Legon.

Preface

The chapters in this collection derive from a conference held at Birkbeck College and the School of Oriental and African Studies in January 1991, under the auspices of the Centre of African Studies, University of London and the Department of African Languages and Cultures, SOAS. The impetus for the conference emerged from a growing sense of convergence between African, American and European scholars of African popular culture, history, music, oral literature and political anthropology, on the nexus between popular expression and power relations.

In examining that nexus the participants emphasised differing contexts and interpretations both of the question of power and of marginality. Assumptions differed among participants about the implications of the notion of *power* as it was to be deployed in our discussions. Aware of the definitional and connotational complexities of the term (see, for example, Fardon 1985, introduction and essays by others therein) participants tended to refer to the ability or potential of one party to be able to influence or affect the actions, words, and occasionally, beliefs and emotions of another. In deploying the term, however, it related sometimes to the capacities of constitutional authority in government, sometimes to the capacity of an individual over other individuals and sometimes to the relation between cultural forms as dominant and dominated.

Similarly, the term *marginality* opened up a number of avenues of debate. While some participants felt that, within the cultural landscape of particular societies, oral literature had been marginalised in comparison with written genres of literature, others saw such marginalisation as illusory, being based sometimes upon the 'literal' preoccupations of observers and commentators within the academic tradition, and sometimes as a reflection of a narrowness of view that sees oral literature as a separate entity rather than a communicative process within an interlocking network of media that includes written and oral forms – in public performance, on television and radio and in the eclecticism of daily cultural life. Within the context of particular power relations, however, marginality was taken to refer to differential positions between social categories, for example, men and women or between the old and the young, and to social distance from a seat of constituted power within a particular society. Importantly, however, such social marginality does not make the artist powerless; it is often precisely such a position that enables the speaker/artist to attack and occasionally to devastate. This perspective is extended from the artist as an individual to the relations between genres such that undervalued, denigrated forms may operate as satirical subversions of dominant forms. Contrasting positions run through the contributions: song that reinforces the marginalisation of categories of people as against song that, from the margins, contests dominant cultural forces, furnishing thereby a vigorous alternative voice; marginal people speaking as against marginal people being spoken about. The focus supplied by the term is upon the relational characteristics of the utterance and upon the people who speak, and who hear, relations of power.

In addition, there emerged two broadly distinct perspectives on the approach to oral literature. In a more traditional vein, some participants concentrated upon the representation of particular types of power relation as portrayed within a body of texts, thus discussing, for example, images of father–son relations and their attendant tensions within a particular culture. A rather different approach set the 'act of speaking', represented by the performance of oral literature, in a broader context of interpersonal dynamics, or within the exercise of power by authorities of one kind or another. This latter perspective is more heavily represented within these pages, though there are variations of scale and emphasis within those chapters.

There were a number of paper givers, chairpersons and discussants at the conference whose names do not otherwise appear in this collection. Ruth Finnegan gave a keynote address reflecting upon the development of the study of African oral literature since her seminal work, *Oral Literature in Africa*, published in 1970. Many of those reflections are drawn together in her 1992 volume, *Oral Traditions and the Verbal Arts: A Guide to Research Practices*. Alongside the presentation of academic papers we wish also to acknowledge the presence of an unexpected and very different event in the conference. It was an experience to which no reference is made elsewhere in this book, but, for all who participated, it constituted a moving, if not disturbing, moment. Reference to it has already been made in Lee Haring's thought-provoking introduction to a recent special issue of *Oral Tradition* (1994), in which there is a paper by Sory Camara. Camara handed on to us, spontaneously, at this conference the words of a *maître du chantier* – words he had kept to himself for some twenty years – a myth about life and death, parts of a cosmology, which became ever more resonant when, in response to a question, Camara added that, in Mandinka, people say *parler, c'est mourir* – to give away information is to give away part of one's life-force. That text, that experience, is not represented here but formed an intimate part of what each participant took away from the conference. We gratefully acknowledge the contributions of the following paper-givers, chairpersons and discussants: Ifi Amadiume, B. W. Andrzejewski, Karin Barber, Szilard Biernaczky, Stephen Bulman, G. G. Darah, Caleb Dube, Lee Haring, Zainab Jama, Russell Kaschula, I. M. Lewis, Virginia Luling, Nhlanhla Maake, Mohammed Abdi Mohammed, J. D. Y. Peel, Alain Ricard, Beverley Stoeltjie, Elizabeth Tonkin, Farouk Topan, Olabiyi Yai.

The editors also wish to thank the British Academy, the Commonwealth Foundation, the A. G. Leventis Foundation and the Research and Publications Committee of the School of Oriental and African Studies for financial support which made the conference possible. Without the help of Jackie Collis of the Centre of African Studies the conference would not have been organised as efficiently as it was. We would also like to thank Janet Marks for assistance with typing, and our editor at the Cambridge University Press, Jessica Kuper, for her helpful guidance and for her sterling efforts in bringing the book through the press.

Graham Furniss and Liz Gunner

Note on transcription

Some special characters have been employed in presenting words in a number of African languages. Orthographic conventions differ from one country to another and between standard orthographies and more linguistically specific orthographies.

In this volume the following special characters are used: ɔ and ọ (for vowel sounds like the English *pot*); ɛ and ẹ (for vowel sounds like the English *pet*); ụ (for vowel sounds like the English *put*); ị (for vowel sounds like the English *hit*); ə for a mid vowel like the one in the English word *the*. Nasal vowels are marked with a superscript tilde as in ã. Additional consonantal characters occur in two chapters: ṣ (representing a phoneme which may also be transcribed by the digraph *sh*); ɲ (for a nasal phoneme otherwise transcribed by the digraph *ny*, and which corresponds to the *gn* in the French word *agneau*, and the ñ in the Spanish word *año*); and ŋ or the digraph ng (for a nasal phoneme like that at the end of the English word *bring*); ƙ represents an ejective k and ɗ represents a glottalised d.

Tone marks generally use the following conventions (illustrated using the vowel 'a'): á (high), ā (mid), à (low), â or áà (falling), ǎ or àá (rising). In the chapter by Moraes Farias and in accordance with the official orthographies of the Republic of Mali, tones are left unmarked in transcriptions of Maninka and Soŋoy. As regards Borgu languages, both Bààtɔ̀núm (a Gur or Voltaic language) and Bo'o (a Mande language) still lack comprehensive studies of their tonal systems. Arabic words are transcribed according to established scholarly practice. Moraes Farias's transcriptions of Bààtɔ̀núm words display tonal marks wherever it has been possible to confirm these in the light of the work of professional linguists. In addition to and differently from the tone marks illustrated above Moraes Farias uses á (top), a (high, unmarked).

CHAPTER 1

Introduction: power, marginality and oral literature

Graham Furniss and Liz Gunner

In a recent guide to anthropological research practice in relation to oral traditions and the verbal arts, Ruth Finnegan, a founder figure in the field of African oral literature, points to the interest that has developed, in anthropology as in many other fields, in local processes of negotiating meaning, the agency of artistic creativity and its relation to social action:

One theme is greater concern with individual voices, repertoire and creativity, part of the move within anthropology and other disciplines from 'structure' to 'agency'. Another is an emerging interest in work on the emotions and in aesthetic and expressive facets of human activity. A more explicit focus on 'meaning' comes in too, both meanings to be gleaned from the 'text' and those expressed through a multiplicity of voices. What is involved, further, is more than just the voice of the composer/poet (in the past pictured as *the* central figure), but also the other participants who help to form the work and mediate its meaning and the dynamics through which this occurs. (1992: 51)

This represents a move towards an appreciation of the role that oral literature plays as a dynamic discourse about society and about the relationships between individuals, groups and classes in society. In particular, this perspective sees oral literature not merely as folksy, domestic entertainment but as a domain in which individuals in a variety of social roles articulate a commentary upon power relations in society and indeed create knowledge about society. There is a substantial body of anthropological scholarship that addresses the issue of oratory, rhetoric and political/ritual language and tropes and figures deployed in discourse (see, for example, Bloch 1975; Sapir and Crocker 1977; Paine 1981; Bailey 1983; Parkin 1984), and as Parkin writes in discussing arguments relating to the deployment of metaphor, metonymy, synecdoche and irony, 'These many particular uses of tropes point, nevertheless, in one direction: it is people who retain the power to name, entitle, and objectify others, who determine the terms of discourse' (1984: 359). Determining the terms of discourse may involve contestation, forcing different individuals and groups to engage in debate over perceived and evolving roles and, at times, shifting identities. Situating a particular speech event within a process of direct debate (or seeing them as juxtaposed alternative expressions) draws attention, when examining the 'text', to the interrelations between that text and other precursor, contemporary or subsequent 'texts'. This interactive dimension between texts is mirrored in the focus upon the relation between performer and audience in the moment of performance. Where Bloch (1975) has seen oratory as the deployment of fixed forms, other anthropologists have foregrounded the adaptability and experimentation that takes place in rhetorical utterances in the face of differing reactions from audiences (Paine 1981; Parkin 1985). In anthropology, discourse has become an extended trope in itself through the work of Foucault and Derrida among others.

In the field of folklore studies, particularly in America, the shift away from a focus upon 'reified persistent cultural items' to 'folklore as a mode of communicative action' was marked by an expansion of the concept 'performance' such that it no longer simply meant gesture, voice quality, etc., in the moment of performance but came to encompass

a focus on the artful use of language in the conduct of social life – in kinship, politics, economics, religion – opening the way to an understanding of performance as socially constitutive and efficacious . . . these critical reorientations relied centrally on the ethnographic and analytical investigation of form–function–meaning interrelationships within situational contexts of language use. (Bauman and Briggs 1990)

The exploration of the term performance and the broadening of its implications has been going on within folklore studies for some time (see Paredes and Bauman 1972; Ben-Amos and Goldstein 1975; Limon and Young 1986). In concentrating attention upon the social action involved in telling a story, singing a song or giving a speech, a number of boundaries previously solid begin to dissolve: the boundaries that delimited a text are replaced by a constitutive notion of textuality (Hanks 1989a); the authorial voice is placed in relation to a variety of other voices both internally and through the intertextuality of external reference, as source, as counterpoint and as 'one side of any particular story'; 'traditional' and 'modern' become not separate categories but current labels under internal cultural debate; 'oral' and 'written' become, '[not] two separate "things" . . . [but part of] the whole communication process in which there may at any one time be a number of different media and processes' (Finnegan 1992: 50), thus directing our attention to the particular communicative processes of 'being oral'/orality rather than objects that are specimens of 'oral literature'. In all this, the concentration on social action demands that the performance, the people, and the 'text' are seen together in their political context. As Finnegan puts it:

Equally striking is the growing awareness of the 'political' nature both of the material to be studied and of the research process itself. This is increasingly appreciated within anthropology, but also runs across many disciplines, from emphasis on the politics of language or of literary theory, to the socially constructed nature of artistic forms or the many-layered nature of human expression. (1992: 50–1)

The concentration upon the broad notion of performance within folklore studies is linked to the movement within linguistics broadly defined to assess the utterance not as a manifestation of underlying linguistic competence but as a 'speech act'. The idea of speech act as social action is not a new one, but the development of speech act theory goes back to Austin (1962) and has been extensively developed (see, for example, Searle 1969, 1979; Bauman and Sherzer 1989) concentrating upon the study of effectiveness, 'illocutionary force' in speech, and intentionality.

Intentionality brings to the fore the myriad, overlapping types of purpose: to amuse, to satirise, to teach, to expound, to warn, to stir . . . the list is endless. In performing these and other functions many speech acts, and the text that flows from them, present a picture of individuals and groups in society and the relationships of power between them. A number of contributions to this volume provide examples. However, people producing oral literature are not just commentators but are often also involved in relationships of power themselves, in terms of supporting or subverting those in power. The forms with which they work are themselves invested with power; that is to say, the words, the texts, have the ability to provoke, to move, to direct, to prevent, to overturn and to recast social reality.

The particular dimension that is most pressing in all orality is the relationship between the fleeting temporary experience and the people who were present at it. Such temporary experiences are nevertheless a class of event that are repeated, even if differently each performance. As such they are socially embedded and have particular relationships with individuals, groups and the state. Not only may the class of event have a particular relationship with external social forces, but all those involved in it have their own longer-standing positions and attitudes to the surrounding society. The 'meaning' of the content of the transmitted messages in the oral performance, complex as it usually is, may yet be only a supplement to the significance of the performer's position in relation to the audience and third parties. Seemingly innocuous jocular moments of relaxation between social equals may yet carry significant messages of exclusion or solidarity to participants and other people. Set outside the parameters of group membership, the performer may articulate unwelcome reflections on the nature of society, or may be looking for inclusion. Lying, therefore, behind the apparent meaning of the text is the complex set of power relations within which the performer, audience and denoted individuals and groups are enmeshed.

Approached from this perspective, then, orality and oral literature raise issues in a number of areas that are represented in the division of this volume into parts. First, at the broadest level, there is the question of the appropriation of expressive forms by the state and the application by the state, or by corporate organisations or social groups, of oral forms to particular purposes. Whether it be through the articulation of patron–client relationships or the co-option of whole artistic movements, the issue addresses both how control is established and maintained and, conversely, how expressions of resistance or alternative views are articulated. In some circumstances, the distinction between supportive and subversive may correspond with genre boundaries, in others even the most narrowly circumscribed of genres may be intrinsically double-edged – praise-song may be, in an instant, transformed into innuendo or vilification.

A second issue is the way in which oral forms articulate and represent to the performer and audience particular visions of existing power relations in society. Whether such representations are supportive or subversive in intent they constitute part of a continuing debate about older versus younger, husbands and wives, mothers and daughters, fathers and sons, one generation and the next, aristocrats and commoners, one ethnic group as against another, elites and ordinary people. The debate is of course in terms of ideas, symbolic representations rather than 'social realities': Azuonye's chapter discusses the representation of kingship in Igbo tales. Kingship is an idea in Igbo debate rather than an immediate reality in Igbo society.

A third issue that emerges is the question of the instrumentality of oral performance in affecting existing power relations. Here the focus is upon the ability of performance to transform and not simply to represent existing power relations or to operate across the margins of praise and mockery. This instrumentality is a dimension of oral forms that is visible most directly at a level of personal or small group interaction. Clearly, when dealing at a more general level with the developing class structure of particular societies or current social transformations, discourse about society is enmeshed in complex social, economic and political forces.

The fourth issue addressed in this volume concerns the relation of gender and genre. Women are constantly redefining the terms by which they are signified within broader social discourses. Thus, for instance, in Durán's essay the emergence of powerful women singers in Mali has not only shifted power relations within the music industry itself but has shifted the discourse on gender and enabled women to produce their own signifying terms. Chimhundu's essay, on the other hand, outlines the enchaining effects of language and popular song which conspire to prevent the emergence of new definitions of women and women's sexuality in contemporary Zimbabwean society. There is thus no clear pattern of an emergent discourse as regards genre, gender and power but rather an ongoing dialectic of positives and negatives.

The final part of the book focuses upon the dynamics of language use in the context of a variety of communicative strategies, related to the wielding of power in society. At the very centre of the exercise of power conventions about speech may inject distance across which communication can take place only in certain ways and through certain forms of mediation.

The chapters in this book encompass different historical moments, current practices, and cover a number of countries in Africa. Oral literature in Africa, as discussed here, is not a discrete and self-contained, inward-looking sphere of human activity but constitutes a field in which the dynamics of political process and the daily representation of social life are central. Song, poetry, popular representations of many kinds, are an integral part of the way in which people in Africa today are commenting upon what is happening to their societies.

A further aspect of the discussion relates to the sometimes unequal status of written and oral texts. The power of the latter is often underestimated in the official discourse of the state. Just as Jameson (1981) simplifies the literatures of the so-called Third World, casting them all as 'national allegory' (Ahmad 1987), so, in a parallel way, oral texts are often regarded within national cultures as texts of the 'other' and thus marginalised.

ORALITY AND THE POWER OF THE STATE

The relation between oral literature and power structures can be viewed in a number of ways. The multiple means of constructing nationalism, of involving and re-using cultural forms, have been drawn out in Hobsbawm and Ranger (1983). Benedict Anderson (1983) has pointed to the fluidity of notions of nation, although he, unlike Hobsbawm and Ranger, overplays the part of print and underestimates the role of oral forms in constructing the nation. A number of essays in the collection point to the interrelation of cultural forms and nationalist discourse. There is, as Ahmad (1992) has usefully pointed out, the danger of a too unitary notion of nationalism. There are, he suggests, any number of different kinds of nations and nationalisms. Certainly the essays in this collection suggest such a multiplicity.

Mlama's chapter suggests a static and artificial use of nation and culture with the latter rigidly used as part of official nationalist practice. She looks at oral art in relation to the Tanzanian State and its political programme as it has developed over the modern period. Post-colonial Tanzania saw a great upsurge of nationalism such that the state itself proposed a major revaluation and endorsement of a wide variety of indigenous cultural forms, thereby striking a position opposed to the colonial 'silencing of the people'. As in many other parts of the world the singular identification of the interests of the state, the people and the party, produced both the reification of tradition and its co-option to the interests of 'the ruling class'.

Mlama's chapter bemoans the monopolistic state control of patronage such that art becomes mere fawning propaganda, on the other hand she stigmatises government for not having a cultural policy with resources to support art. She expresses surprise that the artist does not bite the hand that feeds it in spite of the fact that it very rarely gets fed. The artist is disempowered, in Mlama's view, by being estranged from the 'true' sentiments of the people. But Mlama sees hope in the parallel existence of unofficial art in song and in popular theatre which, beyond the reach of state patronage, attempts to 'empower' the artist and, through the artist, ordinary people.

This broad overview of the place of oral culture in the state raises issues concerning the possibility of benign as opposed to malign policy, the arguments as to whether all oral art is embedded within relations of patronage and whether no policy is the only policy worth having. Nevertheless the Tanzanian example clearly illustrates the way in which issues of 'political correctness' are tightly interwoven into the content and performance contexts of much oral art, and yet oral art has the ability, on occasion, to transform itself out of one political function into another.

Hofmeyr examines the interface between native administration bureaucracy and chiefs in South Africa in the period between 1920 and 1950. The political struggles between those two forces are manifest in many different ways. Hofmeyr's discussion focuses on the way in which each side attempts to mould communication to fit their own familiar and dominant modes of discourse. Overlaid therefore upon the politics of language use, relating to the differential command of English, Sesotho and Seswati, is the struggle by the native administration officials, on the one hand, to impose the authority of written documentation and the styles of language appropriate thereto, and the countervailing strategies employed by chiefs and their people, even within modes of writing, to retain many of the distinctive characteristics of orality, always looking to frame interaction in terms of meetings, debates, spoken promises, recollections of past precedent. These strategies are discussed in more detail in Hofmeyr (1994). Far from seeing the onward march of the hegemony of writing, Hofmeyr documents the repeated frustration of native administration officials as they are required again and again to explain verbally, to exemplify verbally and to justify verbally information whose natural authority, being written, was not accepted by its addressees. In this way, therefore, Hofmeyr's discussion documents the struggle, and the failure to some extent, to marginalise orality in the politics of communication.

Kofi Agovi examines the role of a particular oral performance, *avudwene*, in the situation of a public festival in Ghana. Where Hofmeyr situates the argument between native administration officials and chiefs and their people in South Africa, Agovi looks at the debate between two classes of people in Nzema society, 'chief men' and 'young men'. Young men dominate the articulation of ideas within *avudwene* about the way in which chiefs, and other individuals, do behave and should behave. This articulation of ideas about good governance is undertaken within a structured division of artistic labour: one category of person acts as thinker/author and listener to what people are saying. Their composition is handed on to a category of artistic director who shapes the piece for performance; this second category then train the 'actors' who will actually perform the piece in public. This is not transient, spontaneous material; it constitutes careful reflection upon the ideals, values and expectations of leadership and their relation to observed actions of current leaders. In festival performances audiences indicate their degree of concurrence with the views expressed. Agovi sees the articulation of these ideas not as the forlorn cries of the forgotten and the powerless but as something which affects day-to-day behaviour, and the observation of such modifications of behaviour leads him to view *avudwene* as both a forum for the discussion of constitutional principles and an effective check upon the behaviour of the executive.

Within the articulation of criticism and opposition Agovi sees proverbs as performing a particular role. They encapsulate values and philosophical positions that are part of general popular sentiment. Their deployment in the *avudwene* is part of the articulation of popular sentiment in public debate by one important class against another which cannot afford to ignore that class. Good governance then is not a matter of abstract rules applied to the ruling class but an insistence upon putting into practice these values and philosophical positions. In Nzema society individuals will move from one class 'young men' to the other 'chief men' but the relation remains one of government and 'loyal opposition'. Loyalty to the ancestors and to the people constitutes the perceived basis of the legitimacy of the opposition.

REPRESENTING POWER RELATIONS

Azuonye sets out, through the representation of kings in Igbo tales, a picture on the one hand of legitimate authority and on the other of the abuse of power, two sides of the same coin. His discussion is directed along two lines. First, and most directly, he examines the nature of the picture of power relations painted in the tales insofar as it presents a 'democratic ideal'. Second, Azuonye sees the painting of that picture as part of the propagation of competing visions, 'the power of oral literature to sustain, through the selective process of mythic filtering, a particular type of social ideology against the claims of rival or contending ideologies'. In terms of the image of legitimate authority the tales establish a composite set of criteria – each tale fills in another criterion wherewith to judge an individual – that together constitute a yardstick of approved or disapproved attributes. In this sense, then, the tales both give expression to underlying social tensions such as are explored in the chapter by Görög-Karady, and are self-conscious explorations, through narrative exemplification, of the boundaries of acceptable behaviour by those in power.

Azuonye goes on first to set the representation of kings in the context of relations with the Benin kingdom showing how it is the behaviour of Benin which provides many examples of unacceptable behaviour, and second, in historical terms, to posit a process of democratisation that has led Igbo society from kingship to an acephalous society in which there remains 'a deep-seated Igbo admiration for royalty'. Contentious as this view may be, it indicates that it is not necessary to have a king to be concerned with the parameters that do, or should, surround the exercise of power. In relation to his second concern, Azuonye proposes an overview in which the ideology of 'democratic' restriction on the use of power for the Igbo represents a 'mythic filtering' whereby certain dominant ideas are propagated and maintained through time by being reiterated. What are these dominant ideas? They centre on positive and negative representations of *èzè* which Azuonye generally glosses as 'king' in the tales, but which in society can constitute a 'leader' in a variety of social, political and religious spheres. Tales which focus on negative representations tend to follow a pattern in which oppression leads to resistance which leads to a reversal of fortune/defeat for the oppressor. The tales portray, inter alia, the sadistic king, the jealous king, the king who imitates Benin, the king who is humiliated and the king who does not maintain royal distance. In each of these representations there is the strong presence of the positive alternative, which is made explicit in the alternative set of tales: the amiable king, the moral king, the firm but fair king, the king who investigates fully, the king who rules by persuasion and not by force, the king whose promises are inviolable and the king who maintains distance. For Azuonye the exemplification of good government in these tales is centred upon the restrictions upon the behaviour of the king and it is these restrictions that are the checks of democratic constraint – arbitrary, unconstitutional behaviour is definable through these popular representations.

Görög-Karady examines the representations of power relations between fathers and sons within Bambara society as seen through a body of tales. She sees the tales as a cathartic working through of the inherent tensions and rivalries between fathers and sons in a society where filial obedience and the unquestionability of the parental edict are strongly sanctioned norms. In one story prohibition and transgression relating to a son's sexual behaviour produce punishment and revenge. The story encapsulates both the enduring nature of the conflict over control of the son's behaviour and the necessary transfer, in time, of power from father to son. In another tale, a variation involving a spear motif, there are other dénouements whereby transgression by the son is recognised by the father as a mark of strength and thus of being fit to inherit. The tales weave together, Görög-Karady indicates, inherent tensions between love and arranged marriages, between obedience and revolt, dependency and control. In representing power relations the tales act out the implications of internally contradictory values that remain in contradiction from generation to generation in spite of the momentary resolution of conflict through the transfer of power.

Through an examination of Lyela tales Steinbrich, like Azuonye, sees in an acephalous society a concern with the exercise of power and the accumulation of power in the hands of powerful men. Where Azuonye sees an outside stratified society which provides a model for 'kings' as stereotypes of 'bad' leaders, so Steinbrich sees Mossi as the external influence and source for parts of the Lyela 'debate' on power relations within Lyela society: 'In the divine kingship of the Mossi the peasants had to moderate the outcome of the story. They took care not to enter into conflict with their ruling classes. The Lyela, on the other hand, unfold their fantasies about the elimination of the wicked chief without any constraint.' But in Lyela society the key relationships under discussion in tales about power relate to the temporal power of 'chiefs' outside Lyela and the religious authority of the Lyela Earth Priest, as well as relations between senior and junior and between father and son. In inter-ethnic tales where a Lyela figure encounters an outside temporal authority and is embroiled in conflict it is the magical powers of the 'snake that provides curative medicine' or the 'staff that transforms' which come to the hero's aid. In discussing the symbolic interpretations of these tales Steinbrich also draws attention to the way in which the tales picture a process of transition whereby authority is handed on from father to son sometimes through violent upheaval and sometimes through a more regulated 'inheritance'. Marginal people, destitute orphans, can be the heroes whose defeat of the powerful brings them into the world of influence, wealth and power. Other marginal people, in the case of one tale discussed here, an old woman, can represent dangerous alternative forces. In the debate about the exercise of temporal power the religious authority of elders with their knowledge of alternative sources of power is deployed to counterbalance secular power. The figure of the chief is used as the stereotype of secular authority standing in for the dominant element in a variety of types of relationship, between fathers and sons, rich and poor, families and orphans, young and old, men and women.

Steinbrich sees the tales as restatements of Lyela conscious opinions about the nature of their acephalous society and their desire to be on their guard against a concentration of temporal power in the hands of big men or 'chiefs', a category of persons with which they are familiar through the imposition of colonial chiefs, through an understanding of Mossi society and through recognising the potentially problematic relationships between senior men and other categories of people in their own society.

ORAL FORMS AND THE DYNAMICS OF POWER

John Johnson turns his attention away from the dominant poetic forms in Somali culture to look at a form of song more culturally marginal, the work songs, in which it is possible to observe the deployment of the form to seek redress or to influence, obliquely, daily behaviour. He provides a number of scenarios, taken from experience in Somalia, where the powerless voice their objections and materially affect the situation which then changes. The songs themselves do not discourse upon the nature of power relations in society but rather constitute a voice that affects the interactions between people such that the singing of the songs is part of the exercise of power, sometimes of the inferior over the superior and sometimes more tangentially of an actor, whose authority may not be publicly recognised, over others whose independence of action is under question. It is the apparent simplicity and lowliness of the form which is deceptive. Serious and important messages are expected of culturally 'dominant' forms such as *gabay* and *geraar*, work songs are supposed just to help in doing work. But in one scenario, the playing of one such song on the radio during votes in parliament was credited with influencing the mood of MPs leading to a change of Prime Minister; serious effects ascribed to a form whose allusiveness was an essential part of its position as a voice of the powerless. Indirectness of reference and therefore ambiguity of function are direct correlates of the form's position as a voice of the socially marginal.

In Dyula society some fifty oral genres are identified and named. Political power is differentially distributed by gender, by age and, most particularly, by a distinction between the free and the slaves. Social organisation is by village district and by kin groups. Derive looks at the way in which particular genres are the preserve of particular categories of people and thereby both a pattern of inter-genre relations and a hierarchy of genres becomes apparent. Patron–client relations are manifest through praise genres but also in the 'implicit blackmail' that praise so often entails, either through the withholding of praise or through the many ways of criticism, from gentle innuendo to abuse. While certain forms, historical narratives and Islamic genres, are the preserve of those at the apex of political and religious power in Dyula society, serious ceremonial songs have their mocking counterparts in the obscene slave-caste parodies that Derive observes being paid for and enjoyed by free men. The payment is seen as being both reward and a means of silencing the performer. Historical narratives and moralising genres provide the ideological basis for the 'standard' position on the nature of Dyula society; designed for internal consumption they justify the status quo. Dominated social groups on the other hand deploy oral genres, according to Derive, and exercise 'counter-power' (through vilification, parody), or take to themselves some token of the powers that are denied them through simulation in games or by adopting bits of such things as 'Koranic' doxologies. Derive also sees a cathartic function in such oral expression. It is then in the field of oral genres that the relations between the powerful and the dominated in a variety of spheres are seen to be acted out, ideological assertion being met by a variety of forms of 'resistance'.

The chapter by Furniss treats, in the context of Hausa oral and written literature, issues raised by Derive. He examines the intimate connection between oral genres, such as praise-singing, and the political process. In acknowledging and articulating the basis of the patron's power the singer may also, through his control of the ambiguous borderline between praise and vilification, exercise power over that individual patron's hold on power. Whether within the context of specific patronage/clientage relationships or within the broader ideological context of didactic genres, the language of orature is politically engaged in the sense that it is purposively directed to persuade people of a particular point of view or of the truth value of a particular representation. A second thrust of the essay concerns the relationship between genres in Hausa oral and written literature. As Derive saw patterns of inter-genre relations and a hierarchy of genres linked to the structure of Dyula society, so also Furniss examines the way in which certain genres predominate in urban, male, public culture and how the practitioners of those genres present a particular view of the distinctions between their art form and others and between themselves and other artists. Within the broad spectrum of oral forms there are popular genres, such as burlesque, which operate satirically to subvert the serious intent of dominant forms. In this regard relations of power involving the domination of public cultural space and counter-cultural mockery are linked to the content and the performance of oral literature in Hausa. These relations of power are not static; they undergo renegotiation as fashions change, intellectual movements rise and fall and artists innovate.

ENDORSING OR SUBVERTING THE PARADIGMS:
WOMEN AND ORAL FORMS

The essays in this section show the very different situations that exist for women in relation to their access to meaningful cultural space. The first chapter paints a picture of a discourse of patriarchy apparently largely undisturbed by a recent war of liberation which had as part of its brief, a bid for the equality of women. Thus Herbert Chimhundu argues that the gender behavioural patterns embedded in Shona oral art forms are primarily ones that urge conformity to established roles for women and emphasise virtues such as docility, kindness and generosity and qualities of beauty, fitness and known ancestry. They discourage independence and participation in public life for women and to do this often call up the oppositional images of women as mothers, *madzimai*, and women as prostitutes, *mahure*. The latter is an image associated with women and urban life which runs through Shona written literature.

He argues that written lyric poetry and sung lyrics do not shift the basic norms for gender roles set out in the older sung forms, in fact they tend to repeat and reinforce them. To support his argument he has assembled a corpus of poetry, from older oral forms, written lyrics and the new technological orality of popular songs.

Language is seen by Chimhundu as a conservative factor especially as it is articulated in proverbs and various song genres. He points out that this emphasis on the old configurations undercuts the rhetoric of liberation where equality between the sexes is stated as a goal for the new social order. The emphasis on conformity is also sometimes exploited by African leaders who turn to 'tradition' when they wish themselves to undercut the discourse of democracy which is ostensibly part of their programme. Conformity and patriarchy become particularly sharply linked when politicians refer to the nation as one family thus excluding the possibilities of plurality and co-existing alternative structures. He ends with the example of a statement often made by politicians in calling for a one-party state in Zimbabwe which calls on folk memory, uses the symbol of ZANU (PF) and is couched –

seductively – in the form of a proverb: 'There is no room for two cocks in one chicken coop.'

If Chimhundu's chapter presents a bleak picture of unchanged patriarchal paradigms beneath a fragile surface rhetoric of gender equality Opland's essay tells a somewhat different story. His focus is on a woman poet who seemed for a time able to move beyond the silencing of her sex and who wrote poetry in the Xhosa-language newspaper *Umteteli wa Bantu* in the first decade of its life, 1920–30. Nontsizi Mgqwetho, the poet, engaged with both the large political issues of the day, such as the miners' strike of 1920, and the alienation of her people in their own land. She addressed contentious issues such as divisions in the black ranks and the role of leaders in early anti-pass demonstrations. Alongside these typically male topics she set the concerns of her own sex and wrote more openly as a woman. Thus she stated her support for the activist Charlotte Maxheke, worried about her sisters in the cities, described women's rural protests and defended the place of women in the churches, specifically in their *manyano* prayer unions.

Opland suggests that, in spite of her fire and talent, she was unable to hold together the contradictions of her discourses, wanting both the truth of tradition and of the Bible; wanting and assuming a public persona like a male praise poet and at the same time speaking eloquently of women's issues. Unable to sustain the contradictions creatively she fell back into an increasingly one dimensional discourse of piety and religiosity and finally stopped writing altogether. He concludes, 'Her later poetry lacks fire, her protest is couched in general terms; she yearns increasingly for the gates of heaven.' Whereas her famous male counterpart, S. K. Mqhayi, moved between oral performance and the written word and wove together narrative and praise poetry, she appears to have stayed largely within the domain of written poetry, beset even there by the difficulties of writing as a woman, a marginalised voice attempting to realign the discourses of women and patriarchy and perhaps succeeding for a time.

The marginalisation of this poet would appear to contrast with the stance of the marginal and lonely figure which Anyidoho sees as the self-conscious guise of the Ewe poets, setting a distance between themselves and the centres of power which they may criticise and with which they connect, however indirectly. Mgqwetho appears to have created a space for the private and public concerns of women and to have moved beyond any binary conception of men's and women's roles in her free movement between wide political issues and gender issues. Finally, however, silence claimed her and the issues of *Umteteli* continued to pour out without her disturbing and disruptive voice.

Whereas Opland sees marginality as finally disabling, in the case of the poet Nontsizi Mgqwetho, the chapter by Liz Gunner argues that marginality can offer flexibility and a chance to mock the rigid power structures of the centre or at least to move beyond their prescribed topics. Possibly it is access to the oral form rather than confinement to print which allows for this ability to manoeuvre. Gunner suggests firstly that the genre of *izibongo* has been fundamentally misread by scholars who have failed to see the importance of the popular forms which co-exist with the forms used to praise both royalty and also, over the last decade, new organisations such as the trade unions. Men's popular praise poetry is itself on the margins of power and thus may use the language of militarism and the heroic but may also mockingly undercut it and pay more attention to the autobiographical patterns full of intimate small details of the individual's life. Women's praise poetry is even further removed from the public domain than that of ordinary men and has, therefore, a larger amount of freedom. There is a chance for women to choose their own topics and at times undermine the dominant discourse relating to images of power and the hierarchical status of men and women. They may mock, like the categories of Shona women's poetry referred to glancingly by Chimhundu, but in this case, the genre is the same as that used to underwrite power and status for men – and that perhaps gives them added scope for subversion and alterity.

Gunner discusses the multivocalic nature of popular praises which contrast with the more rigid and monologic mould of the praises of big men. They are ambivalent, sometimes irreverent but men's praises, for all this, never completely escape the warrior and violence nexus. Songs, many with regimental and martial associations, are used as they dance to their praises; these tend to pull them back into the domain of war. Women's praises, on the other hand, have no access to the public domain and they thus have a greater chance to define identities which more completely undermine the ethic of war and the hierarchy of power and gender. Not needing to connect at all with the war ethic, their *izibongo* may lack the rich ambivalence of the men's, which can mock this grand central topic. Yet their praises, also deeply autobiographical, sketch in cliched topics such as jealousy, but also romantic love, the pain of polygyny, the irony of unfaithful husbands who are impotent in their own beds. Women's praises also, predictably, escape the war theme because their dance songs need never relate to it,

instead the women choose songs about jailed lovers in faraway
Pretoria, about having no money, about the heavy yoke of marriage
and, drawing on a multiplicity of discourses, they define their own
topics. These popular praises contain the criss-cross of community
voices often resonant with commentary on urban and rural life, free
from any need to reinforce status and thus free from the inscriptions of
power and authority. They give instead a sense of the multiple voices
of the community. They gesture in the direction of a broad hinterland
of culture which is often overlooked by power brokers within the
society and scholars inside and outside it who focus on militarism and
status. In this version of the art form of *izibongo*, marginality is akin to
flexibility and, as in many other forms pushed to the margins, it
provides a destabilising comment on the seemingly strong centre.

If Gunner's chapter gives a picture of a mocking and vigorous
marginality, Lucy Durán's essay on *jelimusow*, the superwomen of
Malian music, gives a very different picture of power relations in a
patriarchal society. In a society otherwise characterised by male
dominance, women musicians have become remarkably successful
and powerful. The *jeliw*, of Guinea, both women and men, have
proved adaptable to new social and economic imperatives, yet the
form which this adaptibility has taken in Malian culture is a loosening
of the constraints on women musicians, partly because of a shift in
musical taste. The old historical narratives and epics, which have
always been a preserve of male musicians, are no longer as popular as
the shorter lyrics, praises and chorus-like songs which women make
their own. They have thus found a space for themselves and become
popular and wealthy. Durán points out that this is not, however, an
overnight phenomenon. As early as the 1920s and 1930s there were
male–female duos consisting of musician and singer providing a
model from which the present 'superwomen' grew. If, in Southern
African art forms, critics have been drawn to the flamboyant male
forms of the public domain, it is true to say that accounts of *jeliw* or
griots in Mali have also focused on the male artists – Durán's article
redresses some of that imbalance. She discusses early singers of the
1950s such as Fanta Sacko, who travelled with her *kora*-playing father,
and who, as she moved across boundaries with him travelling between
Guinea and Mali, was influenced by the new love lyrics being played
on the guitar. From this crossfertilisation grew her still famous love
song 'Nina'. A later singer such as Ami Koita was able to build on
Sacko's composition and reputation and make her own mark,
showing a blend of innovation and memory, demonstrating that

women too can build on a line of composers and performers and set up an artistic continuity over time. An important feature of Durán's study is the light it sheds on the continuous nature of musical change in relation to gender patterns in performance. The *jelimusow* of Mali have, in a very different way from the women singers about whom Gunner writes, fashioned a new women's discourse. These two essays contrast with those by Opland and Chimhundu which both engage with issues of loss of voice in social space.

MEDIATORS AND COMMUNICATIVE STRATEGIES

The chapters by Yankah, Moraes Farias and Anyidoho set their focus not on discourses linked overtly to gender but on the poet as mediator, on the communicative strategies involved and the crucial relation of mediation with the power of those who govern. Yankah, writing about the art of the poet as intermediary for Akan royalty outlines how formal talk, in the hands of the official poet or *okyeame*, preserves and enacts royal power. It is, as Geertz (1983) puts it, one of the symbolic forms which express that a governing elite is in truth governing. Oratory, one of the modes of formal rhetoric so highly valued by the Akan, is used to minimise the risks in face-to-face interaction between two figures of authority, or between the royal figure and his subject. The complex communicative system allows the *okyeame* room to embellish 'to make complete', but never to parody. The formalisation of the communication means that chief and poet are not in direct bodily or visual confrontation; moreover the *okyeame* has the role of preserving royal dignity; it is he who must recast the speech and edit the content and style of the royal message. The skills needed for this kind of completion are complex, and involve discretionary paraphrasing, elaboration and perhaps proverbial embellishment but never an alteration of its logical focus. What Yankah calls 'the aesthetics of discourse animation' are particularly important to *akyeame* who may have to relay messages back and forth between chiefs and in some cases take a message from a fellow poet, embellish it further and then hand it over to the listening party. They thus play a crucial role, as mediators, in the enactment of royal power. More than that though, their ability to shape the message aesthetically is on some occasions a part of the means of soliciting support from an audience. Persuasion is necessary if concord is to be achieved, and it is the poet, or poets, of the chief who carry his word and make it sweet and palatable. Thus the art of ruling and the art of oratory intertwine, political power and rhetorical skill feed off each other. Finally Yankah points out that the phenomenon of 'answering' and relaying communication from a speaker through an intermediary on to a wider audience is widely used in Africa both in oratory and in other verbal genres and is also found in the New World in African American oratory. Yankah's study highlights the consonance of origin between the poet mediator and ruler, with both working within accepted Akan conventions.

Moraes Farias's analysis focuses on the mediations of self and other in the kingly praise in two societies far apart but linked by the presence of the same category of of 'traditionist' (*gesere*) in both societies, Borgu in Bénin and Mande society in Mali and Guinea. Moraes Farias teases apart the complex relationships between persona and self, office and office-holder, ethnic/professional and personal identity as they are enacted in the ambivalent confrontation between praiser and praisee. At the centre of the discussion is the notion that the discourse of praise is about identification as much, or more than, laudation, 'what praise discourses postulate is their capacity to seize upon the "truth" of the praisee's being, and to activate it and generate acknowledgement of it by the praisee's private self and the public at large'. In his analysis of the process of conceptualising the king and kingship he discusses the way in which, in the one society a musical instrument, the *bala*, and in the other society, drums, serve as an embodiment of kingship alongside the living ruler himself. In the dialogue that takes place in music, language and the visual dynamics of the festival, 'the incumbent ruler is a vessel for kingship as are the drums, but he himself ritually salutes them in the way that that which is self salutes that which is other'. The mediations and communicative processes that take place in the debate about kingship in these two societies are subtly and originally analysed by Moraes Farias in this important essay.

The tight intimacy of poet and ruler, which marks the communicative strategies and the exercise of power in the Akan situation, described by Yankah, stands in contrast with the situation presented by Kofi Anyidoho in his essay on 'The poet as loner in Ewe oral tradition'. In this tradition there is no 'circuit of formal talk', in Yankah's sense, between poet and ruler. What is stressed instead by the Ewe poets themselves is their loneliness. Anyidoho sees the theme of loneliness, which is persistent in Ewe oral tradition, as a metaphor for the poets' chosen isolation, a position which allows them the freedom to criticise powerful groups and individuals in society if they wish to do so. Their position is both secular and sacred, and, in some ways, Anyidoho argues, akin to that of priests, in that devotion to one's talent is seen as a sacred obligation. It is not, though, an occupation that brings wealth as most poets make their living from occupations such as farming and fishing and from these undistinguished social positions they are able to keep the power of the critic and claim the right to speak the truth.

The object of the poets' criticisms are often the wealthy and the politically powerful. The target may also be the creator god himself, or the family group. Anyidoho recounts how the renowned poet Akpalu was, on one occasion, taken to court by his relatives and charged with character assassination. In this social context, unlike the court poets of the Akan and Borgu Béninois, the poet is, in his role, closer to the priest who must expose or exorcise evil whenever it appears. In a quick sketch of the range of poetic forms in Ewe, Anyidoho claims that even in a contemporary popular form such as *bobobo*, the joyful is matched by the contemplative and the philosophical. It seems therefore that Ewe society pushes the poet to the margins, but that does not necessarily mean marginalisation in the sense of silencing, rather it is a collusion of choice between poet and society and it is from the edges that the poet exercises power in the shape of rhetoric and, at times, coercive comment.

The contributions in this volume share an interest in the politics of language use and in the debate about the nature and exercise of power within societies embedded within a variety of national cultures across the continent. The issues being debated here arise in the context of Africa but are manifestly issues that are of relevance elsewhere.

· PART I ·

Orality and the power of the state

CHAPTER 2

Oral art and contemporary cultural nationalism

Penina Mlama

History has witnessed many contrasts in the role of oral art in Africa. Oral art, which here refers to all artistic forms orally presented to an audience, often exalts, but also castigates rulers. Oral art may exhort people to demonstrate strength, courage and prowess and yet lull others into humility and silence before dominant powers. Examples are plentiful of oral art which became part of the colonising process in praising the colonisers and also of oral art as a tool of the anti-colonial struggles.

The status of oral art in Africa has been no less variable. From a prestigious status as a mechanism for criticising rulers, and for producing pedagogues and custodians of community values, knowledge and history, oral art was denied a place in world civilisation during the dark era of colonialism and foreign domination (Thiongo 1986; Fanon 1967). The neo-colonial character of post-independence Africa has meant that the situation in contemporary times has changed little, despite the frequent appearance of oral art performances at state banquets or state visits.

Cultural nationalism, which here refers to a sense of national cultural unity and identity, suggests the overcoming of some of these contradictions. Cultural nationalism was an inseparable companion of the political nationalism of post-independence Africa seeking to free the newly independent states from the humiliation of belonging to colonial empires. Assertion of national identities called for political, economic, social and cultural self-determination, and national cultural identity became a necessary component of nationalism. The 1950s and 1960s witnessed many attempts to propagate cultural identity, including the setting up of national troupes of artists, introduction of local languages in the school curricula and even the flamboyant return to African dress.

In the wake of independence, cultural nationalism was also

23

important in the building up of nations. National political, economic and social structures were seen as necessary to replace ethnic-based systems. A national identity had to replace ethnic identities in order to ensure national unity. A national cultural identity was required to give the citizens a sense of belonging to 'the nation'. This accounts for some of the efforts to revive, promote and develop cultural institutions and artistic activities (Mbughuni 1974).

Cultural nationalism has also become a continuing necessity to combat the onslaught on African culture by foreign cultural influences that dominate Africa through the workings of global social-economic structures including the mass media. Indeed, many African nations are finding it more and more difficult to determine for themselves their national cultural identities (Mlama 1991; Thiongo 1986).

Oral art, as one tool of culture, has received attention in this move towards cultural nationalism. Indigenous dances, poetry, epics, story-telling, work-songs, ritual songs, dirges, recitations and other oral art forms constitute the repertoire of many state-supported artistic groups. State institutions, including universities, research into African oral art and experiment practically with oral art performance for contemporary audiences. Numerous studies have documented various characteristics of African oral art (Lihamba 1985; Mlama 1983; Finnegan 1977; Kamlongera 1989). As a result oral art enjoys more recognition and status today than during the colonial era.

Numerous problems, however, have also confronted the attempts to promote oral art in Africa. A lack of direction is one major problem. Reflecting their economic and political chaos, African culture is barely understood by African governments (Asante and Asante 1985). More than twenty years of independence have not produced defined cultural policies for most African governments. Some of the many problems relating to oral art include lack of resources, an over-emphasis on foreign art at the expense of indigenous oral art and the commoditisation of art. Another problem which needs more attention than has been given to it to date is the manipulation of oral art for the benefit of the ruling classes, leading to its domestication and disempowerment. History provides many examples of attempts to domesticate and disempower oral art when people have recognised its potential to influence the thinking of audiences. Since art appeals at both intellectual and emotional levels, it can educate, inform, convince or persuade an audience for or against an issue or individual. Ruling powers are always aware of such artistic power. The censorship laws of most countries witness this fact. There are many examples of the workings of such laws: witness the numbers of artists in jail or exile. Throughout history rulers have also tried to control oral art through patronising artists. In traditional African societies there are many examples of court artists who sang, recited or danced the praises of rulers and their lineages. Although in some societies court artists had a degree of liberty to criticise rulers denied to other citizens, most court artists presented views that maintained the status quo.

Both pre-colonial and colonial rulers in Africa patronised oral art for their own interests. In 1948 the British Colonial Office, for example, adopted a policy of encouraging the colonies to frequently stage previously denounced indigenous artistic performances for the entertainment of colonial subjects. This was in an attempt to quell rising unrest and feeling against colonial rule (Hussein 1975).

Many contemporary African governments have operated in a similar manner. Although it is often argued that governments neglect oral art, in most cases they do not neglect it as such but rather keep it at a level where they can easily control and manipulate it. On the political stage leaders claim the importance of oral art, but in national planning and development programmes no action is taken to develop it. A well-nurtured oral art could unleash its potential to inform, educate, criticise and influence audiences and thus work against the interests of the ruling classes.

This discussion argues that whereas African governments have claimed that they are building national cultural identities through the promotion of oral art, they have in fact succeeded in domesticating and disempowering oral artists to the political advantage of the ruling classes. This claim is directed, however, at the specific case of Tanzania. The following section gives a historical background to oral art in Tanzania. This is followed by a section discussing the disempowerment of the oral artist in Tanzania and the last part is on the need for empowerment through oral art.

A BRIEF HISTORICAL BACKGROUND TO ORAL ART IN TANZANIA

Tanzania has a rich heritage of oral art within more than one hundred and twenty traditional ethnic groups. Dance, songs, story-telling, heroic recitations, poetry, worksongs, dirges and other oral art forms were an integral part of traditional societies. Like other colonised countries, Tanzania witnessed the disregard for her oral art and her culture in general by the colonial powers: the Arabs, the Germans and the British. The colonial ideological systems, including school education,

Christianity and Islam, discouraged and often suppressed indigenous oral art. The emphasis on foreign literature and art in the school curricula and the complete disregard for Tanzanian oral literature and art placed its development at a disadvantage.

Oral art was, however, significantly revived during the struggles for independence in the 1950s when it was used extensively to mobilise people to fight for independence. See the following two songs, for example:

> Nyerere yaza wahinza
> Chitimile mawanza
> Chimlamuse Chimlamuse
> Nyerere na Chama cha TANU
> Aheeee
> Chimlamuse chimulamuse
> TANU uhuru wize
> Aheeee   (Cigogo)

> Nyerere has come girls and boys
> Let us dance with vigour
> Let us greet him
> Nyerere and TANU [Tanganyika African National Union Party]
> Yes
> Let us greet him
> TANU so that freedom comes
> Yes   (Song in Cigogo from a Nindo dance, Dodoma region)

> Watanganyika njoni tukutanike
> Tujiunge na Chama chetu cha TANU
> Mola akipenda tupate uhuru
> Twalia, Twalia
> Hatutaki, hatutaki
> Kutawaliwa

> Tanganyikans come let us gather
> Let us join our Party TANU
> If God wishes we shall get independence
> We are crying we are crying
> We don't want, we don't want
> To be ruled.
>   (TANU rallying song in Kiswahili from Morogoro region)

Post-independence Tanzania has seen two major phases of oral art. One, a short one from 1961 to 1967, was basically of a neo-colonial character, reflecting the socio-economic structure of the time. The colonial period resulted in many Tanzanians not taking oral art seriously. However, this was also the period when the political movement for African cultural identity swept through the whole continent. Tanzania was part of this movement (Nyerere 1962).

One result of this drive for national culture was the formation in 1962 of the national dance troupe which collected and performed indigenous dances from all over the country. This troupe was disbanded in the late 1970s and replaced by the Bagamoyo College of Art which continues to promote Tanzanian artistic forms until the present day (Mbughuni 1974). However, a lack of direction and clear understanding of the notion of culture prevented further significant action in the development of oral art.

The second phase, 1968 to date, has seen a more active development of oral art. This is the period of the Arusha Declaration through which Tanzania adopted the policy of Socialism and Self-Reliance, *Ujamaa*. Intrinsic to the concept of self-reliance *Ujamaa* was the development of social and economic systems that were applicable and relevant to the realities of Tanzanian society. For example, a new education policy, 'Education for Self-reliance', was introduced, the basic objective of which was to enable Tanzanian children to relate more directly to Tanzanian socio-economic conditions. Relevance therefore became imperative and school curricula changed to reflect this concept.

A similar response to *Ujamaa* was the promotion of Tanzanian indigenous artistic forms and an abandonment of the European art introduced during colonial times. For example, Shakespeare, which once dominated school theatre, was replaced by indigenous art forms such as dances, story-telling, poetry and poetic drama. Outside the school system there was also an upsurge in performances of indigenous art forms throughout the country. Artistic forms once frowned upon by the Europeans or the African elite were now seen as expressions of the Tanzanian way of life. In urban areas *vichekesho*, unscripted and improvised comic skits, became very popular in portraying various understandings and interpretations of such concepts relating to *Ujamaa* as 'capitalist' 'exploiter' or 'parasite' (Hussein 1975).

The *Ujamaa* phase has indeed seen a great increase in oral artistic performances throughout the country. Poets, singers, reciters, dancers and other oral performers have composed and performed numerous poems, songs, recitations, dance songs, comic skits on many issues relating to the construction of *Ujamaa*. In fact, there is no single policy statement of *Ujamaa* that has appeared without an accompanying oral artistic composition. It is indeed possible to document the development of *Ujamaa* through a study of the songs, poems, recitations, dances or comic skits of the period concerned (Mlama 1991; Lihamba 1985).

Such institutions as the ministries responsible for culture, the National Arts Council, the Bagamoyo and Butimba Colleges of Art and the University of Dar es Salaam have, through state support, conducted research, training and performance programmes that have significantly contributed towards the development of oral art. Cultural offices responsible for the promotion of art have also been established at the national, regional and district levels.

The *Ujamaa* phase, however, presents some interesting developments relating to the domestication and disempowerment of oral art and is discussed in the following section.

THE DISEMPOWERMENT OF THE ORAL ARTIST IN TANZANIA

The adoption of *Ujamaa* policy called for much more 'unity of the nation'. There was a perceived need to mobilise all people to participate in the construction of an *Ujamaa* social and economic system. Values and attitudes had to be changed so that people would accept equality, non-exploitation, mutual respect and other principles which would help lead to a more egalitarian society.

At the outset, the ruling party (TANU then, now CCM) recognised the need to employ various ideological tools in order to attain support for *Ujamaa*. In 1968, for example, Nyerere (then party chairman) called the poets together and told them to 'go and publicise the Arusha Declaration and praise our culture' (Mnyampala 1971). The party has, in its meetings, repeatedly endorsed and emphasised the cause of cultural activities for political awareness. For example, the fifteenth TANU congress in 1976 issued a statement emphasizing the importance of 'culture' in portraying the day-to-day life of Tanzanian people (TANU 1976). In the 1988 party programme for the years 1987–2002, projections for culture and art are stated as follows:

> Chama tangu huko nyuma kimetambua
> kuwa sanaa na fasihi ndivyo vielelezo
> vya maisha, fikra na maadili ya jamii . . .
> kinachotakiwa ni kuwasaidia wasanii
> wetu ili waweze kuufikia umma . . .
> Chama kitasimamia ujenzi wa tabia na
> maadili yanayofanana na misingi ya siasa
> ya Ujamaa tunayoijenga.   (Kiswahili)
>
> The Party, since long past, has
> recognised that art and literature

> are portrayals of life, thoughts and
> values of a society . . . what is needed
> is to assist our artists to reach the
> masses . . . The Party will oversee the
> building of habits and values that
> reflect the principles of the policy
> of *Ujamaa* that we are building.
>   (Chama Cha Mapinduzi (CCM) 1988)

Government institutions, ministries, para-statal organisations, especially industrial production units, and the army were encouraged to establish artistic groups. The National Housing Corporation, the National Bank of Commerce, the National Insurance, the Department of Prisons, the Tanzania People's Defence Force, the National Service and the Dar es Salaam Development Corporation sponsor some of the more famous artistic troupes, which frequently perform songs, poetry, *taarab* and *vichekesho* at official party and government functions.

The upsurge of oral art performances in the *Ujamaa* phase was therefore, a result of deliberate efforts by the party and government. Indeed, in Tanzania today oral art performances are very widespread. By 1989 there were some 106 artistic groups registered with the National Arts Council in Dar es Salaam alone. There are also performances at every official party and government gathering including district, regional and national party conferences, festivals or development campaigns on health, education, environment and so on. Most schools have artistic groups that perform both at school and state functions. The majority of these performances is in Kiswahili and based mostly on Tanzanian indigenous oral forms of poetry, song, improvisation and dance.

On the face of it, it can be said that Tanzania has scored a great success in popularising oral art. From a colonial history of disregard for indigenous art forms, these same are now widely popular and recognised as representative of Tanzanian identity. It can also be argued that oral art has played a significant role in bringing about political unity in the country. One example of this is the way in which oral art was used to mobilise national support, military, material and moral, for the war against Idi Amin of Uganda in 1978–9. Oral art has also been a major mobiliser of people during national campaigns such as those against illiteracy, malnutrition, corruption and AIDS.

A major problem with all these developments, however, is the disempowerment of the oral artist. The majority of oral artists in Tanzania are men and women of the peasant or working class.

However, the oral art they produce seldom represents the voice or the viewpoint of the common person. Instead, oral art has become the mouthpiece of the ruling class: oral artists present either what the leaders say or what they want to hear.

There are a number of contradictions in the treatment of oral artists in Tanzania that point to the fact that the Party and the government are interested in oral art only for the political advantage of the ruling class. Indications are that the issue is not so much Tanzanian cultural identity, or unity for the development of the masses, but rather the maintenance of the status quo. Cultural officers at all levels have settled down to nothing more than the organisation of artistic performances for state functions. In fact, the major preoccupation of cultural officers is getting artistic groups to perform at state functions. Artistic groups are often hastily organised a few weeks or days before an official event. After the performance the groups are forgotten until the next event. Often the artists are not paid for their performance and sometimes, after performing, artists from distant villages have been abandoned at performance sites in town without food or transport. The government shows little interest in the welfare of the oral artists, their working conditions, their development or their survival.

Oral artists have remained basically deprived and poor. Because most of them are poor peasants and workers with low education levels, they are not in a position to protect themselves from the misuse of oral art by the government. Surprisingly, and probably because they are a dependent and marginalised group, they continue to produce art, songs, poems or recitations, praising leaders and pledging allegiance to the government and the party. In spite of all their difficulties they continue to show up and perform at official functions even though they get no support to run their artistic groups. Indeed, most of the adult artists willingly participate in these pro-government performances in a general belief that, as citizens, they are fulfilling a duty to their nation. Many groups feel proud to be selected to perform at state functions, especially in the presence of high-ranking officials, even though they are not remunerated. There is a belief that all artistic performances at official functions are part of Tanzanian cultural identity that ought to be supported and a source of pride. A convention has developed in Tanzanian official oral art that sees artistic composition only in terms of praising leaders and supporting government positions. A visitor to Tanzania exposed only to official artistic performances will easily gain the impression that Tanzania's oral art is basically political propaganda.

The government and the party have managed to domesticate artists to a point where they can use oral art not to portray the reality of people's daily lives but to sing the praises of the leaders and to maintain the status quo. It seems, therefore, that the sense of cultural nationalism that has developed in Tanzania is determined by the ruling class, resulting in the disempowerment of the majority and its relegation into a culture of silence.

EMPOWERMENT THROUGH ORAL ART

The apparent success in domesticating and disempowering the oral artist described above should not, however, give the impression that all Tanzanian oral art is simply political propaganda. This is true for the official oral art patronised by the state. There is, however, still a large proportion of oral art outside official art, which portrays Tanzanian life from a non-official point of view. For example, referring to the 'Health for All' campaign, the following dance song was composed about a corrupt doctor in Namionga village in Mtwara region:

> Jamani ee
> Nilitembea huko na huko
> Nikaenda kijiji cha Namionga hadi zahanati
> Nikawakuta watu wengi wamekaa wanazungumza
> Nikawauliza jamani kuna nini hapa
> Wakajibu
> Ewe mganga naomba dawa kichwa chauma
> Mganga akasema
> 'Nyoosha mkono upewe
> Kwani madawa kweli ni adimu.'   (Kiswahili)

> Hear
> I went to many parts
> I went up to Namionga village to the dispensary
> I found many people seated and talking
> I asked them what was happening
> And they answered
> 'Doctor I would like some medicine
> I have a headache'
> The doctor said
> 'Stretch your arm [pay] and you will get some
> You know that medicines are scarce.'

This type of oral art, though, remains marginal and localised. Indeed, it is often dismissed as 'local' and 'ethnic-based' and thus having no role or place in national cultural identity.

The recognition of the extensive domestication and disempowerment of the oral artist has given rise to various moves towards alternative development in oral art. The Popular Theatre movement, sometimes referred to as Theatre for Development, is one such response. Popular Theatre, which has also been extensively practised in other African countries, as well as in Asia and Latin America, refers to a process that involves the participation of the community not only in action for development but also in communicating its own ideas, views and analyses of issues. The process involves several stages. First, members of the community together with 'animateurs' research into what the community believes are its problems. Then the community analyses these problems with a view to pinpointing the root causes and possible solutions. The ideas are then concretised in artistic forms familiar to the community. These are often songs, poetry, recitations, story-telling and dances. A performance is then held, after which a discussion with the audience is followed by appropriate action.

Between 1980 and 1990 some twelve Popular Theatre programmes have been conducted in different villages in Tanzania (Mlama 1991). One important result of these is that, given the chance, oral artists can be empowered to voice their own viewpoints, perceptions and analyses of issues relating to their socio-economic realities. See, for example, the following dance song protesting against bad *Ujamaa* village government leadership:

> Wanakijiji wa Msoga tunayo malalamiko
> Kuhusu mahesabu ya pesa zetu za kijiji
> Tukitaka kuyajua viongozi wanakwepa
> Tingo na nusu rudi nyuma mbele basi
> Wanakijiji wa Msoga nguvu setu zalegea
> Sisi wa Msoga mahesabu hatupati
> Wageni mliokuja mjue tatizo letu
> Huu ndio mwisho wa habari
> Rudi nyuma nenda mbele tingo na nusu
> Wananchi wa Msoga
> Tumechoka na siasa
> Viongozi wa Msoga
> Tupeni hesabu zetu
> Wananchi wa Msoga
> Tumechoka na siasa.   (Kiswahili)

> We residents of Msoga have complaints
> About our village accounts [for projects]
> When we ask about the accounts the village
> leaders avoid the issue

> One and a half steps go forward and stop
> We Msoga citizens are losing morale for work
> We of Msoga are not getting our accounts
> Yes visitors who have come you should know
> our problem
> That is the end of the story
> Go back and forward, one and a half steps
> You leaders of Msoga give us our accounts
> We residents of Msoga are fed up with politics.
> (Mlama 1991)

In most cases members of the community presented 'official' oral art at the beginning of the Popular Theatre workshop, mistaking the 'animateurs' for representatives of the government or party officials. But in the course of the Popular Theatre process they ended up with very different compositions on the issues concerned. See, for example, the following song which changed its content during the Popular Theatre programme in Namionga village, Newala district. Before the Popular Theatre process:

> Twatoa pongezi
> Kwa wahisani
> Kutuletea chombo aa
> Chombo cha uhai na maendeleo ya mtoto aa
> nacho chahimiza mtoto apewe huduma zote
> Apate chakula cha kutosha kabisa na chambo
> zote aa.   (Kiswahili)

> We congratulate the donors
> For bringing us this programme
> The programme of child survival and development
> The programme insists that a child gets
> all the services.
> The child should get enough food plus all
> immunisations.

During the Popular Theatre workshop, after the analysis of the problems relating to child survival:

> Twatoa pongezi
> Kwa wahisani
> Kutuletea chombo aa
> Chombo cha uhai na maendeleo ya mtoto
> Twasema asante aa
> Nacho chahimiza mtoto apatiwe huduma zote
> Apate chakula cha kutosha kabisa na chanjo
> zote aa

                    Chakula tunacho tatizo ni maji pia na madawa aa
Mjue wahusika ndio mnasaidia kifo cha mtoto aa
Wote mlaaniwe oo mlaniwe kabisa wilaya nzima
Twamuomba Mungu mlaanike kabisa popote mlipo aa
                                                    (Kiswahili)

We congratulate the donors
For bringing us this programme
The programme of Child Survival and Development
That programme insists that a child gets all the services
The child should get enough food plus all immunisations
We have the food, the problem is water and drugs
Those of you who are responsible [for the water and drugs problems
  – a reference to leaders]
Are the ones who cause child deaths, a curse to you all
May you be cursed properly in the whole district
We pray god that you be properly cursed wherever you are.
                                                    (Mlama 1991)

What emerges very clearly is that in the Popular Theatre process oral
art is used very effectively by people to analyse for themselves their
socio-economic conditions.

It is clear that contrasts in the role and status of oral art persist to the
present time. Contemporary societies can choose, as the Tanzanian
case shows, to use oral art in the interests of the ruling classes. Yet the
same oral art can be used also to represent the interests of the ruled.
The issue is for us to be able to see through the misuse of oral art and
not to mistake some of our countries' pretended cultural nationalism
for genuine efforts to develop oral art in Africa. The challenge is in
how to enable oral art to empower the previously disempowered.

CHAPTER 3

The letter and the law: the politics of orality and literacy in the chiefdoms of the northern Transvaal

Isabel Hofmeyr

In 1923 the Native Commissioner of Potgietersrus, who was involved in an ongoing feud with Chief Alfred Masibi of Zebediela, wrote to his adversary. 'I do not as a rule,' he said, 'take verbal messages – you must get your secretary to write when transacting government business.'[1] A few years later a new chief, Abel Kekana, took office, but in no time the Native Commissioner was at loggerheads with him too. In May 1929 the Native Commissioner wrote to the Secretary for Native Affairs complaining about Kekana's behaviour:

Adverting to my minute No. 2/1 of the 19th ult., and with reference to your No. 27/55 of the 6th inst. in connection with the conduct of the above named chief, I have the honour to submit [a] copy of my letter evenly numbered of the 8th inst. addressed to this chief calling upon him for an explanation as directed by you. To this letter no response was received other than an intimation that he was busy with his circumcision school and would attend to the matter later. On the 16th inst. I attended the Local Council meeting at Zebediela, and there saw the young chief to whom I at once intimated that I was not there to receive his explanation which he could either submit in writing or personally at my office at Potgietersrust. Further that if I received no response to my letter within seven days of the last mentioned date I would submit the matter for further action by you without his explanation. On the 21st inst. attended by his usual satellites who are mainly responsible for his misguided conduct, he presented himself at this Office. He appeared to be very sullen and on the questions contained in my letter of the 8th inst., being put to him, he gave his explanation, which I took down in writing and a copy of which I attach hereto. His attitude was not at all reassuring, and in the interest of the Tribe I do urge that he be severely dealt with . . . I have seen letters addressed to members of the Royal family urging that this young man be deposed, but an open expression of their feelings [is] stifled by tradition

This essay is extracted from a chapter in Isabel Hofmeyr, 'We Spend Our Years as a Tale that is Told': Oral Narrative in a South African Chiefdom (Johannesburg, Wits University Press, 1993).

and sentiment. However I submit a confidential report sent to me by W. S. Kekana which clearly reflects the true position.[2]

As the letter makes clear, the conflict between the Native Commissioner and the two chiefs was conducted through a variety of media and modes of communication: letters, both public and confidential, public meetings, private appointments, verbal messages, secret reports and speeches copied down in writing. From other letters it is clear that telegrams and telephones were also mobilised in the dispute.[3] It is also clear that the opposing sides attempted to rely on different kinds of communicative strategies to maximise their advantage. The Commissioner generally wanted things in writing or favoured face-to-face situations where he was in charge. Chief Abel Kekana, on the other hand, avoided contact with the Commissioner where possible. But when forced to deal with him the chief engineered an oral interaction while accompanied by his retinue who evidently exercised a somewhat unsettling effect on the Commissioner.

Both sides, then, tried to determine the form and medium of interaction, and while the two parties had access to oral and literate resources, both, in a situation of conflict, tended to turn to the mode with which they were most familiar. Consequently, in this situation of interaction between ruler and ruled, both parties presumably felt there was some political edge to be had from insisting on a particular mode of communication.

This brief sketch of a spat between the chief and Native Commissioner raises a host of questions about the relationship between forms of communication and political authority. There is, however, one issue that emerges particularly clearly and that is the extent to which the forms of communication are a focus of political struggle. This question of struggle is important to stress, since there have been other studies that assume that those with authority can unilaterally dictate the forms and modes of communication between factions possessing unequal power.[4] However, as Fabian in his analysis of language and colonial power reminds us, we should always consider '*simultaneously* local, creative response to communicative needs *and* restrictive intervention from above motivated by a resolve to control communication' (1986: 3).[5]

It is largely the first part of Fabian's analysis that this essay seeks to implement and in so doing, it attempts to contribute to the broader debates on orality and literacy. One principle that this research has established is that there are no automatic consequences that follow from the introduction of literacy. While some have argued that the introduction of written documents – particularly via the agency of literate bureaucracies – will bring about standardisation and depersonalised rule, others have argued that such consequences can never be predicted beforehand.[6] Instead each case has to be investigated individually since literacy as a technology will always be appropriated in different ways and be shaped by the social circumstances in which it operates.[7] The material used to investigate these points is the correspondence that passed between a Commissioner's office in the northern Transvaal and surrounding chiefdoms. In undertaking such an analysis, this essay attempts to show how the chiefdom and its officials responded to and transformed the communicative procedures with which they were confronted.

In this correspondence, written roughly between the 1920s and 1950s, we can observe various ways in which agents of the chief attempted to bend the language of official correspondence and bureaucracy to meet their particular needs. In transforming this language, it was, of course, on pre-existing forms of discourse, knowledge and understanding that correspondents drew. While it is often difficult to specify exactly what such pre-existing forms might have been, there is one consistent theme that emerges and that is an attempt to 'oralise' the written word and make it bear the 'imprint' of the human voices and relationships that necessitated its creation in the first place. Such 'oralising' can be seen in things like an insistence on oral messenger and oral memory; as well as an attempt to subordinate literacy as the medium of ruling to institutions of public assembly, face-to-face government and personal audience. While there may well be a number of ways to interpret these insistences, this chapter construes them as part of the cultural resistance of a community against colonial domination. As in its confrontation with a literate religion, the oral performance politics of the chiefdom challenged the literate institutions of colonial bureaucracy by attempting to 'oralise' them.[8]

In an analysis of the Native Affairs Department during the inter-war years, Dubow illustrates the ideological and administrative shifts that it underwent. Heavily influenced by the Transkeian model of native administration, the post-Union Department followed a policy of gradualist assimilation but subsequently moved to a more rigid doctrine of segregationism. Administratively, the Department initially relied on ideals of government through decentralised paternalism and 'personal rule'. This form of administration was, however, soon supplanted by a much more centralised, purposive bureaucracy.[9] This shift from local paternalism to centralised bureaucracy probably happened more in theory than in practice. In remote areas like the northern Transvaal, the Native Affairs Department could never properly institute the full exercise of depersonalised and distant control that a centralised, literate bureaucracy implies. The areas to be controlled were simply too huge, the people in these areas too numerous and too unwilling to be governed. Under these conditions, depersonalised, distant ruling can never take off and instead, Native Commissioners had to rule through a combination of personal audience, public meeting and oral messenger, or, in other words, the cornerstones of oral government.[10]

In this situation, as Sansom has shown, the Native Commissioner's authority – which was in theory extensive – depended on constant negotiation through which the governed gained a measure of autonomy and freedom.[11] The Commissioner's office, with its risible staff complement and miserable police contingent, had to tread carefully and could not rile its subjects too deeply (1970: 12–53).

In this context of contested authority, the conventions of ruling and protocols of interaction become an important focus of struggle. One such form of interaction was the letter which passed frequently between the chief and the Commissioner. Mostly concerned with the details of licensing and permits for churches, schools and stores, these letters probably formed the major form of communication between the chief and the Commissioner who otherwise only encountered each other for meetings every three months.

For the chief, then, writing letters held several attractions, one of which was that they minimised personal dealing with the Commissioner. Another advantage was that by using such correspondence, chiefs could borrow the power of literacy. Like medieval lords who could use their signet rings to 'sign' documents without themselves being fully literate, many chiefs surrounded themselves with the paraphernalia of writing and bureaucracy and paid great attention to things like letterheads and rubber stamps.[12] Through these accoutrements, chiefs announced themselves entitled and authorised to participate in a documentary culture.

Yet, in participating, however indirectly, in a literate universe, the chiefs and their allies were simultaneously changing the meaning and uses of documents. By bathing documents in the stream of orality, they subordinated them to the prevailing practices and procedures of an oral world. An oft-quoted example of the transformative power of orality is the way in which much writing emanating from paraliterate communities mimics speech. This cross-over is generally cited as an instance of a new technology camouflaging itself in the old (Clanchy 1979: 257). Another, slightly stronger, reading of this situation is to think of the practitioners of the old technology forcing the new to conform to their values and views. Insofar as a technology of communication is woven into a wider set of cultural and political ideas, this clash between forms of representation has a number of implications.

One of these concerns the way in which oral transactions focus attention on a set of social relationships and a group of actors. Literate technology shifts the emphasis away from the actors towards the text which progressively tends to be divorced from both its producers and consumers. This alienation is not something that oral communities easily allow, and in many oral situations there is a struggle to keep documents accountable to the circumstances from which they come. As part of the same process, people also try to make documents ring with the human voices that spoke them and the social relationships that necessitated their creation in the first instance.

The first strategy in this struggle was to write as one spoke. While such a style may arguably be entirely predictable, it nevertheless kept alive the idea of a letter or document as part of a conversation that linked people in particular relationships of power and obligation. In keeping with these trends, most letters to the *komosasi* (Commissioner) bear the 'imprint' of the human voice. Many of these letters also start *in media res*, a technique which inserted the letter in an ongoing relationship. One such letter began, 'My Lordship, allow me please to continue my personal explanation in order to give more light in the matter.' Another said, 'First of all, I greet you very much. Sir, I went on safely out of Mapela's Location . . . My journey took me two days, on account of the scarcity of the buses or that some of the bridges were destroyed by heavy water.'[13] Another letter-writer felt it necessary to imply the social network from which he came and so signed off his letter, 'I am Jeconias Lebelo. Lebelo's son.' Yet another correspondent attempted to remind the Commissioner of his obligations by announcing, 'I am here to inform the commissioner that I have passed carpentry.'[14]

In sending messages, most people still laid more store by the spoken, rather than the written word. Consequently, letters were often accompanied by messengers who would report the substance of the information, embellish the contents of the document they carried or answer any questions the recipient might have. 'Owing to sickness,' a headman in Zebediela wrote (or had written on his behalf), 'I am sending herewith two men of my section who can give you the whole proceedings of the meeting.' Another writer felt it necessary to apologise for sending a letter, 'I am sorry to report this through letter. I wanted to report it personally but unfortunately my bicycle is not in order. Saturday seems too long to come on foot.' Letters could also act as dramatic props, and one chief sent a woman who wanted to apply for a store permit with a document that began, 'By this letter I say the Government may see herewith a girl.'[15]

Another way to embed the spoken voice on the printed page was to reappropriate the written in terms of phonetic spelling. In terms of this practice, one correspondent wrote that 'we spek ablcation to make shop'. Another asked the Commissioner 'why you naver ask awar letter' which had been for a 'lessense' to 'sale soap mill mill and parafin oil'. Yet another letter, which like many others relies heavily on the language of supplication and clientship, combines phonetic spelling, direct translation from the Sesotho and the oral, performance language of the church. The letter concluded, 'The covernorment he will look for [that is, look after] us. Amen.'[16]

The full impact of this 'spoken' writing did not often reach 'the ears of the government' as skilful translation often shrivelled the repetitive and additive style of oral speech into the clipped formalities of bureaucratic English.[17] In expressing their opposition to a new council system, one community wrote as follows:

With respect Sir Amen

I say that everybody at Kamola, they do not like the council and its power at all. Truly we do not like it. The entire *lekgotla* of Doorndraai they do not like it one little bit. You know that we do not like the Council. We are in a difficult position, we are in difficult position, we do not like the Council. You know that we do not like it.
I remain

Johannes Mashishi[18]

A fairly tactful translator got hold of this letter and rendered it as follows:

Sir, with respect Amen. The residents of Kamola Area are very much against a Local Council. Every body at Dorrondrae. Sir I wish to tell you every body hates a Local Council in this area.
I Remain

Johannes Mashishi

Alongside this aural appropriation, many letter writers also reshaped bureaucratic language to their own ends and according to their own understandings. One typical way in which this conversion occurs is by rendering the abstract, concrete, and many abstract nouns beloved of bureaucracy like 'permission', 'notice' and 'advice' were made to render signal service as concrete nouns or transitive verbs. So, letters frequently requested 'advices', 'a notice' or 'a permission note'.[19] Similarly, chiefs requested Native Commissioners to 'permission' applicants 'to make shop'. The noun 'bearer', which appeared on crucial papers like travel passes in the form 'Allow bearer to . . .', was often born again as a verb. 'I also bearer him as far as I know him as a good man', wrote Chief 'Makapan' in recommending a butchery applicant to the Commissioner's office. Elsewhere someone appealed to the Commissioner in characteristically concrete terms: 'I am going about bearing my complain . . . behind my back which I do not know who will take it of from my back.'[20]

Another indirect way in which orality affected correspondence was to render the act of writing and authorship visible. Such a process was, of course, often unintentional but it none the less transferred the performative inflections of oral speech on to written discourse where a letter could 'read for itself', a scribe could 'pen off' or end by saying 'This comes to the stoppage of my pen.' Similarly, one author focused on the physical nature of writing itself when he declared, 'I have this opportunity to draw this few line according to my application.' The verb 'draw' may, of course, be indebted to a phrase like 'draw attention to', but even if this were the case, its use here focuses attention both on the activity of writing and the concrete origins of the metaphorical phrase.[21]

A further strategy through which people used to keep the authority of orality alive was to rely on oral witness and oral contract. The highest statement of trust was to say that someone 'spoke the judgement from his own mouth', and people frequently repudiated written contracts, particularly those made on their behalf by browbeaten or avaricious chiefs.[22] Confronted with such situations, Native Commissioners were forced to abandon the methods of literate government for face-to-face meeting and, at times, police intervention. One such incident arose in the 1930s over the widely hated tribal levy system whereby people were burdened with extra taxation to buy more land to which the rank and file rarely got access. An irritated Commissioner described events as follows:

They flatly refused to pay the Levy, on the ground that their Headman, Lingana Mabusela, (since dead) did not inform them of it; I pointed out that Lingana actually signed the resolution of 6/9/1929 asking for the imposition thereof, but all argument was of no avail. Ultimately it became necessary to invoke the aid of the Criminal law and some 100 were sent to prison for terms ranging from six weeks to two months.[23]

In defying the previous written agreement, the residents of the Mabusela ward were partly relying on the flexibility of oral contract. As others have shown, much oral contract, despite its claims to traditionalism, was quite contemporary in its ability to erase obsolete or unpopular law which generally dies a quiet death. As Clanchy in his study of medieval literacy says, 'Remembered truth was also flexible and up to date . . . the law itself remains young, always in the belief that it is old' (1979: 233). Such flexibility, of course, cannot withstand the relentless record of written evidence, but the residents of the Mabusela ward made a spirited attempt to do so. Two years after the churlish report by the Native Commissioner they were still repudiating any written agreements and refusing to pay the levy. As the members of the *lekgotla* wrote to the 'magerstreet': 'We shill never pay that the trable leve because we never agreed about it when we where there in the meeting we was face to face we have till every thing about this trable leve that we can't pay the thing.'[24]

While literate bureaucrats believed implicitly in the durability and fixity of the printed word, this is probably not how writing must have seemed to many. As Clanchy has pointed out for medieval literacy, in the early stages of writing various forms of forgery flourish. Under such circumstances, it is the malleability and impermanence of the written word that must appear paramount (1979: 209). While the extent of forgery in Transvaal chiefdoms is not at all clear, there is evidence to suggest that there were instances of this 'literate' crime, particularly in connection with the collection of tribal levies. In this regard, literate court messengers often cheated people or bamboozled them with the paraphernalia of receipt books and stamps.[25]

There were other instances in which the malleability of apparently fixed documents emerged. One such instance occurred in 1937 when the self-same Mabusela community hired a lawyer to challenge a levy proclamation in court. As the wording of the levy was ambiguous, it was declared *ultra vires*. It must have been a rather embarrassed Native Commissioner who had to convey this information to the people concerned. At this meeting one apparently ingenuous speaker asked him to explain exactly how many words were wrong in the last Proclamation.[26] One would give a lot to have heard the tone in which these words were delivered but, like so many bureaucratic genres, minutes of meetings do not allow us such indulgences.

As the Mabusela episode shows, an insistence on orality had

powerful political implications. These were further exploited by the tenaciousness with which people clung to any oral agreements made with the Native Commissioner's office. As the Native Commissioner was at times forced to abandon his desk and speak to the chief and people concerned, a lot of agreements in their eyes were oral and, even after years had passed, chiefs or their representatives would continue to insist on various oral promises being honoured. As written records were often lost or burned, and as Native Commissioners changed with great frequency, such requests could safely be embellished or even invented.[27]

While an insistence on orality offered some practical and material advantages, it also offered metaphorical ones whereby the idea and image of the voice became central to much political discourse. People frequently acted on advice spoken to them in dreams (another interesting non-literate form), while the call of the ancestors became a key political metaphor. Again in connection with tribal levies, a group living just north of Pretoria was hit with particularly hefty levy payments in the late 1920s. Some of its more imaginative leaders suddenly recalled that the community had historical links to the chiefdom of Mokopane, which incidentally had much lower levy payments. The Assistant Native Commissioner interviewed the leaders concerned to inquire what had brought this change of allegiance. He reported the interview as follows: 'When questioned by me as to the reason why they now, after this long lapse of years, want to come under the jurisdiction of Barend Makapan, they replied, "That their father is calling them".'[28] This stress on the voice as the basis of much political life also took its surreptitious toll on the procedures of the Native Commissioner's office as officials were forced again and again to explain written documents. It was, of course, the sheer number of non-literates that necessitated this verbal glossing of written documents. Yet in these interactions it was their cultural tastes which prevailed as the arcane documents of a literate culture were baptised in living practice by being explained, interpreted and covered with the spoken voice. It was just such a situation that one Commissioner encountered when he had to explain a bond to an audience that had no desire to finance the land for which their chief had signed. This is how the peeved Commissioner described his encounter in a letter to the Secretary for Native Affairs in which he demanded that the people concerned be forced to apologise:

I strongly resent the attitude taken up by these natives. The Bond was read over word for word by me in the presence of Mr. Attorney Slabbert to some

400 or 500 natives belonging to the tribe of Jonas Makenna. It was also explained by me thoroughly so that there was no mistake about it – I am thoroughly acquainted with the Sesutto language and the interpretation of the Bond by Makenna was not faulty.[29]

This necessity for oral commentary and exegesis was a task that officials often had to undertake. Another Commissioner wrote as follows to his superiors: 'The report of the Assistant Director of Native Agriculture and the Senior Chemist of the Department of Agriculture and the map drawn by the Assistant Engineer, Native Affairs Department was explained to the best of my abilities to the meeting.'[30] This enshrouding of the written document in oral commentary formed part of a complex linguistic situation in which the Native Commissioner's office in Potgietersrus operated. While most Commissioners could speak Sesotho, they were often not entirely proficient and most letters coming into the office were translated into English. Letters sent to the chief were either in Sesotho or English. However, as the chief's court comprised Sindebele speakers (although most were proficient in Sesotho), one could have a situation whereby letters from the chief to the Commissioner could be dictated in one language (Sindebele), written in another (Sesotho), translated, and read in a third (English). Similarly, if a letter went from the Commissioner to the chief, it could be written in English, translated into Sesotho and read out in translation in Sindebele. All of this was extremely time-consuming and often formed a source of annoyance to officials.

In its response to the tactics of performance politics, the Native Commissioner's office often behaved as one would expect of a literate bureaucracy. Much of its energy went into trying to promote the kind of literacy that it believed would make people governable. This battle to impose 'orderly government' on the performance politics of the theatre state was waged in joyless campaigns centred on issues of protocol, grammar, procedure and etiquette.[31] In endless letters and meetings, various Commissioners at the Potgietersrus office nagged and threatened on how to give speeches and compose letters (*always* with a date, *never* in pencil). Vexed by the apparent flexibility of customary law, Native Commissioners frequently requested that laws be codified and printed. In the end, most chiefs came to request such books which, along with things like date stamps and letterheads, were the few visible performance accoutrements that literate power allows.[32]

Yet, try as hard as they might, the dream of making the subordinate more pliable through literacy was a far-fetched one. Apart from having a hopelessly patchy presence, literacy, if not flatly resisted, was furthermore appropriated and domesticated by the subordinate in selective ways. It was not a situation to encourage the smooth exercise of power. Or, as Benita Parry phrases it: 'the fracturing of the colonialist text by re-articulating it in broken English, perverts the meaning and message of the English book . . . and therefore makes an absolute exercise of power impossible' (1987: 42).

NOTES

1 Transvaal Archives (hereafter TA), Transvaal Archives Depot (hereafter TAD), KPT 2, 1/1/3, Native Commissioner (hereafter NC) to Chief Alfred Masibi, 12/12/23. Unless otherwise specified, all officials are attached to the Potgietersrus office.
2 TA, TAD, KPT 2, 1/1/2, NC to Secretary for Native Affairs (hereafter SNA), 27/5/29.
3 See correspondence in TA, TAD, KPT 2, 1/1/2.
4 For a discussion of this point see Grillo (1989: 14–17).
5 See also Opland (1989) for a fascinating discussion of how, in Xhosa oral poetry, literacy is perceived as part of colonial oppression. My thanks to Jeff Opland for making this reference available to me.
6 On this point see Goody (1986: 89–90, 105, 110, 114, 124).
7 The major works here are Clanchy (1979), Street (1984), and Finnegan (1988).
8 On this point see Scheub (1985), who discusses a range of points on such 'spoken writing'.
9 See Dubow (1986). The issues discussed here are more fully treated in his book, Dubow 1989: 77–127.
10 On this point see Goody (1986: 89–90, 105, 110, 114, 124).
11 For details of the powers of the Native Affairs Department and Native Commissioners see Lacey (1980: 84–115).
12 For examples see TA, TAD, KPT 3, 2/3/2, Anon. to Assistant Native Commissioner (hereafter ANC), Zebediela, 1/12/30; Special Justice of the Peace (hereafter SJP), Zebediela to F. Madisha, 24/12/30; SJP, Zebediela to Abel Kekana, 17/3/31; and SJP, Zebediela to NC, 5/12/32. For a comparative perspective see Clanchy (1979: 184).
13 TA, TAD, KPT 16, 2/3/3/4, P. R. Seboa to Sub-Native Commissioner (hereafter SNC), 18/6/37; and KPT 16, 2/3/3/4, J. Madisha to R. M., 26/2/34.
14 TA, TAD, KPT 29, 2/4/3/48, J. Lebelo to NC, 24/11/38; and KPT 18, 2/4/3, A. H. P. Mako to NC, 16/5/48.
15 TA, TAD, KPT 16, 2/3/3/4, P.M. Kekana to NC, Zebediela, 31/3/34; KPT 16, 2/3/3/8, D. Malepe to an unspecified recipient, n.d.; and KPT 26, 2/4/3, Chief A. Kekana to SJP, Zebediela, 20/4/32. See also KPT 16, 2/3/3/4, P. Kekana to SJP, Zebediela, 10/5/34.
16 TA, TAD, KPT 16, 2/4/2, J. Ngwepe to NC, 13/11/50; and Anon. to NC,

7/1/51; and Headman F. Maeteletsa to NC, 15/10/47. 'Mill mill' is mealie meal.

17 Phrase from TA, TAD, KPT 32, 2/9/2, 'Chief' to NC, 19/4/26.

18 TA, TAD, KPT 54, 10/1/2, J. Mashishi to NC, 22/6/48.
    The letter which is in a Sindebele-tinged Sesotho with Afrikaans echoes reads as follows:

>   Kaboikokobetso Morena Amen Kere Lekhutla le kamola gaberate eseng kakgonthe garerate kgarebeso la Councerl. Ruri garerate lekgotla. Kamoka far Dorrondrae gabaerate eseng legaele garajani. Otsebe gore garerate Councerl. Reapatana Reapatana garerate Councerl. Otsebe gore garerate.
>
>   I Rimain
>   Johannes Mashishi

My thanks to Kgomotso Masemola for help with translation.

19 TA, TAD, KPT 2, 1/1/2, C. Leolo to W. S. Kekana, 19/11/28; KPT 16, 2/3/3/7, Chief P. Seloane to SJP, Zebediela, 2/6/40; and KPT 15, 2/3/2, W. D. Seshoka to NC, 5/9/35.

20 TA, TAD, KPT 18, 2/4/3, Chief P. Makapan to NC, 1/10/48; and KPT 29, 2/4/3/48, D. Lamola to NC, 24/11/38.

21 TA, TAD, KPT 2, 1/1/2, W. S. Kekana to NC, Zebediela, 23/11/28; KPT 54, 10/1/2, T. Monene to NC, 22/6/18; KPT 16, 2/4/2, C. Makhubele to NC, 11/9/49; and KPT 15, 2/3/2, J. P. Kekana to SNC, 2/10/28.

22 Phrase from TA, TAD, KPT 31, 2/8/2, SJP, Zebediela to NC, 6/5/31.

23 TA, TAD, KPT 45, 4/3/3, NC to SNA, 18/10/32.

24 TA, TAD, KPT 44, 4/3/3, 'Lekgotla' to 'Magerstreet', 12/12/34.

25 Gurr, *Daniel Heese: Ein Lebensbild aus der Mission in Makapanspoort in Nord-Transvaal*, 89; and TA, TAD, KPT 45, 4/3/3, undated, unsigned document headed 'The present state of affairs in Valtyn Location'.

26 TA, TAD, KPT 44, 4/3/3, Minutes of a Tribal Meeting of the Langa Tribe under Chief Mankopane Masibi, Bakenberg Location, 28/6/37.

27 For insistence on oral promise see TA, TAD, HKN 46, 47/15/38, NC, Nylstroom to Chief Native Commissioner (hereafter CNC), 25/6/37. For allegations of invented claims see TA, TAD, KPT 14, 2/54/3/21, A. Gilbertson to NC, 30/9/50; and KPT 15, 2/3/2, H. S. Robinson to NC, 23/5/35.

28 TA, TAD, KPT 32, 2/8/2, Additional Native Commissioner (hereafter ANC) to NC, 21/10/29.

29 TA, TAD, KPT 32, 2/9/2, SNC to SNA, 19/3/20.

30 TA, TAD, KPT 41, 2/11/6, ANC to CNC, 8/9/39.

31 Phrase from Geertz (1980).

32 Paragraph based on TA, TAD, KPT 31, 2/8/2, SJP, Zebediela to NC, 6/5/31; KPT 12, 1/15/4, Pitsu [*sic*] of Native Chiefs and Headmen held at the NC's Office, 16/2/34; and KPT 32, 2/8/2, Moses Kgobe to NC, 6/12/29.

CHAPTER 4

A king is not above insult: the politics of good governance in Nzema avudwene festival songs

Kofi Agovi

Avudwene satirical songs are performed in the Nzema annual Kundum festival. The festival is celebrated by the Ahanta and Nzema people of south-west Ghana (Agovi 1979), who occupy a contiguous coastal strip of land from Sekondi-Takoradi to Half-Assini in the Western Region of Ghana. They are members of the Bia language group (Kropp-Dakubu 1988: 50–76) and share the same Kundum festival as a common cultural event.

Since the early seventeenth century when the festival was first recorded in European records (Bosman 1967: 158), writers have always drawn attention to its dominant religious focus and links with other festivals in Ghana (Rattray 1924: 151–5).[1] On the other hand, its singular feature of satirical songs significantly reveals a concern with secular issues. It deals exclusively with historical, political and socio-economic developments in Ahanta–Nzema society. For this essay, the socio-political concerns of the songs have been isolated for analysis.

Several writers have drawn attention to the close relationship between African orature, politics and the traditional state. According to Ruth Finnegan (1970: 82), the patronage of poets in centralised political systems in the past led to the creation of a 'poetry of profound political significance as a means of political propaganda, pressure or communication'; such poetry includes songs of insult, challenge or satirical comment used as 'politically effective weapons' (1970: 172). Similarly, Izevbaye (1971: 146) has contended that 'in West Africa, at

This chapter, originally presented at the conference in London on power, marginality and oral literature in 1991, has meanwhile appeared in *The Literary Griot: International Journal of Black Oral and Literary Studies*, 3 (1): 1–18. The original material was collected at various times between 1976 and 1989 as part of an extensive research project on the dramatic and literary aspects of the Kundum festival.

least, the earliest important tradition of poetry has its source in political action'. During the period of Shaka, Mazisi Kunene writes, 'Zulu literature changed to become a powerful vehicle of social and political ideas', and poets and singers became central 'democratic agents to reaffirm the approval or disapproval of the whole nation. It was through the poet and singer that criticism and evaluation of the heroes and rulers was fully and freely expressed' (1979: xxv).

The politicisation of literature in African society was inevitable because literature, or artistic forms, became the nerve centre of a network of complementary institutions which were 'integrated into the state machinery by virtue of their pursuit of similar or related goals and ideals' (see Agovi 1995). Such institutions were made to owe allegiance to a common body of ideas and values that gave rise to a sense of humanism in African society. Artistic forms were well placed to undertake this task because they had an intellectual content. Themes of immediate philosophical, religious or social significance were always consciously made the intellectual basis of each performance (Nketia 1964: 57–62). Moreover, the practitioners of the arts themselves, poets, singers, rhetoricians, dancers and composers, enjoyed an enormous reputation as a class of intellectuals, who were respected for their wisdom and profound thought. According to Kwame Gyekye, such people in Akan society, for example, were not only creators but *onyansafo*, 'wise men/women' or *odwendwenfo*, 'thinkers'; they were considered to have the ability and the disposition for creating or originating philosophical ideas (1975, 1978). The institution of the arts became the data bank of the society's sense of humanism and it ensured that all the fundamental institutions in the society owed a common allegiance to it. The foregoing considerations are relevant to my examination of the *avudwene* as an instrument of political definition in Nzema society.

BACKGROUND OF THE *AVUDWENE*

Bosman seems to have been particularly impressed by its songs, as he writes in his account of the Kundum festival he witnessed in 1704:

a perfect liberty is allowed and scandal so highly exalted, that they may [the artists] freely sing of all the faults, villainies and frauds of their superiors as well as inferiors, without punishment or so much as the least interruption; and the only way to stop their mouth is to ply them lustily with drink, which alters their tone immediately, and turns their satirical ballads into commendatory songs on the good qualities of him who hath so nobly treated them. (1967: 158)

Bosman's description of the songs is still valid today in every detail except that, during the actual performance, drinks are not used to 'alter the tone of the singers'. As we shall see, the nature of the event does not admit of any kind of influence or intervention in the course of the performance.

Bosman also notes that the government of the Nzema country consisted of two parts, 'the body of Caboceroes, or chief men', and 'the Manceroes or young men', and that while the former were vested with 'small power', the class of young men seemed to wield actual power in state affairs (1967: 162). Meredith writes, in the early nineteenth century, that, 'the whole [Nzema] country is vested with the king ... his power is absolute' (Meredith 1967: 27). But according to the oral traditions of the people, even during the reign of their most dictatorial king, Kaku Ackah (1833–51), the basic constitutional power of the 'chief men' and 'young men' remained unchanged. It is important to note in this regard that the creators and performers of the *avudwene* are recruited from the ranks of the young men. In fact, during the performance of the *avudwene*, these young men sing the songs with a certain consciousness of their power as 'the young men' of the society. In almost every song, there are constant references to the singers as the young men who are called together by the ancestors and entrusted with their messages to the society of the living. The power enjoyed by the *avudwene* performers in the course of performance has, therefore, a political and religious base, which contributes greatly to their sense of moral assertiveness and apparent postures of self-righteousness.

THE CREATORS OF THE AVUDWENE

The creation and performance of the *avudwene* depends on three related categories of artists: the *ezomenlema*, the *kodokuma* and the *awuakama*. According to Asua Ngema of Bonyere, 'the people who compose the subject matter of the songs [the *ezomenlema*] tell us [the *kodokuma*], and we in turn tell it to the *awuakama* or teach them'. Each category of artist is very clear about its role in the process of creation and enactment, but each is also aware that his role is meaningful only in the context of co-operation with the others. There is therefore a healthy spirit of mutual co-operation and respect among poet, cantor and singer, based strictly on each artist's talent and contribution to the total process of creating and transmitting the *avudwene*: the *ezomenle* originates the poems, the *kodokuma* rearrange and set them to music and the *awuakama* perform them.

As their name suggests, the *ezomenlema* are the 'silent rememberers' of the society. They are 'poet-intellectuals', gifted with a profound knowledge of the language, history, psychology and value system of the culture, and are regarded as custodians of the 'original' Nzema language, and the 'inheritors' of the collective wisdom of the ancestors. They are highly respected for their knowledge of men and events, and their linguistic competence. Their primary function is to 'remember' events and people, then, in the 'silence' of their thoughts and hearts, 'weave' the *avudwene* songs (*be sinla avudwene*). 'As the year draws near', says Komenle Ndabia, a renowned *ezomenle* of Adoabo, 'I keep thinking of the subjects about which to compose the songs. I begin to think of the songs along the patterns I have been taught by the old men. Then I think of the changes and replacements.'[2]

As is the case with poets generally, the *ezomenle* goes about with his eyes and ears open, alert and sensitive to the pulse of his society. It is normal for individuals to offer information, ideas or themes for specific songs to be composed. If these individuals' ideas are used, the composers name them and give them credit in the songs. But the *ezomenle* is ultimately responsible for the creation of the songs, because he is the one who arranges the proffered material in a coherent form, selects the appropriate creative idiom and provides the apt social or historical frame of reference. Since he does not take part in the actualisation of the songs, the *ezomenle*'s creativity is of a special kind: whether information, ideas and themes are volunteered or not, it is his sole responsibility to give form and meaning to otherwise disparate material for communication with his public.

The *dawuasivoma* 'those who "pitch" songs' or *kodokuma* 'owners of "bag secrets"' are poet-cantors, who mediate between the 'silent rememberer' (*ezomenle*) and the *awuakama*. They receive the songs from the *ezomenle*, and proceed to set them to a music rhythm. They rearrange the words in accordance with a fixed form or structure which makes it easy to remember and articulate in a flowing and uninterrupted manner. In setting the words to music, great care is taken not to change meaning or alter the original words. A great deal of imagination is also needed to formulate the songs into chorus and response patterns, and to introduce usages which will retain the interest and attention of the audience. The poet-cantor is not expected to improvise in this process, but he must have the ability to convey total meaning in a recognised and memorable form.

After the poet-cantors have created the 'new form', they teach it to the *awuakama* during the rehearsal or *sienu* period. They maintain discipline and ensure that the group attains an acceptable standard of voice articulation in their interpretation of the songs. Subsequently, the poet-cantors direct and produce the entire public performance; they thus act as stage managers, regulating the utterances, gestures and movements of the *awuakama*. They 'pitch' themselves in front of the songsters and recite each song line by line as a guide for the *awuakama* to follow.

It is believed that these poet-cantors are the guardians of the 'bag' which contains all the 'secrets' embodied in the songs performed in public, hence their name, *kodokuma*. The term *kodokuma* also defines the role of these artists and, to some extent, conditions their relationship to the performance as cantors. Similarly the names *ekpunlibaka* 'group stick' and *awuakama* 'survivors of the dead', which are used to describe the songsters, reveal the latter's relationship to the activity they perform. Since they are held together by means of a 'group stick', the name *ekpunlibaka* suggests the unity of purpose and the common voice with which they dramatise the ancestral wisdom of the songs. Their verbal actions, gestures, facial expressions and body movements are all co-ordinated to express the content of the *avudwene* songs and emphasise ideals of morality and virtue.

Awuakama membership is open to all males who are willing to learn the songs. Since vacancies are limited, prospective candidates are subjected to an audition conducted by the poet-cantors. According to Komenle Ndabia, *ezomenle* of Adoabo, 'if one has a good voice, we accept him. But what matters most is one's ability to learn and pronounce the words distinctly. If a person has difficulty in pronouncing the words distinctly, he is asked to back out and he is immediately replaced.' And in Beyin I was categorically told that 'voice quality' alone did not count, 'We listen to the content of the songs. If a person is able to verbalise clearly the ideas in the song, we take him. Even if you have a beautiful voice and you can't enunciate the words properly, we shall dismiss you.'[3] In effect therefore, a songster remains a member of the group only as long as he is able to understand and remember the words of the songs in addition to enunciating them clearly. The emphasis on clear enunciation rather than on quality of voice is important because the *avudwene* is designed to be listened to and heard properly, hence the importance of delivery.

THEMES OF THE *AVUDWENE*

All the informants interviewed during fieldwork agreed that the *avudwene* is primarily a means of social commentary. In its broadest sense, it evaluates and interprets significant values, traditions and circumstances of the society from year to year; but it is also expected to be an instrument for providing a critique of individuals, groups and institutions within the society. According to Asua Ngema:

Some of the songs advise, some concern what things people ought not to do, others direct our attention to things done during the year. Some of the songs also tell of the history of the Kundum itself, remembering those who were once with us but are gone and the lessons that are derived from their exemplary behaviour. We are also inspired by our desire to derive some good examples from the songs for our own lives in the world. (Asua Ngema, personal communication)

In Adoabo, poet-cantor Akesson said, 'through the *avudwene* we are able to tell people of their bad deeds which otherwise could not be told them in the face, so that when they feel disgraced in public they will put a stop to it'.[4] J. K. Quaw, another poet-cantor from Ezinlibo addressed the psychological dimension. 'Things change. It is like a thief and prison. The emotional tension of being in prison is a deterrent to those who have experienced prison conditions.'[5] However, because of the sensitive nature of public criticism and the wide range of interests expressed in the *avudwene*, its language is consciously designed to effect a certain distancing from the immediate emotional situation of the performance. Hence the songs are heavily allusive. When the song is critical of society, persons and institutions, the poet uses the technique of indirect reference to great effect. Much of the allusive quality of the *avudwene* is therefore derived from a combination of proverbs, allegory and imagery. 'In the olden days', laments a poet-cantor, 'we used to flood our songs with a wide range of proverbs, allegory and concrete imagery. The use of language was rich, but nowadays, the youth do not understand classic Nzema, so we try to explain in the songs. Otherwise, our songs are always full of proverbs.'[6]

Proverbs in the *avudwene* are not only referential, they also encapsulate thought and emotion in a vividly synthesised and pithy form. In addition they extend the scope of the verbal action by evoking a wealth of meaning and association well beyond the immediate confines of the performance. This feature of the songs is greatly exploited as the poet expatiates on principles through which political action and governance are judged during the performance.

AUTHORITY TO PERFORM

The *avudwene* is concerned with weighty matters of history, politics and social conflict. This fact leads one to believe that the complex burden put on its form demands credibility and authority for a totally successful performance. The artists are fully aware of this and take care in trying to convince the public that their songs tell nothing but the truth and that they, as artists, are non-partisan messengers. The following lines are in fact a standard formula that prefaces each major theme of the *avudwene*:

In the beginning, at the time of creation, there were wise men in the land. They called us together and sat us down. They said to us, 'listen to our words'.

In this brief introduction the performers identify themselves as recipients of the ancient wisdom of the land. Such wisdom is perceived as being central to the tradition handed down to them directly by the ancestors:

When our ancestors of old invoked this proverb, they left it to posterity. They said, 'when a bird's feather falls off another grows in its place'. Thus they blessed the torch and handed it over to us. Then they told us – the ancestors told us, the youth – to listen again, 'may this torch be yours forever. If you are guided by it, you shall be forever blessed'.[7]

As the bearers of the 'torch of posterity', the performers have no need to lie; they have no need to be afraid or be partisan in pursuit of temporary interests. Their allegiance is solely to the truth, or knowledge of the truth, as we find in the following song collected in 1989 in Ezinlibo:

We will wear our hat to the public square and sing our songs; bastard deeds and historical truth we will reveal; we will do so in proverbial wisdom so that all and sundry may learn from it; so that gossip and hearsay may cease to hold sway. Thus are you forewarned!

In addition, the songsters are very careful in establishing evidence and facts as the basis of their criticism. Targets of insult are named in the texts, and the reason for the attack is outlined and the sources of the information are acknowledged. At the end of each song, the songsters always attest to the veracity of the testimony by swearing on either a known deity, a mythical figure or ancestor: 'May the public listen to what we say. Our witness to all this – today is Thursday – is Kaome Koasi, the ancient grindstone of Nawule!' So important is the need to establish credibility, authority and allegiance to a superior power that no song is performed that does not reveal all of these attributes. The cumulative effect of all this is a performance in which fearlessness, frankness and openness in dealing with weighty matters are very important. The artists create the impression that they are not obligated to any constituted authority or to any power lower than the combined authority of the ancestors and the wise men of the land.

POLITICS OF GOOD GOVERNANCE

A direct concern with political matters relating to the problem of 'good governance' is a major preoccupation of the *avudwene*. As Judith van Allen argues, the handling of political matters requires a 'system in which public policy is made publicly and the relevant knowledge is shared widely'; in another sense, it entails the 'settling of questions that concern the welfare of the community in a public way [and therefore] necessitates the sharing of "political knowledge" – the knowledge needed for participation in political discussion and decisions' (1987: 64). Accordingly, the deeds of rulers are brought into the open forum of the songs and examined in order to determine the extent to which they promote the people's collective aspirations for stability, peace and orderly development. Good governance, from the point of view of the Nzema, is the orderly organisation of government to respond effectively to the people's aspirations. This, in effect, means that the people have clear notions of what is an orderly, effective and organised government. They also have clear ideas about what constitutes their collective aspirations. The constant juxtaposition of these two perspectives in the songs informs the politics of good governance in the *avudwene*.

Indeed, the interplay of these aspects in the *avudwene* takes place against a background of publicly acknowledged principles of political conduct. Principles of leadership, the uses and abuses of power and the relationship between ruler and the ruled are constantly evoked as a measure of good government. In this regard, no state official, institution or political action is ever deemed to be above scrutiny. There is no attempt to 'cover up' or rationalise away political shortcomings from any quarter, as we find in the following texts:

> We are certain of what we say
> In their naivety, the people of Ananze[8]
> have behaved like fools;
> they have chosen a nincompoop
> and entrusted him with power.
> That is why they are suffering for it,
> May the public listen carefully
> to what we say.[9]

> Come out, come out, our chief,
> may you come into the open,
> if you are still a living being.
> This town is dead,
> a town where there is no leader,
> Busua town has no leader,
> so this town is dead,
> this town is dead.
> Busua town has no leader,
> so this town is dead.[10]

The targets of criticism in the two texts are fairly obvious. The first text is an attack on the people of Nzema for selecting a ruler who is anything but wise and effective. Similarly in the second text, the Omanhene of Busua is accused of providing no leadership to the state. The irony of a living chief whose town is dead for lack of leadership is particularly scathing. In each case, however, accusations are levelled with certain assumptions in mind. In the first text the political assumption is that power should go with responsible leadership. Accordingly, those who select fools for leaders are bound to suffer for it. In much the same way, the second text suggests that a weak leader gives rise to a weak state. The personality of a state is defined by the strength of its leadership. That is why it is often said that, 'a town does not live with the chief, it is the chief who lives with the town'. These assumptions or principles are not stated but emerge by means of implication.

In another text collected in Bonyere, the chief of Ezinlibo[11] is portrayed as an imbecile:

> Why do you do what no one
> else would dream of doing?
> When our elders of old
> created this proverb they left
> it to posterity. They said,
> 'One cannot build a town
> on the loyalty of strangers.'
> Can you pretend not to know of
> this, Koasi? You have barricaded
> yourself with strangers like a
> fortification of snares . . .
> The downfall of Ezinli[12] town
> is all your fault, Afum Koasi;[13]
> all the cement blocks already
> cast are lying idle and decaying.
> This has greatly displeased the men
> of Ezinli. Who does not see it?

Because of coconut trees
all the buildings we have planned
remain a dream.

Eventually, when complaints from the citizens become too loud for
comfort, the chief is summoned to Kumasi by his head of family who
lives there:

Apaso[14]told Afum Koasi,
'Listen to me. I have heard
of all your misdeeds at Abelamo,
that is why I called you here.
The elders of the land have created
this proverb and left it to posterity.
They said, "A child may skin the snail
but not the shell of the tortoise."
You have made coconut trees
a thing of value: as soon as
you buy some of it, you
acquire the land on it.
May the public listen to what
we say. And this is the
place where you build your house.'[15]

This apparently simple narrative tells the story of a chief at variance
with his people. He exchanges state land for a project that clearly does
not represent a priority item for his people. He is, therefore, out of
touch with his people's aspirations. As I remember, in the course of
this particular song, there was intermittent applause from the audience.
At the end of it, there were prolonged cheers of acclamation. Indeed, at
the time in 1976, the subject-matter of the song was a particularly
sensitive one. By virtue of their wealth and connections, some
well-known individuals had virtually appropriated most of the arable
land in the area and turned it into large-scale coconut plantations
(coconut remains the most significant economic crop in Nzema). The
result was that overnight, food crops such as cassava, plantain,
cocoyam, corn and other items either vanished or became scarce and
expensive in the market. There was general apprehension concerning
an imminent famine in the society. Thus when this situation was
evoked in the song, there were cheers of instant approval from the
crowd. Some of them clapped or gave out money while others shouted:
Ngya mo, ngya mo, 'Our men, thank you, thank you'. These were all
gestures of appreciation based on opinions shared by the audience.

These indicators of audience–performer rapport in the performance mark the effectiveness of the *avudwene* as an outlet for the shaping of public opinion on policy and political action in Nzema society.

While the story is told in a straightforward narrative, other issues are raised in the form of proverbs. The first proverb questions the propriety of a ruler who builds his town 'on the loyalty of strangers'. The proverb is intended to raise the problem of popular participation in governance. Can a ruler afford to ignore participation of his own citizens in the affairs of state? The consequence of such an example of poor governance is captured in the second proverb: by surrounding himself with strangers, the chief has excluded his own citizens and thus entrapped himself in a 'fortification of snares'. The chief has cut himself off from his people; he can neither go to them nor will his people come to him for fear of falling prey to the snares. There is, therefore, total alienation between the ruler and the ruled. To warn against such a situation, the third proverb prescribes that 'a child may skin the snail but not the shell of a tortoise', an apt description of how a chief's power is limited by the sovereign will of his people, like a child's *vis-à-vis* his father's.

These concerns of the poem are thus brought out by two corresponding language structures, a narrative structure and a proverbial structure. The latter is intended to reinforce the former. While the narrative structure tells a simple story without distraction, the proverbial structure advances an argument and engages the mind in a debate. From one proverb to the other, one notices a logical relationship being developed between the proverbs, which corresponds to the flow of an argument. Political ideas and principles are formulated through this proverb structure. In the end, the two language structures are fused together to present one coherent picture of reality.

When the offence is grievous, the language of the songs tends to be more direct, declarative and aggressive:

> Useless chiefs, you have
> done well in this realm;
> You promised to create a stable society.
> Instead, we have become slaves to your misrule.
> May the public listen to our story;
> while they offer us a helping hand
> they drag us in the mud as well.
> We are determined to install
> educated chiefs so that we benefit

from their vision, but our trust and
confidence have been misplaced.
As soon as the chiefs tasted *kutuku*[16]
they made it their eternal inheritance.
That is why you don't see
any meat when you skin
konglobesa, the small inedible crab.
May the public listen well
to our word.[17]

Once again, proverbial statement is used to seal the main point of view
of the song. The image of a crab without any meat buttresses the view
that there is nothing to the bad chiefs; they are useless and have
nothing to offer by way of leadership. The draining effect of alcohol,
emptying the chiefs of any strength of vision or leadership, is
concretised also in the image of the crab as an empty living shell.
Because of their addiction to material things symbolised by the
kutuku, the chiefs lose their sense of balance and their sense of
spiritual vision. This critique of corrupt and ineffective leadership is
reiterated in the song below:

It has been said that people show
courtesy to chiefs out of respect;
we agreed to respect your office
in anticipation of exemplary leadership.
In this alone, we knew what we were doing.
You have done well,
Koasi Amakyi[18] the imbecile,
you have done well in this state.
Since you have put on
a fool's carrying-pad, you will
always carry a fool's burden!
May the public listen to what we say;
our ancestors invoked this proverb
and left it to posterity. They said:
'If you ensnare gossip, you trap litigation.'
The backwardness of Nzema
is all your fault, Koasi Amakyi.
It was in earnest when it was said
that truth is an eternal tree.
Since you abhor the truth,
we are suffering for your misdeeds . . .
Because you only pursue the purse,
you have created your own chiefs . . .
Truly, Koasi Amakyi,
you have done well in the state;

> may you uphold the truth this year
> so that we have peace again.[19]

As in other instances, the story line argues that the king abhors the truth, he is in love with the purse, a symbol of addiction to material things. He is, therefore, no longer in a position to provide the expected 'exemplary leadership'. He is advised to uphold the truth so that peace may reign in his kingdom. The central issue of principle, the fact that in politics as in life, one always reaps what one sows, is highlighted through the network of proverbs in the text. Related to this point is another consideration: is such a king entitled to obedience and respect? Indeed, at what point does he forfeit respect and loyalty? The answer to these questions is provided in the text through the process of proverb discourse and analysis. The immediate effect is that several points of view are brought into play. In the above extract, we have the points of view of the performers, the public, protagonists and the points of view of tradition, so that one is not merely confronted with a simple understanding of the situation. The listener is able to explore the implications of all these points of view.

A KING IS NOT ABOVE INSULT

A general view of traditional African political practice has been that a king is above insult but not above being disagreed with. In all the texts examined in the Nzema case there is both insult and disagreement, very often violent, with those in authority. In addition, there is noticeable anger in the unrestrained manner in which disagreement is often expressed. Epithets such as 'fool', 'nincompoop', 'useless' and 'imbecile' abound in texts where they are freely hurled at those in authority. All of these carry decided impressions of insult. However, there is also an indication that, as far as issues of governance are concerned, the language of insult is deliberate. The spirited candour with which political issues are treated emphasises that no matter how much power and authority a political figure may wield, he is certainly 'not above being disagreed with'.

The *avudwene* performance raises into an act of principle the freedom to disagree. The spirit of candour in the performance seeks to drive home the lesson that freedom of expression is a right that ought to be cherished as a necessary condition for good governance. So, in the course of the performance, when freedom of expression is advocated, the poet uses powerful language to demonstrate that it is a right which transcends temporary restrictions. One cannot fail to be struck by the relish and ardour with which this right is exercised during the brief period of the performance. Paramount chiefs and other political figures are deliberately subjected to relentless attack, criticism and insult in order to drive home the value of openness. What we have in the *avudwene*, therefore, is not just a catalogue of gratuitous insults arising from the simple fact that the occasion demands and guarantees immunity. Rather there is a conscious attempt to raise insult into a serving instrument of public policy.

The *avudwene*, in effect, constitutes a public forum at which both rulers and ruled are brought together to deliberate, consciously, on issues of governance. The people allow the performers to represent their interests at this assembly because they are aware that their opinion will be voiced. The process of collating information for the performance, as already indicated, ensures a deep-seated level of public involvement. Moreover, the creators of the *avudwene* enjoy credibility as thinkers for their society, creative people whose mediating role rests on their ability to offer leadership in originating ideas, insight and principle. Such performers do not go into the arena merely to articulate 'repressed feelings' on behalf of the general public (Piersen 1976: 167–8); they perform in full knowledge of the political aspirations and priorities of their people and with a mandate to argue their case. Words such as *ndene*, 'dispute/disputation', and *anee*, 'story/defence', occur constantly in standard refrains such as: 'May the public listen to our story/defence.' These refrains are reinforced by a verbal array of facts, evidence and 'witnesses' (Agovi 1979: 245–77). Moreover, the singers conduct their case in accordance with familiar legal and political principles. Thus it is in the context of a semblance of a court or palace procedure that the deliberative discourse of the performance is carried out.

As we have also seen, the main issues are issues of governance. There are discourses on leadership, on sovereignty and power, and on the place of consent in political relations. There are issues of freedom of expression, openness, accountability and probity as understood by the Nzema. Such serious concerns are expressed on behalf of society in the shared belief that public interest, and not the narrow interests of some constituted political authority, provides the main impetus for the performance always. Indeed, to quote Mazisi Kunene once more, the poets and singers of the *avudwene* are, in this regard, true 'democratic agents' through whom criticism and evaluation of Nzema rulers are 'fully and freely expressed'.

NOTES

1 Rattray specifically refers to Bosman's accounts of the festival, and relying on aspects of Nzema oral tradition, comes to the firm conclusion that the Kundum festival is descended from the Apoo of Tekyiman in the Brong-Ahafo Region of Ghana. While the broad motivation and orientation of both festivals may be the same, the forms they take are different. For example, the concept of organisation and performance of verbal insult in the Kundum is radically different from what obtains in the Apoo festival.

2 Komenle Ndabia, *ezomenle* of Adoabo, personal communication.

3 Amanzule Kese, *tufuhene* of Beyin, personal communication.

4 I. G. B. Akesson, poet-cantor, personal communication.

5 J. K. Quaw, poet-cantor, personal communication, Ezinlibo.

6 J. K. Quaw, personal communication.

7 Text collected from the Adoabo *awuakama* group on 25 October 1976.

8 The old name of the Nzema state, it exists now only in poetic texts.

9 Collected from Adoabo, 25 October 1976. It was sung to chastise the late Omanhene of Western Nzema, Awulae Kwasi Amakye II.

10 Collected from Busua, the traditional capital of the Ahanta state in the Western region of Ghana. It was sung at the palace in the hearing of the Omanhene, Nana Baidoe Bonsoe XV, 26 August 1976.

11 Ezinlibo and Bonyere maintain two separate corps of performers, poet-cantors and poets. During the Kundum festival the group from Bonyere visits Ezinlibo to perform on a Thursday, and the following day, Friday, the other group from Ezinlibo goes to Bonyere to 'reply' to the songs of insult from the Bonyere group.

12 This is the shortened form of Ezinlibo town.

13 The name of the present chief of Ezinlibo town who was the target of this vilification.

14 Apaso is the name of the Head of Family of Chief Afum Koasi.

15 Text performed by the Bonyere group, 28 October 1976.

16 The name of the local alcoholic beverage brewed from the wine of the raffia palm.

17 Sung by the Bonyere group, 28 October 1976.

18 Name of the late Omanhene of the western Nzema State with its traditional capital in Beyin.

19 Bonyere group, 28 October 1976.

· PART II ·

Representing power relations

· CHAPTER 5 ·

Ìgbò énwē ézè: *monarchical power versus democratic values in Igbo oral narratives*

Chukwuma Azuonye

The Igbo people of south-eastern Nigeria are well known to history and the social sciences for the democratic and republican character of their social organisation (see Basden 1921; Leith-Ross 1939; Green 1948; Ejiofor 1981). The saying, *Ìgbò énwē ézè* 'the Igbo have no kings', which appears in the title of this chapter, epitomises this ethos. The saying is perhaps not a denial of the presence of 'kings' (*ézè*) or types of leaders who go by that title in the Igbo social system, now or in the past. Indeed, the linguistic, literary and archaeological evidence before us suggests very strongly that both the institution and the title of *ézè* have been part of the Igbo experience from remote antiquity and that, despite what appears to have been a far-reaching transformation of the institution and title over the years in favour of a democratic ethos, royalty (in the sense of the majesty of the king as an embodiment of sovereign power) has remained one of the most highly cherished values in Igbo thought in a situation in which monarchy (in the sense of the monopoly of power by one man or one family) is viewed as anathema. It would, therefore, appear that the saying, *Ìgbò énwē ézè*, is better translated as 'The Igbo abhor monarchical power'.

The present chapter has grown out of the discovery that folktales appear to be among the most powerful of the numerous forms of traditional artistic expression in Igbo culture which reflect and serve to perpetuate this fascinating tension between monarchical power and democratic values. In both the two major categories of Igbo folktales – fictional tales, *ákúkó-àlà*, literally 'tales of the land', and historical tales, *ákúkó-ífó*, literally 'tales of the imagination' – we are again and again confronted with two diametrically opposed images of actants who go by the title of *ézè*. At one end of the pole is the ideal *ézè* who personifies royalty and reigns by deferring to communal consensus while at the other end of the pole is the deviant *ézè* who personifies monarchy and who, because he epitomises the abuse of power in all its

65

aspects, is in the end tamed, or as Okoh (personal communication) has put it, 'humiliated, deposed or beheaded'.

One tale that captures these paradigmatic contrasts between royalty and monarchy and to which I refer in this chapter is a type that might be called 'The taming of the cruel king'. In one telling of this well-known tale, entitled 'Àkàánụ̀, ọ́kpárá Ọ̄bā àlá Ìdúù', ('Akaanu, son of the Oba of Ìdúù') (Iwe 1963: 41–8), an ideal king is succeeded by a cruel king who is either ignorant of, or chooses to ignore, the democratic values of his people. He marginalises the traditional council of chiefs and elders and the entire populace and imposes mindlessly cruel laws on the people. In the face of resistance spearheaded by a pauper who gains the support of the elders and the entire populace, the cruel king gets lost while riding in a forest and in the course of his wanderings is enslaved and put through worse sufferings than those imposed by his sadistic rule on the people. In the end, he returns to his kingdom, wiser, more humane, and more attentive to the rule of law and the voice of the people. Through the taming of the cruel king, the democratic ideal is reasserted against the autocratic claims of deviant monarchical power.

Within the limits imposed by the filters discussed in the last section of the chapter, it is assumed throughout that folktales, irrespective of their sources, are a true reflection of aspects of the life, culture and history of the society in which they flourish. But to see the power play in Igbo folktales in its proper perspective, it is necessary to give a brief account of relevant aspects of the institution of *ézè* in Igbo culture and history before the presentation and analysis of the tales themselves. The analysis of the tales suggests that what is reflected in them is not reality in the raw but reality passed through certain filters of communal interests in order to distil 'a myth to live by'. By and large, the essay is conceived, not only as a study of the power relations as reflected in oral literature, but of the power of oral literature to sustain, through the dynamic process of mythic filtering, a particular type of social ideology against the claims of rival or contending ideologies.

THE INSTITUTION OF *ÉZÈ* IN IGBO CULTURE AND HISTORY

The term *ézè*, commonly glossed in the literature as 'king', 'chief', 'chieftain', 'ruler', 'headman' or, more generally, 'leader' in any field of human activity (see Thomas 1914, IV: 192; Basden 1921: 255–6;

Onwuejeogwu 1981: 84; Ejiofor 1981: 157; Ifemesia n.d.: 39–40; Ebeogu 1989: 84; Chukwuma 1990: 8–10; among others), seems to derive from the verb root *–ze–* 'fear; defer to; avoid; revere'. Basically, therefore, *ézè* means 'one who is feared, deferred to, avoided, or revered'. But there is a qualification here. The fear of the *ézè* is contingent upon his achieved position, power or other significant personal attributes which set him apart from other men. In this sense, the connotations of *ézè* include expertise, professionalism and, above all, heroism. Cognate terms in the language, include *ǹzè* 'lord; titled man; chieftain; or member of the traditional elite' and *ǹzèrè* 'respectability, venerable status, dignity associated with a fulfilled life', as defined in Nwoga (1983). *Ézè* itself seems to have originally referred to a ritual head or chief priest – a person who, by reason of his closeness to the gods, spirits, and other supernatural powers or because he was believed to be a repository of the collective life-force of the community, was held in great reverence. The title is still used in this sense when referring to the chief priests of various deities. Well-known examples from the novels of Chinua Achebe include Ézē-Ànị (chief priest of the earth-goddess, Ànị) in *Things Fall Apart* (1958) and Ézè-Úlù (chief priest of the communal deity, Úlù) in *Arrow of God* (1964). In contemporary local politics and administration, the title has come to be reserved for traditional or so-called 'natural' rulers who derive their legitimacy from being direct descendants of the putative ancestors of their communities as opposed to three major categories of non-traditional rulers in the Igbo experience, namely warrant chiefs, money chiefs and honorary chiefs. The warrant chiefs (see Afigbo 1972) are a very recent phenomenon. Called into being by the British colonial government during the first quarter of the century, as part of their system of indirect rule and on the mistaken or mischievous assumption that Africans are best governed under some kind of centralised and authoritarian system, they were recruited mainly from among outcasts, slaves, ne'er-do-wells and dissidents in the traditional society since it proved difficult for the alien power to recruit from among the traditional elite. The warrant chiefs, therefore, represent a subversion of the traditional social order. The so-called money chiefs, on the other hand, are symptomatic of a process of decay in the institution of *ézè* which appears to have been going for some generations before Igbo contacts with the British. They are men or women of means on whom chieftaincy titles or positions have been awarded for hard cash by cash-starved or avaricious *ézè*. It would appear that the phenomenon of 'money chieftaincy titles' has existed since the first quarter of this century, and it appears to have been sufficiently problematic even at that time to have elicited the following comments from Basden (1921: 256): 'In modern times the dignity of the chieftainship has been degraded and the tendency is to bring the whole system into disrepute, owing to the indiscriminate sale of titles to any youth who can produce the stipulated fees.' The honorary chiefs are closely related to the money chiefs, but they owe their titles not to money or payoffs to an *ézè* but to their influential social positions or remarkable personal achievements. In recent years, however, honorary chieftaincy titles have habitually been awarded to political office holders by many an *ézè* in the hope of some preferments.

By and large, the *ézè* occupies, not the apex of a hierarchical social order (as is suggested by the title, *Ígwē*, which implies 'the one with the gods who dwell in the sky'), but the centre or heart of a closely woven social system (as suggested by the title, *Òbí*, which implies 'the one who occupies or represents the centre'), surrounded by an inner council of *ǹzè* or minor *ézè*, with the populace occupying the outer fringes of the circle but operating within the same egalitarian and republican order in which the possibility of movement into and out of the inner circles or the centre itself is never foreclosed. Thus, as Basden (1921: 255–6) has observed: 'It is the ambition of every free-born youth to rise to chieftainship and in this democratic country the highest honours are open to every freeman equally.' But, inasmuch as the Igbo social system recognises 'the king in every man' (to borrow the phrase from the title of Henderson, 1972), no incumbent *ézè*, if he is true to tradition and not an alien imposition, can afford to rule without the consent of the ruled.

The tales examined in this chapter suggest a clear distinction between the ideal type of *ézè* cherished by Igbo culture and various categories of deviant or alien *ézè* apparently imposed by outside powers or modelled on the kingship institutions of proximate kingdoms and empires, notably the ancient Edo kingdom of Benin which is commonly described in the tales as *Ìdúù* (a term possibly derived from Edo). As Chubb (1961: 6) has rightly observed, 'The main characteristics of the Ibo are marked individuality, self-assertion, adaptability, and *a strong dislike and suspicion of any authority other than their own*' (emphasis added). The last of these characteristics is indeed crucial in appreciating what we shall see presently to be a combatively denigrative image of *Ìdúù* (the Benin kingdom) and its kings (*Ǭbā Ìdúù* or *Ǭbā n'Ìdúù*) in many Igbo folktales. The tales, typified by 'The taming of the cruel king', suggest that the Igbo would have nothing to do with monarchical power of the kind associated with the Benin kings, be it in the form in which it is exercised in the Benin kingdom itself and in the Igbo and other vassal kingdoms under Benin dominion, or in the form in which it exists in those Igbo communities which have at one time or another established themselves as kingdoms modelled on the Benin kingdom. In this sense, the saying, *Ìgbò énwē ézè* would seem to represent a traditionalist rejection of the power and influence of imported types of *ézè* in favour of the people's own democratic institutions.

The true *ézè* of Igbo culture is one bound by taboos or what have been described as 'ritual prohibitions' (Thomas 1914, IV; Onwuejeogwu 1981). Such 'ritual prohibitions' (e.g. those listed for the *Ézē-Nrì* in Thomas 1914, IV and Onwuejeogwu 1981: 52–3) seem to have been deliberately cultivated, not only to restrain the king from tyranny but also to protect his dignity. Thus, the verb-root *–zè–* defines the king not just as one who is to be 'avoided' (feared, revered or deferred to) by reason of the authority and dignity he commands but also as one who is expected to 'avoid' (fear, revere or defer to) a whole range of things in order to be deserving of his authority and dignity. What we have here is probably a ritualised equivalent of the Gallic idea of *noblesse oblige*. In the ideal democratic society of traditional Igbo thought, the consequence of an efficient operation of this system of reciprocal avoidances, deferences and reverence is a kind of tightly knit balance of power which makes for social harmony. As reflected in the tales examined here, the essential basis and outcome of this social harmony is a species of democracy which admits of the centrality of a 'father' figurehead who possesses the outward radiance of a king (royalty) but is in actual fact a *primus inter pares* (Ejiofor 1981: 157) and in some cases a glorified servant or slave of his people. As the saying goes, *Ézè nwé ọ̀hà, ọ̀hà nwé ézè* 'The king owns the people, the people own the king'. By the same token, another palindrome says: *Ézè zèéré ọ̀hà, ọ̀hà ézèéré ézè*, 'As the king defers to the people, so do the people defer to the king'. An *ézè* who keeps within the bounds of the prescribed system of deferences or avoidances in his relationships with his people is sure, by the force of the reciprocal obligations on which Igbo social relationships are founded, to carry his people with him.

THE KING, THE PEOPLE AND POWER RELATIONS IN REPRESENTATIVE IGBO TALE-TYPES

Seen in the light of the expectations of the democratic society, Igbo tales about kings and their exercise of monarchical power fall into the two major categories outlined above. The first, represented by 'The taming of the cruel king', is concerned with the deviant or delinquent *èzè* who operates outside the boundaries of traditional ritual prohibitions. His oppressiveness and folly are resisted and in the end, he is tamed, punished, or disgraced. The second category of tales presents the ideal king, who operates within the boundaries of traditional ritual restrictions and represents in his relations with his people the highest standards of dignity, generosity, honour, truthfulness, justice and, above all, respect for reciprocal obligations. In many instances, tales of the first category, including 'The taming of the cruel king', begin by presenting the ideal king who under external pressure or personal psychological degeneration is transformed into a negative force that must be brought under control.

TALES OF THE DEVIANT *ÈZÈ*

Most of the tales in the first category are set in the ancient Benin kingdom (*Ìdúù*). It would appear from the major thematic patterns of these tales, that somewhere in the course of Igbo–Benin relations, the Benin kings (*Èzè Ìdúù*) came to represent to the Igbo mind the epitome of the much-feared deviation from taboos restricting monarchical power. It is not known for certain when and how these taboos originated, but Achebe has speculated that the Igbo had previously had kings and through a bad experience somewhere in their history had decided they were either not going to have kings again or were going to severely limit their power.

From the Igbo point of view, *Ìdúù* – a proximate power with dominion over parts of Igboland – appears to have developed autocratic kingship patterns which turned it into a major threat to their evolving democratic institutions. Benin historians, like Egharevba (1968) acknowledge the reality of the autocratic excesses of the Benin kings. If this was the kind of bad experience the Igbo once had with their kings, as speculated by Achebe, it seems only natural that every effort should be made by the custodians of Igbo culture to create powerful structures of the intellect and of the imagination to help protect their democratic values from as many potential negative influences as possible. Tales about *Ìdúù* are thus detailed in their gory portraiture of the brutalities of *Èzè Ìdúù* and the humiliation with which he must of necessity be visited in the end by the levelling forces of an uncompromising republicanism.

One of the most representative of the tales in this category is a type which may be called 'The sadistic king'. Described in various local tale-type classifications as 'The narrative of *Ọbá Nkpêzè* (tooth-plucking king)' (Anene-Boyle 1979: 75–84; Okpewho 1985: 36–8) or 'The king of *Àtùmà* and the king of *Ìdúù*' (Iworisha, 1978: 36–38), this tale is in many ways the same as the story of the Isoko epic of *Omofbhon* recorded by Akegwure (1978: 4). In it, the king of *Ìdúù* is a sadist who takes pleasure in forcibly plucking one tooth from one of his vassal kings (in this case, the king of the Igbo state of *Àtùmà*) during each of his festivities. As the cruelty grows in intensity and the vassal king loses most of his teeth, he begets a wonder child who grows up rapidly, equipped with magical powers with which to avenge the wrongs. The sadistic king is not only restrained from unleashing further barbarity, he is dethroned, enslaved with his wife and children and subjected to cruelties similar to those meted out to the avenger's father.

Other tales focus on encounters between the cruel king and his subjects both within *Ìdúù* itself and within its vassal states. In these tales, the king appears as a sadistic taskmaster, a monstrous predator on his own people and an uncompromisingly aristocratic exploiter of the weakness of the marginalised masses. Apart from the motif of the impossible task often set by the king on pain of death in many different tales, it is not uncommon for the king to dream up gargantuan but ultimately useless projects which take a great toll in human life and suffering. The story-within-a-story in 'The endless tale', recorded by Okeke, describes such a project:

Once upon a time there was a king called Ọbā of Idúù. He was very powerful. In fact, he had powers of life and death over his people. The king's *Ògbú-ńgwá-ngwà* 'fast killers', executioners, were ready at all times to do his will. Ọbā of Idúù ordered his subjects to build an extensive grain store with mud walls as high as the tallest Iroko in all the land. For ten years all toiled night and day and the end of the great store was not in sight. Life became very difficult and uninteresting. Men died like fowls, but the work continued. At long last the giant granary was completed. The king then ordered that the granary should be filled to the brim with grains and maize. This took much more time than building the great store. (1971: 85–6)

In some cases, over-concentration on the king's sadism leads to destructive digression – a narrative that begins with the opening formulae of tale decomposes into an oral essay on tyranny and oppression. A typical example is contained in Ogbalu:

Once upon a time in a country called Iduu, a great king named Igwekaala reigned. All the surrounding countries were greatly afraid of this king. The kings of these countries were afraid of the great king because he was more powerful than them all and had a large army of ferocious soldiers. It was with the decrees given by Igwekaala, the king of Iduu, that all these countries were governed. It was also only those selected by the great king that could reign as kings in all the nations surrounding Iduu. All the able-bodied men that lived in that country worked for Igwekaala once every month so as to be able to live in peace. (1974: 219–20)

At this point, Ogbalu, the Christian evangelist, takes over from Ogbalu the folklorist and the story is turned into a sermon against the barbaric customs fostered by the rule of a despotic pagan king! But despite its Christian colouring, the picture that emerges of the king as a monstrous predator who preys on his people is a constant theme in Igbo folktales, a theme which in animal tales assumes wider significance within the framework of an allegorical reconstruction of aspects of culture history. In 'Ágū̀ nà ụ́mụ̀ ánụ́māānụ̀' ('Leopard and other animals') (Iwe 1963: 58–68), King Leopard preys on his subjects and they flee the animal kingdom, leaving the predatory king and his family to face starvation. Shortly after the flight of the animals, the king feigns death and arranges for the animals to be lured back to the kingdom, but the animals are suspicious and send rodents too small to be eaten by leopard to go and survey the ground, but they return with confusing messages suggesting that the king was really dead. The trick is discovered when leopard kills and devours antelope who is sent to confirm the stories of the tiny rodents. In the end, tortoise succeeds in tricking the king to his death. Through this triumph of the intellect over brute force, tortoise eventually arrives at a riverside where he succeeds in dispersing a community of snakes under King Python, becoming king of the riverside.

Leopard is not only a symbol of the predatory king of the law-of-the-jungle situation of the very early stages of human evolution, he is also a symbol of the aristocratic arrogance and exploitativeness of the feudal systems of the supposedly more civilised stages of the evolution of human social institutions. In 'Leopard and goat':

All the animals and men are making farms. Leopard goes to where goat has cleared the ground for a farm and says, 'This is the place where I came the other day and said I would make a farm; perhaps, Òlìsè (God) has had mercy and cleared the ground for me, working a little while and going away.' At dawn, goat comes to the place and sees that someone has planted crops in the middle of it and says: 'O, what luck I have; who else can claim that Òséb[ū]ùwà (Lord of the sky) ever worked for him in this world? Aha! Òlìsà who does what puzzles men, thank you because of the work which you did for me.' At dawn, leopard comes and is full of joy and declares: 'Oko! Chúkwú ('God of Light' as popularised by Christianity) loves me too much; he has worked for me again and brought and planted yams.' When dawn comes again, goat comes and says: 'O, it's Òséb[ū]ùwà that plants yams and goes away.'

Three days later, leopard and his people and goat and his people all come together to the farm and leopard is quick to say to goat, 'What do you want in my farm?' And goat bleats, 'Ma! When one is bigger he takes things for nothing.' And they quarrelled, and leopard took hold of goat and killed him; and the kids ran away, and that is why if a goat sees the leopard, he runs away. (Adapted from Thomas 1914, IV: 90)

Here again, as in some of the tales discussed above, the aetiological conclusion is hardly germane to the story. The real conflict in the story is that between the complacent and powerful aristocracy which presumes absolute ownership of all for nothing and the poor, hard-working masses with simple faith in the providence of God who are frustrated by the naked power and arrogance of the aristocracy. Conflicts of this kind can be seen in many tale-types from the *Ìdúù* corpus, confirming our allegorical interpretation of the tale.

The motif of the great suffering which awaits the king who fails to avoid certain kinds of behaviour informs 'The king who desires to experience suffering', the second part of 'The taming of the cruel king' which exists as an independent tale-type. Once upon a time, a prosperous *ézè*, feeling a strong desire to experience suffering, consults a *díbìà áfā*, 'diviner', who instructs him to go and catch a certain kind of bird which always appears to be perched near at hand but keeps hopping away as the seeker seems to be on the verge of catching it. In the *ézè*'s attempt to catch this bird, he is struck by the wander-leaf (*ákwúkwó-ǹjù-óhīā*) and wanders off into a faraway land, remote from his kingdom, where, unrecognised as *ézè*, he is forced to eke out a living by begging, slave-labour and other kinds of strenuous menial services. In the course of these, he experiences suffering to the fullest, bearing through the pangs of starvation, the humiliation of penury and of different kinds of abuse. In the end, he wanders back home unrecognised to his own kingdom now ruled by a tyrannical usurper. At the palace, he is met with an arrogant indifference, condemned to imprisonment for daring (in his impoverished state) to pretend to be the lost king; but in the end, he is recognised by a birthmark by one of his servants. The tyrannical usurper is dethroned by the loyal servants and legitimacy, sobered by the experience of the lot of the marginalised masses, is restored as in 'The taming of the cruel king'.

Some other common tale-types comprise materials which seem to have diffused into Igbo culture from far and near through oral reactions to the *Arabian Nights* or Biblical stories. From the popular

Oxford English Readers of the pre-independence years have come tales from African traditional monarchies of East, Central and Southern Africa. Other tales have diffused by oral transmission from the oral traditions of the proximate Igala, Edo, Yoruba and other monarchies. In considering these tales, it is interesting to note how in some tale-types, which in cultures with monarchical traditions present positive images of kingly power, the image of the king is filtered through the Igbo democratic sieve. The tale, 'One beggar trusts God, the other the king' (AT 841) is one such example. In the form popular in Europe and Mexico, which as Thompson (1946: 141) observes derives ultimately from medieval and oriental exempla, 'the two beggars are given loaves of bread by the king, who sees to it that the loaf of the one who trusts him is filled with coal. Ignorant of this, the beggars exchange their loaves and thus show that luck attends the man who trusts God' (p. 142). It is not surprising that this tale-type should be found to be of evangelical value to the early Christian missionaries on the Niger who included an Igbo version of it in their 1860 primer, the first literary work in Igbo to be published. The 1904 version is a typical Christian parable:

Once, there were two brothers. Their mother and father died soon after they were born. One old woman took them and fostered them. When they grew up, one of them decided that he would keep faith with the Oba (king) while the other said that he would keep faith with Chineke (God) who created man.

The one that kept faith with Oba laughed at the one that kept faith with Chukwu, saying, 'Chineke, will he throw down what you will eat from heaven?' But he told him to go away, that he must continue to trust in God.

Everyday, Oba would send food and all manner of good things to that person that trusted in him. After having his fill, he would send the dregs to the person that trusted in God, laughing at him, saying, 'Chineke, does he give you what to eat?'

The person that trusted in God kept quiet; but he persisted in his farmwork, became a well-accomplished man, built up a family of his own, married a wife, begot children and prospered.

But the person that put his trust in the Oba did not know how to farm; there was nowhere he had acquired any skill for any kind of work; he had no family, had no wife, had no money, was unable to do anything. He went on begging for food from house to house until he died.

The lesson is this: trusting in God is better than trusting in Oba no matter how great the Oba may be.

Since the publication of this tale, numerous oral versions have evolved in which the motifs and plots have been varied to fit into the Igbo democratic mythos.

TALES OF THE IDEAL *ÉZÈ*

The tales examined so far stress the qualities which the Igbo find undesirable in the exercise of royal power. The second major category of tales now to be examined specifically contrast such qualities with those deemed to be desirable. They distil the image of the ideal king in a democratic society. Many of these tales are animal tales and as such are allegorical explorations of the theme. In 'The king of birds' (Basden 1921: 280–1), a tiny, self-effacing bird is elected king in preference to a richly adorned but proud, vainglorious and powerful bird with an overbearing manner because of his well-known qualities of amiability, generosity and concern for honourable conduct.

But more than moral probity, intelligence and resourcefulness are frequently stressed in tales as the qualities most treasured in an *ézè*. The achievement-oriented ethos of the Igbo allows for a great deal of machiavellianism and pragmatism: thus immoral conduct may be condoned in a candidate for the position of *ézè* where he displays a capacity for personal achievement through the exercise of the powers of the mind (see, for example, Basden 1921: 257). It is against this background that we can better appreciate the triumph of fraud and deception in most variants of the type 'How the tortoise became the king of animals' (Okwesa 1979: 74–6; Oguine 1974: 191–2, 112–14; Ugochukwu et al. 1977: 191–2). Here, the trickster (tortoise), discovered in the belly of the king's cow which he kills by cutting up its entrails, claims the whole meat for himself. Leopard, the incumbent king of the animals, is detailed to decide the case, but on arriving at the scene, he falls to gustily, eating the flesh and throwing the bones to tortoise and his family whom he covers up with a basket. But soon, tortoise manages to convince leopard that eating too much flesh softens the body while eating a lot of bones gives strength. Frightened at the prospect that tortoise and his family would soon emerge to be stronger than him and his family, leopard begins to deliver the meat to tortoise while he eats the bones. When the rest of the animals reassemble at the scene, they are disgusted by the folly of their king and chase him out of the kingdom. Tortoise is declared king in his stead in appreciation of his intelligence and resourcefulness.

The ideal *ézè* commands the loyalty and respect of his subjects, not by inspiring fear in them but through the display of humane concern for the dignity and worth of every individual no matter how small. Only rarely do we come across the motif of the community 'working for the king' on pain of death (Nwasogwa 1983: 55). Such forced labour would normally provoke the kind of opposition found in 'The taming of the cruel king'. In most tales, the king would normally plead with people to work for him, offering very handsome rewards ranging from cash and yam-seedlings to even his daughter's hand in marriage (Iworisha 1978: 56–8, 87–90; Okwesa 1979: 131–3). In some cases, however, the worthy conduct of the king so impresses the populace that working for him becomes an expression of love and gratitude. In 'Why the tortoise has a checkered shell: I' (Egudu 1973: 37), the conflict is set against the background of a decision among the animals of the forest to contribute money to build a befitting palace for their amiable king.

The requirement that the king must rule by persuasion and not by force does not, however, mean that he is expected to function as a completely powerless figurehead. Many tales do indeed recognise his power and authority but within carefully circumscribed domains within the basic law of communal living (*òménààlà*) under which he must operate. He is often described as *ézè-ná-áchị-òbòdò*, 'the king that rules the community' (Ogbalu 1966: 41); but these appellations are valid only so far as he is portrayed as a custodian and interpreter of the basic law of communal living. For instance, a stranger would normally be taken to him and he may set the conditions for allowing him to reside in the domain. In 'Tortoise and the maize grain' (Ogbalu 1966: 41), the king sets an impossible task for tortoise: wed a beautiful princess with a grain of maize, not for sadistic pleasure as in the case of the cruel king but to ascertain whether the intelligence and resourcefulness of the newcomer is really in consonance with his fame. Tortoise accomplishes the task and in the end, 'The king made him a big man in the domain and gave him land and money' (p. 44). But in the times of emergency, the king can rightly assume the powers of an absolute law-giver so long as the laws enacted are not oppressive or discriminatory and pragmatically solve the problems at hand. In 'The big test' (Umeasiegbu 1969: 72), Chief Nkapi 'Shrew', responding to many reports of murder, enacted a new law that 'no animal had the right to kill another animal' and goes ahead to enforce the law in the case of the pig accused by his wife of killing the duck. In 'A wrestling contest' (Umeasiegbu 1969: 84) a diametrically opposite law is enacted during a great famine. The king organises a series of wrestling competitions with the rule that 'Any competitor that defeats his opponent is free to kill the latter and eat him as food. If, however, the defeated wrestler offers a ransom, he may be released if the victor so wishes.' Emergency powers are of course recognised in all democratic regimes, but in more normal times, as in the emergency situations themselves, the king is expected to administer the existing laws with firmness and fairplay.

By and large, the king not only submits to the democratic principles of his society but also operates as the conscience of his people. In 'Ézè-ènwè' ('The king of monkeys') (Ugochukwu et al. 1977: 151–2), the king of monkeys invites all monkeys in the land to work for him. He shows them a fruit-laden tree under which they would assemble for refreshment at the end of the work. His purpose is to test the morality of the monkeys. But while others are working, six monkeys go secretly in turns and eat up all the fruits. Their guilt is detected through pit-jumping, a form of oath whereby guilty ones fall into a pit while the non-guilty are able to jump over safely. The six guilty monkeys are buried in the pit. The king's objective is served by the incident. The cheats and frauds in the community are sifted from the good. As the king declares at the end of the trial by ordeal, 'Have you seen why it is important that everyone should speak the truth always?'

In as much as the king demands that his subject should 'speak the truth always', he himself is expected to be their role model *par excellence* in this direction. His word must be his bond. The point is stressed hyperbolically in many tales in which the king is presented as keeping his promise no matter the sacrifice involved. Usually, the king pledges his extremely beautiful daughter or throne to anyone who can accomplish an impossible task. Sometimes what is demanded is 'the rarest thing in the world' (AT 653) as in 'Nwáàgbọ́ghọ̀-na-árọ̀-dī' ('The young woman that rejects all suitors') (Mbaeme 1983: 69–73, 162–6) where the king promises his beautiful daughter in marriage to any person who can perform the greatest feat in the world. In this dilemma tale, however, a problem arises in the end: but all the same the king must make good his promises. Of the four skilful brothers (AT 653) involved in rescuing the beautiful daughter from the monster who abducts her and raising her from the dead, the king picks the medicineman and gives his daughter in marriage to him.

The inviolability of royal promises is the main point of variants of the type, 'The trickster accomplishes an impossible task and weds the king's daughter'. In the Ikwerre Igbo story 'Tortoise and the seven princesses' (Okanlawon 1990: 8–9), the king promises his seven exquisitely beautiful daughters away in marriage to anyone who is able to unravel their secret names known only to the king, the queen and the princesses themselves. Numerous 'handsome and excellent princes' try and fail. But tortoise succeeds. Though shocked by this turn of events, the king is forced by the power of tradition to keep his promise.

It is the ideal king who possesses the qualities examined so far that is depicted, as noted by Okanlawon (1990: 8), 'as possessing enormous, if not exaggerated wealth, power and health'. Tales about such kings usually begin by highlighting their wealth and power (Egudu 1973: 33; Ogbalu 1973b: 20). Everything around them glitters with gold and in the Igbo Cinderella cycle of tales (AT 510) they appear as a symbol of marital security, the ultimate in feminine dreams of fulfilment (Iroaganachi 1973: 7; Nwaozuzu 1985: 136; Mbaeme 1983: 93–6, 187–190; Ugochukwu et al. 1977: 34–6). Usually the Cinderella is transformed into an exquisitely beautiful princess from an oppressed or rejected orphan in a beauty or dance competition organised at the behest of the king for the selection of a bride. In the royal household itself, everything is unusual in excellence betraying what is essentially a deep-seated Igbo admiration for royalty. The king himself is ever tolerant, patient and benevolent as illustrated by the story of 'The blindman, the cripple, the poor man and the king' (Thomas 1914, IV: 81–2).

In the midst of the great famine, a blind man goes to the king and asks for food and is given yams and meat but warned not to reveal the source of these things. He walks away, rejoicing, and meets a hungry cripple who he tells to go to the king and receive things, for the king is aiding the helpless. The cripple goes to the king to ask for food and is asked who told him to come to the king and he says it is the blind man. Nevertheless, the king gives him yams and meat and warns him not to reveal the source of these things. Again he walks away rejoicing and meets a hungry poor man who he tells to go to the king to receive things to eat, for the king is aiding the helpless. The poor man goes to the king to ask for food and is asked who told him to come to the king and he says it is the cripple. Nevertheless, the king gives him yams and meat and warns him not to reveal the source of these things. Again, he walks away rejoicing and meets a thief who begs him to tell him where he got yams and meat but the poor man refuses. Nevertheless, the thief goes to the king who asks who he met on the way and he say it is the cripple. The king asks him if he told him anything and he says no. He tells the thief to go to the blind man and cripple and steal what they have but leave the poor man alone, 'So that he does not report you to me.'

The moral drawn at the end of the story seems rather inconsequential: 'That is why thieves rob the blind man and he does not see; they rob the cripple and he does not follow them; but if they rob the poor man, he foliows them to report them.' What is of consequence here is the favourable image of the king as a patient provider and arbiter of social morality which the story distils. The king never loses his patience despite the repeated failure of his helpless beneficiaries to keep to the terms of this benefaction.

DISCUSSION AND CONCLUSIONS

It seems clear from the foregoing that, despite their numerous sources and aesthetic realisations in various contexts, by various artists in the oral performance, all Igbo tales about *ézè* in each of the two categories examined maintain the same mythic structure informed by what is essentially a powerful ideological purpose. The basic motifemes of the mythic structure of the first category of tales which present the cruel king are OPPRESSION › RESISTANCE › RESTITUTION. Oppression is a delinquent deviation from the democratic norms on which the institution of *ézè* is founded. The true *ézè* rules by divine grace and the commonweal and his goal should be to protect and care for all, not to exploit or plunder them and their land. Such a delinquent deviation inevitably provokes resistance towards the restitution of the God-ordained status quo. The low-born hero, symbolising the democratic weal of the populace, is always successful in resisting the oppressive monarchical power and bringing about a reversal of fortunes towards the restitution of the contravened democratic ethos. The ideal order is that represented in the second category of tales examined in which the image of the ideal king is represented. Here the structure is reversed. An initial problem or dilemma is resolved through the display of one royal virtue or another.

The persistence of these monomythical structures in all the tales examined, irrespective of their sources and modes of transmission calls attention to the mechanism of their creation in the light of their ideological significance. To do this correctly, a brief reflection on some pertinent literary and oral historiographic theories seems in order. Such a reflection will centre on the validity of relating literary images to the realities of the culture, history and social life of a people. The question before us then is to find out the extent to which the images of kings in Igbo tales examined are actually related to the realities of Igbo culture, history and social life.

Literature is a reflection of reality, both the phenomenal and the imaginative, but it is not a static 'holding the mirror up to nature', but a dynamic process of recreation of the facts of experience for specific ideological purposes bearing on the directions of growth of society. Its ultimate purpose is the creation of 'a myth to live by', and the creation of that mythos involves the filtering away of ideas and experiences which run counter to the myth. A parallel process in the mass media has been discussed by Herman and Chomsky in their book, *Manufacturing Consent: The Political Economy of the Mass Media* (1990). The Herman–Chomsky model has been described as 'a propaganda model that passes reported information through five filters: ownership concentrated in the hands of a small number of people who can afford it; advertising which keeps the product (newspapers, radio and TV news shows) widely available, but also influences its content and slant; reliance on government and other establishment sources for timely information and credibility; a desire to avoid controversy, negative public response, or "flak"; and the tendency to frame all issues in terms of a communist menace' (Levinson 1990: 20). Through these filters, the American media, according to Herman and Chomsky, is able 'to reinforce the values and interests of the wealthy and powerful who control them' (p. 20). They do this by restricting or negating 'the context in which information is given' and defining 'narrowly what constitutes "the story"' (p. 20).

This process of mythic filtering may be conscious or unconscious; but in whatever form it manifests itself it is an expression of the power of the dominant elite in the society to shape the direction for the future. Conscious mythic filtering will usually be directed by totalitarian regimes, monarchical or republican, secular or religious, rightist or leftist, and the themes to be developed in literature will be determined by bureaucratic fiat and presented in a 'consciously sanitised' (Levinson 1990) form. Unconscious mythic filtering on the other hand, takes place in free democratic societies as part of the popular weal to defend and sustain democratic freedoms usually won after long historical struggles. The structures of the imagination created by minds nurtured in such an environment will naturally sift away images which have the potential of threatening democratic freedoms. This process, which generations of oral historiographers describe as 'the selective process of folk memory' (Lach-Szyrma, in Dorson 1972: 215), seems clearly operative in the Igbo folktales examined. It operates as a dynamic instrument of social control, by using all the available aesthetic–rhetorical resources to create images intended to ensure that oppressive monarchical power is kept at bay and that democratic values are strengthened.

The fundamentalist–ideological view of the mythic structuring of oral art has wider implications for historiography. The old 'debate over the trustworthiness of oral traditional history' (Dorson, 1972: 199–222) cannot glibly be resolved in favour of one party or the other. Oral narratives subvert history, yet they are rooted in historical facts and direct the movements of tastes, manners and actions of men in society. Their themes and motifs do not add up to reliable documents for the reconstruction of events, rather they constitute programmes of sanction which can enable us to interpret the course of events. To rely on Igbo oral narratives for data on the lives and careers of particular *ézè* in Igbo history would be an exercise in futility. The images of *ézè* presented in them are a monomythic condensation of all that is objectionable or worthy in the actions of the various categories of kings and chiefs in the Igbo experience.

The following categories of kings and chiefs appear to have emerged at various stages of Igbo history: ancestor-kings (founding fathers recognised as *ézè* after migration to a settlement in a new environment); hero-kings (great warriors, hunters or achievers in other fields recognised as *ézè* following their victory over the enemies of the community or in recognition of other contributions to the security of the land); priest-kings (chief priests of deities who assume political powers as a result of the centrality of the deities served by them in the political life of the community as in the case of the *Ézē-Nrì* of Nri); title chiefs (holders of the title of *ézè* who serve as members of the cabinet of the paramount *ézè*); vassal-kings and chiefs (kings and chiefs appointed and controlled by an external power such as Benin); warrant-chiefs (chiefs appointed arbitrarily by the colonial government and given the warrant to rule in pursuit of that government's indirect rule policy); money-chiefs (holders of chieftaincy titles purchased for hard cash from natural rulers in modern times). Of these, only the ancestor-kings and their descendants appear to be *de jure* or natural rulers while all others are essentially *de facto* rulers who assume power through what amounts to *coups d'état* (as in the case of the hero-kings and warrant chiefs). Basden (1921: 255) refers to 'the autocratic state of former chiefs'. Heroic legends suggest that while the earliest ancestor-kings ruled with the benevolent despotism of patriarchs, the latter-day hero-kings introduced terrorism and predatory despotism into governance. These and the excesses associated with vassal kings acting on behalf of outside powers seem to have necessitated the emergence of democratic polities and the need to bridle monarchical power through the elaborate system of ritual prohibitions evolved over several centuries.

The tales examined in this essay uphold the value of these ritual prohibitions in maintaining the democratic ethos of Igbo society. Clearly, the statement *Ìgbò énwē ézè* should not be taken literally to imply that the Igbo do not have kings now or that they have never had kings. There are numerous pieces of archaeological and ethnohistorical evidence (notably Shaw 1970; Onwuejeogwu 1981) to confirm that not only have the Igbo always had kings but that the kingship institution is indeed regarded as a socially stabilising institution which should be guarded against all corrupting alien influences and negative internal developments. This is the position summed up in Achebe's comment quoted earlier on. In the effort at severely limiting the power of their kings, folktales appear to have served and continue to serve as a powerful ideological support to the elaborate ritual prohibitions created from remote antiquity for the same purpose. By their constant denigration of oppressive monarchical power and the tendency to frame all relationships between the ruler and the ruled in terms of the threat of aristocratic exploitation, they constitute a powerful mythic filter through which the democratic values of the society have been sustained and reaffirmed over the generations.

CHAPTER 6

Tales and ideology: the revolt of sons in Bambara–Malinké tales

Veronika Görög-Karady

If we may make general statements about the nature of West African tales or, more particularly, about the tales of the Bambara–Malinké group, we can say that they carry rather simple explicit ideological messages which conform to prevailing social norms. They show in most cases a protagonist acting against established laws of society and who will be punished accordingly. In fact the most productive narrative pattern found in the Bambara–Malinké corpus is based on misdeed followed by retribution, the latter being as serious as was the misdeed. An inventory of misdeeds occurring in the tales reveals the major internal conflicts that arise between members of the group. The degree of retribution inflicted upon those who transgress social norms is an indicator of the more or less coercive character of the norms concerned, as well as of the degree of tolerance with which they are enforced. However large the disparities may be, Bambara–Malinké tales are always about the confirmation and inculcation of the system of law, exemplifying for the narrator and his audience that anti-social conduct necessarily leads to the ruin of the transgressor.

It is worth mentioning here that the ideological messages carried by European tales, though similarly simple and conformist as to social norms, are differently formulated, since they are much more often conveyed by the positive hero. The central figure in European tales is indeed generally the positive hero who succeeds in his enterprise which comprises the defeat of evil. The stress is regularly laid here on his (or her) heroic action and glorious deeds, though the punishment of anti-heroes is also part of the denouement. In Manding tales on the other hand, the being responsible for retribution or punishment – be it a supernatural being (a genie) or a human being (a husband or a king) – does not usually have an active role in the story or such a role is limited to the conclusion. If one finds a positive hero in Manding tales, it is distinctly less often than in European tales. One should add though, that such triumphant heroes abound in Manding epics.

FATHERS AND SONS

The Bambara–Malinké tales I discuss below are different in that they are more complex than those mentioned above. The two stories to be dealt with, especially the second, present a violent confrontation between protagonists who both uphold, separately, some of the most fundamental and respected values in society.

Since for each tale several versions are at our disposal, it is possible to evaluate whether the social message conveyed by it is of a consensual nature. In this respect the concluding sequences are particularly relevant. In fact, two kinds of tales can be distinguished with regard to the denouement. There are tales whose concluding section is always identical, while in others the denouement takes on various forms. Such disparities are important for the ideological content – showing the existence of different views in these fields – and, for that matter, for the importance that the topic currently has for the Bambara–Malinké public.

Among the numerous tales dedicated to the problems of alliance by marriage and to kinship relations in Bambara–Malinké oral literature, two rich groups may be distinguished according to their relevance to the subject. In the first one the pair of protagonists is composed of a father and his daughter of marriageable age, while in the second the father appears with his son (or sons) of marriageable age. The third protagonist – necessarily involved – is the suitor or the potential bride (who chooses her bridegroom herself). He or she plays a more or less active, though always essential role in the story. Obviously the first group of tales is much better known in West Africa – as well as in Europe – than those of the second group chosen here for presentation, and whose rarity is matched only by their astonishing composition. Still, both groups of tales rely upon a traditional narrative stock, even if they stage a pattern of conduct which might appear as 'revolutionary' in terms of Bambara social values. Their interest resides precisely in the extent of conscious knowledge they reveal concerning the emotional conflicts and affective contradictions generated by the prevailing and generally accepted hierarchical order and matrimonial rules.

In order to understand the scope of social conflicts staged in these tales, I start by presenting some features of the relationship between fathers and sons as well as some major matrimonial rules and the customs governing pre-marital love and sexuality.

THE RELATIONSHIP BETWEEN FATHERS AND SONS
IN SOCIAL LIFE

In Bambara–Malinké society, as well as in many West African groups of patrilineal type, the son is expected to show deep respect to his father. He never utters his name. Even if he refers to somebody in the family circle having the same name, he calls him 'the one holding the same name' (*n'fatoma*). Father and son have only a very limited verbal exchange, the former giving orders or advice and the latter not being supposed to say anything in his presence, unless he is asked. This state of dependency and submission of sons is maintained even after their marriage. As long as the father is alive the son remains his inferior in all social hierarchies. A strong rivalry is established between them when the son arrives at the age of adolescence. This rivalry is consciously experienced by those concerned as is testified in the Bambara proverb: 'Our first rival is our father.' The conflictual relationship among fathers and sons, and the consequent tension emerging within the household, is well expressed in the Bambara language. The word used to designate the concept of 'conflict' is *fadenia*, meaning 'sons of the same father' (but not of the same mother). In everyday life the father habitually deprecates his sons' performance, whether in agricultural work, in the wars of earlier times or in other matters.

SOCIAL ORDER AND MARRIAGE

Among the Bambara, as in other West African societies, social order relies on the organisation of authority according to the principle of age (in the sense of genealogy: fathers and sons, or seniority: successive age groups) and sex. The main pattern of domination is that opposing the old and the young, the hierarchical relationship between men and women being just a variant of this. According to the striking definition suggested by Elisabeth Ranc (1987) the power of the seniors is based on their special relationship with gods, men and the ancestors as well as with knowledge and with things. Power is thus determined by social condition, status and age (primogeniture).

Within this system the matrimonial institution is one of the major instruments of domination since the elders have full command of the matrimonial arrangements to be made for the young of the family; these arrangements are considered as an undertaking involving the interests of the whole kinship group. The head of the family is exclusively responsible for the common goods, he takes care of the payment of the matrimonial compensation alone, his brothers and sons having no autonomy whatsoever in matters concerning finance or food production.

Traditionally, a married woman becomes 'the common property' of her husband's family. The transmission of the 'rights of property' is operated between her father's family and that of her husband via marriage councils and through the payment of matrimonial compensation, sealing thus the permanent transfer of the girl and her future children to the family of her husband (Ranc 1987: 96). A married woman, however unhappy in wedlock, has no means of breaking the matrimonial link against the will of the men (father and husband), the latter having the liberty to beat her till exhaustion to make her accept her matrimonial situation.

In order to secure the proper functioning of the matrimonial system and to keep control of the young, Bambara and Malinké societies make a fundamental distinction between two types of relationships, that is between love relationships based on personal mutual attraction between partners (*kani*) and matrimonial alliance proper (*furu*). The former are permitted and even arranged in institutionalised forms before marriage. The latter is not based on personal affinities but on the declared interests of the groups concerned. Love and matrimony are in fact opposed in social practice. To marry a partner of a *kani* relationship is seen as something to be avoided since it leads to the individual-emotional overcharge of the marriage, detrimental to the unity of the family and conducive to the weakening of kinship cohesion (Ranc 1987: 150).

Some forms of marriage are institutionally outlawed, such as between a free man and a slave, between a free man and a woman of caste or between individuals descended from kin allied by the ritual exchange of blood. Traditionally marriage with foreigners and outsiders is also forbidden.

Conversely, some unions are socially recommended as preferential matrimonial choices. Such are matches between a young man and a daughter of the mother's brother: she is called *bereninmuso*, 'woman of the little nephew', given by the uterine uncle. Another example of preferential marriage is that contracted between a young man and the daughter of the father's sister, named *kalumemuso*. Considered as sacred unions, such matches are not liable to end in divorce.

PRESENTATION OF THE CORPUS

The two tale-types presented here are both well attested in the whole Bambara–Malinké region. In both, the main character is the domineering father using force to prevent his sons from establishing sexual and matrimonial ties:

'The son confined'
The king forbids his son, a very handsome young man, to have relations with women and confines him to the top floor of a house. The prince, watching from above, and a young woman who passes by and looks up, become interested in each other. They show it by signs with the hand. At nightfall the prince uses a rope to let his beloved one join him. At dawn, all the animals of the city spread the news about Nyanyé's (the name of the prince) having spent the night with the girl. The father gathers the people and bids his son come, together with his lover.

Once they arrive, the king hands a knife to a slave and orders him to slay the prince. The girl declares that she wants to die with him. The slave tries to kill the prince, but his hands tremble and he fails in his task. The same happens to the other slaves who are entrusted with the job. Finally the king himself takes the knife but it stops three times in his hand.

The king orders the people to disperse, frees his son and the girl. The young people get married.

Moral: 'Since that day a father has never said to his son that he should not take a wife.'

In all three available versions of the tale (Görög-Karady and Meyer, 1988: 34–7; Camara 1978, III: 625–9, 638) special stress is laid on the beauty of the protagonist. If, in a similar confrontation between father and daughter, the motif of beauty appears to carry particular weight, this is not, or is less, the case in a confrontation between father and son. Is the king incapable of admitting that his son surpasses him in any field, including in terms of physical attraction? One can suppose that 'beauty' often stands for moral qualities as well. It is also arguable that the 'beauty' of the prince is just a rhetorical feature here, analogous to the daughter's beauty in the other set of similar tales. In any case it helps to stress the theme of paternal cruelty when the father is determined to have his disobedient son executed. Finally, the beauty of the prince is also instrumental in inspiring the girl's love to the point that she accepts death with him.

The second and more important focal point of the story concerns the confinement of the son. Condemning a young man to seclusion and depriving him of relations with women, as well as incidentally with others, is an act against the natural and social order. Such an enterprise amounts to an effort by a father to bring the normal course of time to an artificial halt: by analogous existential reasoning, if sons do not mature as they should, fathers may not grow old and need not leave their place to the upcoming generation. By the same token this act is obviously based on jealousy: it is a symbolic expression of sexual rivalry between father and son. But such sexual rivalry is linked here to a social antagonism detrimental to social order. The father's desire to keep his son in a state of submission and minority, including an incapacity to procreate and become adult appears as an attempt to destroy the social order which implies that fathers are replaced by their sons. Fathers as well as kings have to abandon power to their sons, that is to their heirs.

Such an enterprise by a father must meet obstacles. These are both natural and supernatural. The young people, moved by their natural impulses, dare to violate the father's law. Secondly, an immanent supernatural justice prevents the father and his substitutes from executing the fatal sentence passed on the young couple. Supernatural forces will compel the father to modify his behaviour and cease to maintain his son in the state of 'social death' to which he had been sentenced.

The tale stresses the fact that the union of the young couple is based on mutual attraction and on their personal determination to face danger (including death). This passionate commitment is exemplified by the decision of the young woman to follow her suitor in death. Such a strongly individualised liaison is reminiscent of the European model of romantic love. This Romeo-and-Juliet-type love relationship represents the very transgression of the traditional pattern of arranged marriage in accordance with family interests, as it is accepted in Bambara society. It refers much more to the *kani*-type lover relationship, based on personal choice and individual attraction permitted before marriage. Thus the story not only confirms the norm of the 'natural' succession of generations (as opposed to the father's arbitrary action) – as a fundamental aspect of social order – but indirectly conveys an apology for the individual's right to choose his marriage partner, in opposition to Bambara customs. Thus, in two important instances the social norm is contested: the father should accept his being succeeded by the son; the son should not insist on marrying his personal choice of partner.

If the tale – just like its equivalent 'the confined princess' – ends well and the conflict reaches a peaceful solution, the message conveyed is that the 'natural' law of libido (as expressed in individual sexual choices) is superior to the arbitrary law of those in power.

THE FATHER WHO IMPOSES UPON HIS SONS THE ORDEAL
OF THE SPEAR

In several African societies a lance is considered a guarantee of justice, just as it is often the symbol of virility. In a second variation on the tale dealt with above the lance is the instrument that ensures respect for the father's arbitrary decision. Three Bambara versions of the story are attested (Görög-Karady 1976: 15–17; Görög-Karady and Meyer 1988: 34–7; Görög-Karady, unpublished ms). together with five Malinké versions (four in Camara 1978: 647–9, 656–8; and one in Meyer 1987: 47–53). The tale differs in many respects from the story of 'The son confined'.

There are a number of protagonists (two twins, three or seven brothers). Physical coercion – confinement – is replaced here by verbal prohibition. The threat hanging over the young men refers to moral law: sons must respect the father's order, whatever its nature. Finally, there is an institutional 'ordeal' to ensure obedience to the father's prescription. The tale can be summarised as follows:

The king forbids his sons to have sexual relationships but allows them to attend a funeral or a circumcision feast, meeting places for young people of both sexes. Before leaving, the father warns his sons: upon their return, they must jump over a spear and the one who has disobeyed will be pierced to death. The older sons follow the father's orders but the youngest deliberately flouts them and gets involved with a girl. Upon their return, he is transfixed by the spear and the father in his rage throws his corpse onto the rubbish heap. The girl arrives and brings her lover back to life thanks to medicinal leaves she has received from an old woman (or, in one case, from a helpful animal). The resuscitated son takes his revenge.

Here again we have a father using his power to enforce an arbitrary decision against the 'natural law' stipulating the son's right to sexuality. He never in any way justifies his attitude which, formally, corresponds to the absolute authority fathers in Bambara–Malinké society exert over their offspring. Still, his motifs are implicitly suggested as above, and Bambara–Malinké audiences would well understand them. He refuses to give up his place to his heirs by forbidding his sons to become adults in biological as well as in social terms. The rebellious son is in each case the youngest one. Such an opposition between youngest and older brothers is a permanent feature in Bambara–Malinké narrative literature (and quite often elsewhere too). The older offspring are closer to adult status, closer to the power position of the fathers and are consequently supposed to have more fully accepted the system of norms, and thus to be less liable to question it, let alone revolt against it. The older brothers are thus, in a way, closer to the other side of the generation-barrier which formalises the dominance of the older over the younger.

This domination of the older is nonetheless strongly challenged in the tale, especially in its final sequence. In three versions the younger son, once back to life, takes his bloody revenge: he kills his father, or has him killed or else makes him commit suicide. As soon as his father is dead, he makes himself king, or, in one version, offers the kingdom to his oldest brother. Now such a form of revenge, hardly tolerable in terms of the ideology upon which social practice is based, is presented here as a legitimate act of punishment. The logic of the story stresses the principle of justice. The father perishes by the same means he used to put his son's life at stake. Though disputing the father's authority is inadmissible in traditional Bambara–Malinké ideology, the tale allows for an exception – the son's revenge gains a measure of justification by its retributive character in punishing the anti-social and anti-natural way in which the father attempted to take his son's life. Of the two evils, the preference expressed in the tale is for the righting of an injustice, working to the benefit of the son's right to life, sexuality and inheritance.

Following the logic of both social and narrative action, the first killing by the father gives justification for the second one, committed by the younger son. But the latter carries a supplementary meaning too. Since sons are normally called upon to succeed their father, the means they use to do so, however violent they may be, have an ultimate justification. Conversely, the elimination of children by a father, exclusively for the perpetuation of his privileges, is considered intolerable.

We can identify here a parallel to the cathartic psycho-sociological dimension of works of fiction, especially important in oral literature of traditional societies. Through such stories some of the most hidden forms of internal antagonism, current in such in-group sociability as family life, are revealed and in a way psycho-dramatically reacted against (*abreagiert*, to use the German psychoanalytical expression). In patriarchal and patrilineal societies (with extended family systems) the domination of the head of the family provokes a deep-rooted but publicly suppressed hostility from offspring. The tale offers a fictional elaboration of such a theme of structurally determined violence, in-built in the family arrangements of the Bambara–Malinké. The violence opposing father and sons, though inherent in social reality, cannot be expressed publicly. It is reserved for narrative fiction. Its cathartic function should nevertheless not be underestimated for the audiences and the narrators of these tales.

One of the versions of the tale presents a distinctive denouement compared with the others. The younger brother, after having transgressed against the father's order, returns home unharmed, the spear remaining ineffective against him. He reproaches his father for his false threats: 'You deceived us . . . your word inflicted useless suffering upon my brothers' (by condemning them to sexual abstinence). There is no explanation in the tale why the spear was harmless, even if allusion is made to modern times when traditional magico-religious powers tend to be viewed as inoperative. At any rate, this instance of the father's failure to mobilise occult forces upon which, normally, his authority relies, may point to a reversal of the hitherto prevailing power relationships in the family.

A different situation arises in another version of the tale where the father turns the disobedience of the younger son to the latter's advantage. Instead of being punished, he receives the inheritance and succeeds the father, while the obedient older sons are punished and killed by the father. Such an unexpected inversion of the social and narrative logic of the story can be interpreted in at least two ways. First, the theme remains within the realm of the father's absolute power, even if it is used apparently in contradiction to his announced intentions. Yet, in a way, the events conform to obvious social practices. Young men should not be forced, and have no reason, to accept sexual abstinence. Those who assent to it show weakness and an unmanly attitude. The one who refuses is entitled to due recognition for his adult behaviour. This is the sense of the father's final decision to endow him instead of taking revenge on him.

The tales ending in divergent or even contradictory denouements – such as those we have just examined – do not result from the fancy of various individual narrators. On the contrary, they indicate the importance of the topics for members of the community in two senses: those concerned are either perceiving conflicts within their own values or are reacting against the oppressive nature of their laws. Antagonisms of this sort may arise through the colonial and post-colonial experience of values both new and alien to the tradition. Narrative fiction is a field of social space where such controversial issues may find legitimate expression.

CHAPTER 7

Images of the powerful in Lyela folktales

Sabine Steinbrich

The Lyela are one of the numerous smaller ethnic groups of Burkina Faso, the former Upper Volta. They are one of the 'Gurunsi'-speaking people; and the Mossi, the dominating ethnic group in the country, call them somewhat contemptuously by that term (Köhler 1975: 186–9). The Lyela live in the south-west of the country, about 120 kilometres from Ouagadougou, Burkina's capital. Their northern neighbours are the Samo, a Mande-speaking people. In the east they are bordered by the Mossi, in the south by the Nuna and in the west by the Bwa (for the linguistic and ethnic composition of the Gurunsi see Duperray 1984: 13–29). In 1983 Réo, the largest settlement in Lyela country, became the district capital.

THE 'TRADITIONAL' SOCIAL STRUCTURE AND ITS DISTRIBUTION OF POWER: THE EARTH PRIEST

Lyela villages are loosely settled parts of cleared bush. The single compounds are constructed at a distance of 100–300 metres from one another, and between them the Lyela have their gardens and 'housefields' (kǎlsε, pl.). The oldest man of the senior generation is usually the compound chief (kèlέ-cɔ́bal). The other family fathers, his junior brothers and sons, stand under his authority, as well as the women, unmarried relatives and the children. The compound chief represents the people of his kèlέ before the outside world, he is responsible for sacrifices and other religious activities. The size of a compound varies between a handful and over one hundred people. The average number of compounds in a 'bush village' is between twenty and thirty. Several compounds form a *clan section* of all patrilineal descendants of a

The field trips, upon which this discussion is based, were supported by the Deutsche Forschungsgemeinschaft (DFG). I also express my gratitude to Prof. Schott for his support and encouragement in this research.

common ancestor who came once to a particular village. These members of a localised patriclan who have the same clan name should ideally revere one single clan shrine (*kwálá*, pl. *kwálsɛ*). Rituals at the clan shrine are performed by the *kwálá-cɔ́bal*, another important person in Lyela social organisation who, among other functions, has to settle clan disputes and conclude marriages.

Among the clan sections living together in one village, old clans have to be distinguished from new ones. The old clans are said to descend from the village founders; they have a legitimate claim to a part of the big animals that are given as sacrifices to the village's Earth shrine (*cɔ-kú*). Even more important are rights over a *bono* (pl. *bandɛ*), their clan land which stretches out from the centre of the Earth shrine into the bush. The members of the younger clans are 'sitting' on the ground of the older clans. They only have a right of usufruct granted by the *bono-cɔ́bal* of the older families.

The decisive factor for membership of a village community is subordination under the *cɔ-kú*, the Earth shrine, which may be considered as the spiritual 'middle' of a Lyela village. The priest of this shrine (*cɛ-cɔ́bal*) is the most powerful man in a traditional Lyela community. His title is translated into colonial French as *chef de terre*. People say that he is a direct descendant of the village founder or of the second arrival in a new settlement. The Earth Priest has to punish the transgression of certain laws of the Earth, such as bloodshed, theft, adultery and sorcery (Schott 1984).

Besides his judging and punishing functions the Earth Priest has to perform fertility rites, rain sacrifices and harvest rituals. Communication between the Earth Priest and the other compound chiefs is facilitated by the work of the *copyaa* (sg. *copyal*), the elders of the ancient clans. Duval makes the following comment concerning the Nuna which holds also for their northern neighbours, the Lyela:

One can not say that 'the power' is distributed among the whole male population. The Nuna only grant the status of an 'adult' to men over thirty-five. Taking into account the low life expectancy in rural West Africa it becomes clear that an important part of the adult male population is discarded. From the beginning women, adolescents and children are not considered. So the exercise of power is reserved to males on or over the compound-chief's level. (1985: 22)

Duperray (1984: 39) believes that the Earth Priest, who has an important socio-political function among the different 'Gurunsi' people in Burkina Faso and Ghana, was the only form of authority among the Lyela until the arrival of the French colonialists. She found no earlier evidence of a political post above village level. The *pyɔ* or *peo*, a pre-colonial chief over one or more villages, never previously existed as a hereditary office among the Lyela.

It is very often the *pyɔ* (chief) and sometimes the *cɔ-cɔ́bal*, the colonial village chief, who is made protagonist of folktales. With the exception of a few (rather hidden) allusions, the Earth cult or the role of the Earth Priest is not mentioned in Lyela folktales. The Earth Priest is not shown either in his role as a judge, nor as calling upon supernatural forces to intervene for his village in case of war or other sort of crisis. The Lyela say:

One does not talk frivolously about the Earth. The matters of the Earth are severe, they are dangerous. The Earth will punish anyone who does not speak the truth in every word. Tales, after all, are full of lies. They are told for entertainment and amusement.

THE VILLAGE CHIEF AND THE *CHEF DE CANTON*

Bayili traces the division of political power versus religious authority in one single village back to the domination of the Mossi over large parts of Lyela territory in the nineteenth century. Contrary to Duperray, he reports a divison of power between the Earth Priest and village chiefs in northern Lyela country *before* colonisation:

the village chief is responsible for judicial questions in his village, but he is closely subordinated to the Earth Priest. He (the village chief) has been chosen and installed after the consultation of the soothsayers. He takes over the role of 'first minister' for the Earth priest who remains the most important authority. (1983: 59)

But it is certain that after the arrival of the French, the 'village chiefs' (*cɔcìnɔ́*) were charged with a number of new tasks, and that they were paid for these additional duties (Ponton 1933: 106). They had to appear before the *commandant de cercle* from time to time, they had to collect and deliver taxes, to maintain order and cleanliness, they had to recruit young men for the police, the army and private firms in Ivory Coast, they had to collect and deliver tributes of millet, chicken, cotton, wood and livestock.

In the villages of Pwa and Sanje, where I obtained most information on the structure of political power in Lyela communities, the Earth Priest is regarded as the 'father' of the village chief. Both men come from the same clan, so that the village chief is a classificatory 'son' of the Earth Priest. In theory village chiefs should be elected by the villagers and it is in principle possible that the *cɔ-cɔ̀bal* (village chief) could be chosen from another clan than that of the Earth Priest but that is rarely done. The Lyela concept of authority is fundamentally determined by the principle of 'relative age'. So the Earth Priest as the 'father' occupies a position of superiority over the 'son'. Conflicts between the religious power of the Earth Priest and the village chief's claim to political power are neutralised by the father–son relationship between the two men.

Following Bamony (1984: 434), the first chief (*pyɔ̌*, pl. *pyǎ*) over thirty-eight Lyela villages was installed in 1910. At that time he was still under the supremacy of the Mossi–Naba Larlé in Ouagadougou. The first *chef de canton* over the whole of Lyela country was *pyɔ̌* Banyini Bassolé in Réo. He was made 'king' over the province of Réo ten years later and he 'ruled' his country so well that he even exceeded the amount of cotton that had to be grown by *travail forcé* for the French (Duperray 1984: 201). In 1926 Lyela country was divided into three *cantons* that correspond roughly to the three dialect groups of Réo, Batondo and Didyr. Each of the three new *chefs de canton* (*pyǎ*) had weapons, and he was charged with judging cases between the villages of his district (Bamony 1984: 438). The *chef de canton* had, for instance, the right to beat the abductor of a married woman as well as the adulterous wife. Following older informants' accounts, the *pyǎ* had horses and servants (*sona*, pl. *sonɔrh*). They imitated the clothing, status symbols and behaviour of the Mossi *nabas*, a lifestyle that was likewise copied by several village chiefs. The possession of horses was their most important status symbol.

In Lyela oral literature the *pyɔ̌* (chief) and the *cɔ-cɔ̀bal* (village chief) are used as scapegoats who have to absorb all kinds of tensions between different social groups in Lyela society. They are symbols for social and political power on very different levels: they rule over a fictitious kingdom, over the inhabitants of a village and last but not least, over the members of one compound.

Out of about 1,000 folktales (*soswala*, pl. *soswalsɛ*), that form the basis of my collection, roughly one hundred, that is every tenth tale, has the 'chief' (*pyɔ̌* or *cɔ-cɔ̀bal*) as the main protagonist. Often the figure of the chief is secondary to a conflict in the family between father and son. Another popular theme is conflict at village level where the 'chief' is called upon to punish a 'traitor'. Finally we find fictitious 'kings' (*pyǎ*) whose attributes are reminiscent of Mossi rulers governing a whole country. They are described as being 'very powerful', possessing horses, guns, lots of women, servants and the right to judge over life and death. As indicated earlier, colonial village chiefs and *chefs de canton* were also very eager to acquire these status symbols.

How can one explain the contradiction between an acephalous social structure in 'reality' and the frequent concern with a powerful ruler in fiction? Are these very powerful chiefs (*pyǎ*) only described in tales in order to attack, at the level of imagination, their power? Perhaps it is one of the functions of Lyela oral literature to warn against the accumulation of too much power by one man over other men. In my discussion here I consider the relationships portrayed between powerful chiefs and marginal persons. Subsequently, the discussion turns to power conflicts inside the family where the 'king' takes on the role of a super-elevated father figure.

'THE CHIEF AND THE ORPHAN'

The first tale (in my collection numbered LYE-E893) has an orphan and *homme de brousse* in the hero's role. A helpful animal is present as a minor motif. The tale finishes with an open end, the established ruler and the youthful challenger separate when conflict threatens to arise:

A young man and his sister lose their whole family and live in the bush all alone. The siblings are very poor, they have to feed on bush rats hunted by the brother.

One day he is going to catch the last rat. The animal tells orphan that it is the last of its species so that the boy should not kill it. In recompense the animal gives him a magical wooden stick.

With the help of the magical stick orphan is able to transform one sort of livestock into another (oxen into donkeys, etc.) so that the proprietor of the herds does not recognise his animals any more, and orphan can chase them away to his homestead.

Oxen started to fill his compound, he (orphan) took the livestock to marry a wife and to get wives for the people of the compound. He became rich. He was in the bush, the village moved over to join him there. The villagers came to construct their houses next to him. The compound of the ancient chief was left behind. A traitor (*shetana*) stood up and said: 'This man over there, he is going to take over the power (*pyè lè*). If he is not killed, the whole village will be lost.'

The chief summons orphan and tells him that he should be killed for trying to contest his power. Orphan says that the village chief should show him the person who brought forward such an accusation against him. Then he transforms the traitor into a donkey.

Traitor and orphan are once more summoned to the chief's court. The traitor, transformed into a donkey, does not show up. The chief says that he is not able to judge that case without his witness, and he sends orphan back into the bush.

Since that time donkeys have been beaten with a stick, because they are transformed *shetana*.

The motif of the magical object (a stick, a cow's tail, a flute) acting in a way to balance justice is quite frequent in Lyela folktales. This kind of magic robbery of the chief or rich man's possessions is not considered illicit among the Lyela. One of my informants put it as follows:

In ancient times people [the Lyela] went as far as Bobo Dioulasso [the second largest city in Burkina Faso, about 350 km from the Lyela region]. There they have 'looked for things' for their village. This is no theft. In ancient times we did not know theft.

Bayili documented the significance of the spear, the club and the hoe as symbols of power in the investiture ritual of a new Earth Priest:

In the northern Lyela territory and on the western river of the Black Volta the new Earth priest was given a bended club or a herd boy's stick. That meant that he had become the guardian and the herdsman for the villagers. (1983: 67–72)

This interpretation makes sense for the present tale too. The proprietor of the magical club does not only get extraordinary wealth in livestock, but through the distribution of cattle he arrives at the next stage of prosperity in achieving power over people. At the end of this tale the old chief has to accept the young man who took his cattle and his people over to the new village in the bush. The two rivals agree finally on a silent partition of power. The old king wanted to kill the man who took his cattle and people away. After the liquidation of the traitor however, the conflict is not pushed forward to an open confrontation, but the old chief accepts the loss of his power and lets the young man return to his homestead in the bush.

The theme of the traitor setting up two parties against each other, disrupting peaceful village life, is very prominent in Lyela folklore, as in the following text:

'THE MAN WITH THREE TUFTS OF HAIR ON HIS HEAD'

This tale was recorded in seven rather similar variants (LYE-E078, LYE-E142, LYE-E523, LYE-E610, LYE-E822, LYE-E853, LYE-E968) and one more original version (LYE-E305):

A (young) man shaves his head leaving three (or four) tufts of hair. Each of them represents a piece of worldly wisdom, expressed in a proverb. (In a Mossi variant the man is a close friend of the chief.) The proverbs say:

A good friend is better than a brother (LYE-E078, LYE-E142, LYE-E610, LYE-E822, LYE-E968, MOS-ETIE)

Sleep is stronger than the fear of being killed (LYE-E610, LYE-E822, LYE-E853)

Even a king can kill another person only with God's consent (LYE-E610, LYE-E822, LYE-E968)

The chief only knows his own will (MOS-ETIE)

The king (a rich man in LYE-E523) tries in vain to guess the significance of the proverbs (*noms devises*). He has to give ten cows for every wrong guess.

The furious king goes to see the hero's wife and blackmails her into revealing to him her husband's secret. In LYE-E968 the hero has to find a pair of ear-rings that have been flung into the river.

The hero's wife refuses sexual intercourse (LYE-E078, LYE-E523, LYE-E822) or she does not cook any more for her husband (LYE-E853, LYE-E142) and so she learns his secrets.

The hero is summoned before the chief and tied up for decapitation. His brothers take away his clothes, and the first proverb is proved right when a Fulani-friend of the hero gives him his clothes so that his friend may die in dignity. In LYE-E968 it is the friend who retrieves the ear-rings out of the river in the stomach of a big fish.

In three variants the hero falls asleep just before his decapitation (LYE-E610, LYE-E822, LYE-E853), in one variant he is overwhelmed by fatigue when he has to dig his own grave, and so another proverb is proved right.

In four variants the unfaithful wife or an old traitress is killed (LYE-E523, LYE-E610, LYE-E822, LYE-E968). In other variants (LYE-E078, LYE-E142, LYE-E853), including the one from the Mossi, the hero is pardoned because the chief has learnt the truth of the proverbs.

Considering the multitude of Lyela variants of this Mossi tale set in a Mossi environment at the Naba's court I asked myself the same question which Platiel posed when she tried to analyse the tale of the *enfants malins* in Samo oral literature, 'Pourquoi tant de variantes autour d'une histoire qui semble avoir été empruntée?' (Görög et al. 1980: 174).

The hero's haircut for instance is inappropriate for a Lyela but it is significant for the Mossi, where in earlier times the young men wore their hair in three tufts before marriage. Their hairstyle distinguished them at once from the older married men who shaved their heads completely. So the present tale may be understood in part as addressing a conflict between different generations, a conflict which is fundamental in Lyela society as well. The young unpropertied man provokes the well-established compound chief who has women, children and livestock and who resides within a big compound. The term 'king' (*pyɔ*) marks up the figure of the compound-chief (*kɛlɛ-cɔbal*) and accentuates the contrasts.

The motif of the faithful friend standing by his comrade while the brother is not even willing to support his sibling at the moment of death, allows the articulation of negative feelings at the level of imagination against the closest of relatives. In reality the Fulani are most unpopular among the Lyela; this special Fulani accentuates a 'best friend' image as the contrasting figure to the mean brother. Brothers have to spend their whole lives together in one spot in patrilineal societies, and so it is little wonder to find tensions between them in the tales (I have no space here to address the important topic of witchcraft between brothers which is a major vehicle of envy, jealousy and hatred among blood relatives). The tale describes a friendly relationship between two strangers in order to contrast with the bad feelings towards a brother.

The 'king' symbolises a threat from above, the dangerous attack by a superior, a situation where the help of equals is needed. Other tales are concerned with the mutual assistance of two friends in the face of a dangerous tyrant. The seduction of one of the chief's wives is a favourite motif in this context (cf. LYE-E394, LYE-E498). The king wants to kill the impudent adulterer, but he is rescued from danger by his close friend.

The recurrent rivalry between a ruler and an antagonist concerning 'knowledge' and 'wisdom' is a motif found in very different tales about chiefs. The story about the hairtufts is strongly moral: the antagonist believes himself in the possession of truths ignored by the ruler. For instance in LYE-E822 it is said at the beginning, 'Un chef qui n'est pas intelligent ne doit pas avoir la chefferie (*pyɛ̀lɛ̀*)'. In the story of the *garçon malin* the hero provokes the chief's anger by naming himself with another *nom devise* saying: '[My] Intelligence is stronger than the chief's.' Magical, supernatural knowledge is the key to power, and the legitimation of authority. In no tale is the established ruler able to resist the antagonist's provocation. The appeal to his curiosity emanating from the antagonist's challenge to guess the content of the tied-up fetish package is too strong for the chief; he must find out the significance of the hairtufts, he absolutely wants to know what is in the fetish bundle.

'THE "MEDICINE" THAT MAKES PEOPLE ABLE TO EAT
RAW CEREALS'

A boy has lost his parents, and he has no one to cook for him so he has to eat all cereals raw: white millet, small red millet, corn, sesame and peanuts (LYE-E049, LYE-E536, LYE-E725).

The chief watches orphan chewing his grain, and he believes that he has a 'medicine' with the help of which people can eat cereals without first having to cook them. In one variant the king is told of the 'medicine' by an old woman.

The king claims orphan's 'medicine'. The boy tells the king to fill his sacks with millet, sesame, corn, etc. To get the 'medicine' they have to go out in the bush for a period of time.

Deep in the bush orphan leaves the king under a tree and returns home. The king waits for him to return for a long time. Then he gets hungry and starts to eat up one bag of cereals after the other. When it starts raining the king retires into a cave, where he meets some wild animals: lion, panther, monkey. When the king reaches behind his back to kill a mosquito, all the animals flee in panic. They believe that he reached out for his arrows to shoot them. Cat (LYE-E049, LYE-E725) or monkey (LYE-E546) stay with the man and bring him back home.

In two variants the orphan gets the king's daughter in marriage so that he does not have to eat raw grain any more.

The Lyela stories design the 'clever boy' or the 'strong boy' as the stereotyped counterpart of the 'king' or 'chief'. As in numerous animal tales, of hare and hyena for instance, the weak teaches the strong a lesson by resorting to a ruse. The ruler over a village suspects the poor orphan of having a strong fetish he has no right to possess. The same theme of the king claiming a supernatural object from orphan, because he, the king, regards the possession of magical agents as his own privilege, turns up again as a 'serious' motif in a number of tales.

The present funny tale makes a fool of the chief. The audience roared with laughter at the description of the stupid chief sitting alone under his tree in the bush unable to find his way home crunching one bag of hard grains after the other. At the same time it pokes fun at the Lyelas' strong belief in 'medicines' and 'fetishes'. Orphan and king are types representing antagonistic poles in the status spectrum in a village community:

Orphan	*King*
Young	Old
Poor	Rich
Powerless	Mighty
Without wife/mother	Has many wives
Raw food	Cooked food
Walks around in the bush	Stays in the village
Clever from hard life	Weak from comfortable life

Orphan is not punished at the end of the story; on the contrary, he gets the king's daughter in marriage, so that his marginal position at the bottom of the village's social hierarchy is raised. The tale mediates between the oppositions, and in this respect it proclaims an 'acephalous' moral. The king lacks dignity, wit and wisdom, and it is his wisdom before anything else which is regarded as legitimation for a chief's power. The chief's role as a clear-sighted judge forms the basis of his power over the people of his village.

ORPHAN, KING AND OLD TRAITRESS

In the following tale we find three classical protagonists of Lyela oral literature acting together in one tale: orphan, king and old traitress/old woman. They come into conflict after the discovery of magic pots producing unlimited food that will end man's fight for existence once and for all. The tale talks about one of the most important topics in Lyela society: mistrust and insecurity among members of different clans living together in one village, tensions provoked by gossip and intrigue. The following synopsis is the résumé of eight variants (LYE-E196; LYE-E212; LYE-E225; LYE-E805; LYE-E826; LYE-E863; LYE-E906; LYE-E983):

A young man (orphan in most variants) who has nobody in the world to take care of him, finds two clay pots in the bush. They ask him to repeat a certain formula and then the one fills with millet-porridge and the other one with sauce (the daily food of the Lyela). Orphan eats his fill and hides the two pots.

An old woman comes to his house under a pretext, she sees the pots and orphan has to share his food with her. The old woman goes to the chief's court and tells him about the pots. The chief confiscates them.

Orphan returns to the bush and finds a couple of whips. They tell him to repeat a formula, and then they beat him thoroughly.

Old woman finds the whips, is beaten after the pronouncement of the formula, and once more she goes to the chief and tells him what orphan has found.

The king confiscates the whips as well and is beaten. He orders his people to bring old woman. She swallows a clay pot and says that she is unable to come in her advanced stage of pregnancy. The king tells his people to tie her onto a bicycle and to summon her. He forces her to repeat the whips' formula, the old woman is beaten, the clay pot in her stomach breaks into pieces, the old woman shits them out and dies.

The old woman is the focus of the listeners' attention in all variants. She forms a 'marginal couple' together with the poor orphan, but in contrast to him living on his own hiding in the bush, she does not keep away from the mighty. They both have their faults: orphan hides his nourishing pots and behaves in an anti-social and selfish manner, while the old woman is a reprehensible traitress. The Lyela have various expressions for persons talking behind other people's backs: a *jewal-cə́bal* is, as the Lyela say, a tell-tale, broadly implying a 'spy'. These people play an important role in Lyela folktales. *Yewal zɔ̀mà* are *paroles prononcées en temps inopportun*, lies or gossip which bring two parties against each other. The focusing of the old woman's aggressive and destructive behaviour in the Lyela tales stands in contrast to what Calame-Griaule and Görög-Karady (1972: 54) said about the same tale-type in six other West African societies:

> Toutes ces figures féminines réelles ont un point commun: quels que soient leurs défauts, elles sont *nourricières* et font profiter leurs enfants des bienfaits de l'objet magique (ce qui est d' ailleurs logique, étant donné la symbolisation maternelle de celui-ci). Seule exception: la vieille femme du conte gouro qui vole la nourriture pour elle-même. . . Nous avons ici le personnage classique de la femme frustrée de sa féminité par son âge, devenue une charge pour la société et se conduisant de perturbatrice.

Orphan does not only eat his fill but he takes the magical pots home and hides them in his hut. Although people have to share their food with others, Lyela housewives usually hide the rest of a meal in the back of their houses. Food is kept under a *kúlpú*, a meat safe made of clay. It protects the food from insects and hides it from the neighbours' curious looks. So the woman is always in a position to say that there is nothing left to eat if somebody comes along and asks for food. Old woman in the tale finds a pretext to enter orphan's room and to search for food in every corner.

Despite his initial refusal orphan has to share his food with old woman, but she has nothing better to do than to tell the chief about the magical pots. Her action appears unreasonable; after all she could easily eat from the pots forever. The comment was made to me that old women expect presents of tobacco or money, and that they are ready to give away even the most important secrets for immediate advantage. Her compulsion to divulge the secret of the magic pots is stronger than her hunger, even in a time of famine. In variant LYE-E683 old woman tells the king, 'My king, orphan has things that are too big for him, they should be yours, they should not belong to a poor person.' Finally the king confiscates the two magical pots and orphan as well as old woman (the contrasting marginal pair) have to live in hunger and misery again. Orphan has lost his mother substitute, the nourishing pots. It is the old woman (a contrasting figure to a real mother) who provokes the final loss of the food-producing pots. In one variant old woman is called a *shetana* (from the Arabic word *sheitan* 'devil or bad spirit'). That is why her elimination has become the king's duty.

Paulme and Seydou stress the importance of the traitor (traitress) in their analysis of the tale about the 'Grateful animals'. They say that in general the members of acephalous societies, *societés villageoises*, react very sensitively to a disturbance of peace and harmony in their communities:

Nous nous trouvons ici dans des sociétés villageoises où l'entraide, la paix sociale, sont des vertus essentielles; y provoquer gratuitement, par simple jalousie, une discorde est une faute grave qui compromet l'ordre public, menace la vie du village; aussi nul ne défendra le traître lorsque le héros exigera son élimination; en débarassant la communauté d'un élément dangéreux le héros (ici le chef) affirme son rôle dans la société humaine. (1972: 85)

The role of the wicked traitor is most often transferred to social categories 'qui sont les plus chargés de signification défavorable dans son contexte sociologique' (Paulme and Seydou 1972: 95). The social devaluation of old woman follows her loss of fertility after menopause and of her working power. The loss of her former role as caring, food-preparing mother is expressed in strong terms in our tale. Not only has the old woman become too weak to cultivate food crops and to process hard grain, in the tale she deliberately causes the loss of the magical food-producing pots. Her wantonness seems to be regarded as worse than the abuse of power by the chief. In the Lyela tales, like in the versions of the Wolof, the Dyiwat and the Dogon, the chief is beaten up by the magical whips, but he punishes old traitress with death.

Finally in this section, I want to summarise a last variant of the 'Magic objects' told by an old woman more than sixty years old (LYE-E212). She re-writes the power relations between marginalised and powerful and concentrates on 'her own' confrontation with the ruler:

A chief had killed animals for a sacrifice. He distributed the meat among the women of the compound, but he omitted one old woman to whom he gave nothing.

She went out into the bush where she gathered wild potatoes. She distributed them among the people of the compound but she gave nothing to the chief to whom she replied when he asked her: 'Oh, I thought that you don't eat any potatoes just as you thought that I don't like meat.'

Next time in the bush she found two clay pots producing food after the pronouncement of a certain formula. She hid the pots in her house. A traitor told the chief about the magical pots, he summoned old woman and took her pots away from her.

Next time in the bush old woman was beaten by magical whips. She broke them into pieces and put them behind her grinding stone. Her new find was also confiscated by the chief who thought that this magical object could also produce something valuable. He pronounced the formula and was beaten thoroughly.

The chief ordered his people to summon the old woman. He tried to force her to pronounce the formula. She started hesitatingly, he tried to speed her up, they talked to and fro, and finally it was the chief who spelled out the complete formula. The whips seized the chief and beat him until he ran away to hide in his house.

Juliette Kanzie, a woman in her sixties who told the story, identified strongly with the hero of the tale. Another woman of only eighteen years had also told the story and included the motif of the swallowed and defecated clay pot in the tale. The audience was roaring with laughter about this end to the story. The older woman on the other hand was obviously not happy with this ending and she felt the need to transform the final episode.

In Juliette Kanzie's version, on the other hand, old woman defends herself with wit and intelligence. She can not recover her fertility, but she can fight against her social devaluation by her efforts to fulfil her role as a producer as long as possible. She continues to gather food in the bush and she distributes what she obtains among the other people of the compound. She has something to give, her only chance to secure the respect of her companions.

When old woman finds the food-producing pots the chief regards the possession of the magical pots as his prerogative and takes them away from the marginal persons in six out of seven variants. In the old woman's version it is the old woman's verbal skill which gives her victory over the chief as he becomes the victim of whips which had been intended for the marginal old woman.

THE CHIEF AS ELEVATED FATHER FIGURE IN THE TALE 'CLEVER BOY'

It seems to me that in addition to intra-village conflict and more general inter-generational conflicts between seniors and juniors it is the father–son relationship which furnishes the most important focus for tales about chiefs among the Lyela. Three tale types are significant in this respect: the almost 'classical' Oedipus tale, the story about 'The king who ordered the killing of all the old men in the country', and the tale of 'The clever or strong boy and the male who is delivered of a child'. My discussion here is limited to the last of these types.

In the 'Clever boy' tale the father is shown in the role of a big chief, symbol for his superiority over his son. The son on the other hand is still stronger than the most powerful chief, he is shown as clever boy, *garçon malin*, or strong boy with supernatural faculties. The son, along with his mother, sets himself against his father. A Lyela youth growing up does not feel the necessity to sever his ties with his mother. Social norms insist on his fulfilment of economic and social duties toward his mother. He has to take care of her until her death. I present nine Lyela variants of the *garçon malin et le mâle qui met bas* (see Paulme 1976) in a short summary:

A long-time sterile woman becomes finally pregnant. In some variants she has been severely humiliated by the other women of the compound. She gives birth to a supernatural or a very intelligent child.
In seven variants either,
  the child chooses its own name provoking his father, the chief, by the act of self-designation or by the name itself (LYE-E112, LYE-E161, LYE-E204, LYE-E596, LYE-E597, LYE-E894, LYE-E946)
or,
  the king has numerous sons, one of them unloved, who does not get a wife from his father. The son finds himself a very beautiful wife and the father desires her for himself (LYE-E596, LYE-E736).
The chief gives clever boy an impossible task to do:
  brewing millet-beer in one day (LYE-E115, LYE-E204, LYE-E597, LYE-E894, LYE-E946)
  the preparation of huge amounts of rice in one day (LYE-E204)
  drying of fish or meat without any loss in weight or volume (LYE-E115, LYE-E894, LYE-E946)
  spinning and weaving of enormous quantities of cotton in a single day (LYE-E204)
or,
  the king gives the boy a single male animal to breed from (LYE-E161, LYE-E481)
  the boy has to forge an imagined object from iron without any description of what the object is (LYE-E894)
  he has to find a sheep without legs but able to walk (LYE-E597)
  he has to guess the name of a girl in order to marry her (LYE-E736).
Clever boy responds to the impossible task as follows:
  with a clever answer: he tells the chief that his father needs immediate help after the delivery of the baby (LYE-E161, LYE-E481);
  with an impossible counter task: calabashes have to be grown from seeds in one day (LYE-E115, LYE-E481, LYE-E597, LYE-E894, LYE-E946), or a

bag filled with shea fruits must be filled to the rim with the nuts from the eaten fruits (LYE-E115, LYE-E894, LYE-E946);

he gets the support of a supernatural helper: the boy is helped by a supernatural mosquito, a snake, a frog, a ghost, his own strong wife (LYE-E204, LYE-E596, LYE-E597, LYE-E736, LYE-E737, LYE-E897).

The chief tries to kill clever boy in eight out of nine variants: he tells his people to dig a deep ditch, and the opening is covered with a cowskin or a covering. Clever boy digs a tunnel into the house of his mother (LYE-E894, LYE-E946, LYE-E976) or of his wife (LYE-E596) and saves his life. Other attempts to kill clever boy are:

Burning in a huge fire (LYE-E596, LYE-E736, LYE-E737, LYE-E897)
drowning in the 'sea' (LYE-E115, LYE-E894)
poisoning (LYE-E121)
tearing to pieces by wild animals (LYE-E204, LYE-E976).

Clever boy lures a naive victim to his place (a Fulani, the chief's own son), or he entices the king into an exchange of clothes so that the chief is caught in his own trap (LYE-E112, LYE-E115, LYE-E161, LYE-E596, LYE-E736, LYE-E894, LYE-E946).

Clever boy marries the king's wives and usurps him in his office (LYE-E115, LYE-E204, LYE-E596, LYE-E597, LYE-E894).

In six out of ten Lyela variants the audience is explicitly told that the chief is clever boy's father. In one case (LYE-E736) the teller calls the hero by his own, the teller's name. Three variants apply the method of the 'split image' and the own good father is opposed to the wicked chief. In one case (LYE-E112) the chief kills his eight sons instead of the clever boy (see Paulme 1976). Following Paulme's analysis, the tale or the episode of the 'Male Giving Birth' is told in societies with very different forms of social organisation and systems of kinship. But everywhere the powerful person abusing his superior position of authority is overturned in this tale.

Almost every motif of the Mossi variant (cf. Tauxier 1917: 494–6 in Paulme 1976) can also be found in the Lyela tales though not in one single variant. The motif of the supernatural child born to an unhappy mother after a prolonged time of sterility is of course an expression of the desire for a child felt strongly by every Lyela woman. But it also symbolises the distance between the mother–son dyad on the one hand and the father on the other. After the unhappy woman has had to live for a long time with an unfulfilled desire for a child, suffering from the scorn of the other women in the compound, she is finally compensated by God himself (LYE-E946; Tauxier cf. Paulme 1976: 199) or by one of his messengers (LYE-E204). A child is born from her foot, her knee or her thigh.

In numerous West African variants clever boy provokes his father's anger by choosing his own name and especially by choosing a provocative, disrespectful name. In Mossi and Bulsa variants clever boy's mother does not miss an opportunity to call out her son's name, 'Intelligence is stronger than the chief', in a loud and penetrating voice (cf. Paulme 1976: 196). In a Lyela variant (LYE-E204) the boy is called Okɛlɛ, 'the power has come back into the world'. The boy's *nom devise* 'slogan name' implies that he is one of the returned ancestors, the old Okɛlɛ, who is reborn into the world as the clever boy. The Lyela treat children identified by the soothsayers as reborn ancestors with special generosity. They are accorded more liberties than 'normal' children (see Dinslage 1986). If the clever boy of the story is really a reborn ancestor his rank in the age hierarchy is higher than the chief's. As a reborn grandfather or greatgrandfather he is 'older' than the chief and is not obliged to submit himself to the chief's authority. Another moralising name chosen by clever boy says (LYE-E112): 'If you do something good you do good to yourself, if you do something bad, you do bad to yourself.' This name hints at the chief's bad character, suggesting his injustice and arbitrariness.

Ten of my eleven Lyela versions of clever boy and his fight against the vicious chief end up in a satisfactory way for the Lyela audience. The chief is killed, and the young hero inherits his wives. Strong boy's victory over the king is again supported by the holy power of the Earth. In variants not included in the summary the king attempts to get rid of his dubious son and pushes him into a deep ditch, but the boy is not even injured. The wicked king does not manage to kill the boy sitting in the well either with boiling hot millet-beer or with burning logs. Strong boy has the judging power of the Earth on his side, the underground tunnel offers him protection and enables him to escape (see Paulme 1976: 196).

In the end the king is drowned (two versions), burned (two others), shot with guns (four versions), and in two versions no details are given about his death. Paulme shows that the Mossi tellers took care to choose an innocent ending so as not to provoke the powerful (1976: 199). Mossi society is strongly stratified, the peasants are in the lowest stratum, and the noble lineages (*nakomse*) are used to defending their superiority by force of arms. In the kingdom of the Mossi the peasants had to mitigate the outcome of their stories. The Lyela on the other hand unfold their fantasies about the elimination of the wicked chief without any such constraints. Bayili reports that the Lyela were courageous enough to rebel against submission under district-level chieftaincies (*chefs de canton*) after their armed revolt against the

French had been suppressed with the help of artillery in 1916. A colonial officer gave the following characterisation:

De caractère frondeur et individualiste, le paysan Gourounsi est toujours prompt à répondre à son chef: 'Qui t'a fait roi'? (unp. ms.)

I interpret such Lyela stories as supporting the community's conscious decision to maintain the acephalous structure of society and to guard against the accumulation of too much political power in the hands of a chief (*pyɔ̌*). Following Lyela ideology it is the individualistic power of the self-made leader as an economically and politically powerful individual which has to be limited. The religious power of the elders in their diverse traditional offices is, on the other, hand strengthened.

In contrast to other West African traditions Lyela chiefs are *not* given explicit political and juridical tasks in the tales. They are *not* shown as belligerent conquerors who endeavour to expand their orbit of power. In these few examples and in other tales not discussed here (see Steinbrich 1987) the chiefs are used as symbolic scapegoats who have to absorb all kinds of tensions in the community: between rich and poor, young and old, men and women and especially between father and son. The analysis of Lyela tales, where one can find a 'chief' in every tenth story, shows once more, that folktales are not simply reflections of the social order. It shows rather how much people who seem determined to keep an acephalous, segmentary social order are occupied with the problem of power, its accumulation, proper use and its abuse.

PART III

Oral forms and the dynamics of power

CHAPTER 8

Power, marginality and Somali oral poetry: case studies in the dynamics of tradition

John William Johnson

The performance of Somali oral poetry on the Horn of Africa is not limited to formal presentations to defined audiences. Many instances of the performance of verse occur in non-formal situations, often overlooked and considered culturally insignificant by scholars of the past, who have concentrated their efforts on the highly prestigious classical genres used to debate political and social issues overtly in this East African, Cushitic society. Among the powerful, which means for the most part, elder men, work songs are considered to be of low prestige, and thus study and analysis of them has been neglected by scholars, both Somali and foreign alike. In so doing, a large body of traditional lore has been overlooked, both from the point of view of aesthetics and of social interaction in very interesting contexts. Moreover, the most recent genre to develop in Somalia, called *hees* or *heello*, began its career with low prestige, because it, too, was the voice of marginal segments of the society. As an urban-based genre, *heellooyin* have always been composed and recited by the youth of the country and even by women. In fact, it was with this genre that public performances by women became socially acceptable.

This chapter describes some common situations of work and illustrates how poetry is employed as an act of communication and even defiance between individuals and groups which are marginal in the power structure of Somalia and those who hold power in that country. This communication often happens in situations that are very delicate and even socially volatile. Indeed, in the case of work poetry, the message may not even be related to the work being conducted to its rhythm, the work only lending itself as a convenient activity during which to facilitate communication on very sensitive issues by individuals otherwise excluded from the main power structure of the society. I illustrate this activity by describing four scenarios, in which I ask you, the reader, to imagine yourself as the key role player in each of these situations.

In the first scenario, you are an urban housewife in Muqdisho, the capital of the Somali Democratic Republic. You were raised in the countryside, as was your husband, but you have moved to the city with him because he has obtained a post in the burgeoning bureaucracy of the federal government. You frequently have house guests, and many of them are members of your husband's extended family. In fact, they flock to him because he has employment and lives in the capital city. One such house guest is Bashiir, a nephew – your husband's sister's son – who has come to live with you whilst attending a local middle school. He is very loyal to your husband, but since you are a member of a different lineage, he does not feel such loyalty to you and is insensitive and often rude to you, at times nearly intolerable. He takes things without asking. Such is his right by custom, but he over-indulges his matrilineal rights, and takes advantage of his maternal uncle and his uncle's family. For instance, after the noon meal one day, when many people rest because of the heat near the equator, you are exhausted. The heaviest work of the day has been done, namely the morning shopping and preparing the main meal. As is the custom in Muqdisho, you want to lie down and rest from about 2:30 or 3:00 until about 4:00 or 5:00. Bashiir wants you to play dominoes with him. You indulge him for a while because he is your husband's kinsman, but finding yourself unable to break loose from him, an argument ensues. And your husband walks in on the fight unexpectedly, overhearing only the end of the verbal exchanges. He accuses you of disrespect for his blood kin – you are doubly frustrated, but a good wife does not talk back to her husband! Society does not give her the power to directly confront the authority of her husband.

Relations between you and your husband are strained for several days, and he even refuses to take his noon meal with you, upsetting the daily routine in the life of the family. Brooding for some time, you compose a poem reserved for women's affairs, in a genre called *buraambur*. Next evening while your husband is resting in the courtyard, and you are sweeping the day's fallen leaves into a pile, you sing the poem within his earshot. You sing it several times, as though just passing the time away whilst working. . . Is he listening? . . . Did he hear? . . . You sing it again . . . Did he hear it this time?[1]

> Anoo tukadayoo sariir gogladay,
> Bashiir baa iigu soo boqooloo belo dhigay,
> Dibnaduu ii keenay baa naa dareen i galay,
> Dacwada yaa iga bogsiiyoo dad iigu xiga,
> Duhurkii inaan kala didnaa waa dabeecad xumo,
> Dunida maantiyo da'deenoo dhan waa ku ceeb,

Sabniyoo weeyiyo sanadahan wax laga ilbaxay,
Sowjadaada soorteeda laga tago,
Sabniyoo weeyiyo sanadahan wax laga ilbaxay,

  Anoo tukadayoo sariir gogladay,
  Bashiir baa iigu soo boqooloo belo dhigay,
  Dibnaduu ii keenay baa naa dareen i galay,
  Dabeyshii caafimaad buu dagaal dhaxdhigay,
  Dacwada yaa iga bogsiiyo dad iigu xigaa,
  Duhurkii inaan kala didnaa waa dabeecad xumo,
  Dunida maantiyo da'deenoo dhan waa ku ceeb,
  Inay doodeeniyeey derisyadu maqlaan,
  Dunida maantiyo da'deenoo dhan waa ku ceeb,

Whilst I did pray and make the bed for sleep,
Bashiir came in at noon and angered me.
The dominoes he brought caused consternation.
Who can restore my health in this complaint;
  who is closer kin to me than other people?
To disrupt our family life at noon is very bad.
In the world today our peers frown on divorce.
Through the years the public changed their attitudes
About forsaking meals their wives prepared.
Through the years the public changed their attitudes.

  Whilst I did pray and make the bed for sleep,
  Bashiir came in at noon and angered me.
  The dominoes he brought caused consternation.
  He brought dissension to our healthy home.
  Who can restore my health in this complaint;
    who is closer kin to me than other people?
  To disrupt our family life at noon is very bad.
  In the world today our peers frown upon divorce.
  Our neighbours often hear the quarrel here.
  In the world today our peers frown upon divorce.

The next morning your husband seems short-tempered with his
nephew. Finally an open fight breaks out, and you listen as your
husband chastises his nephew for a multitude of sins, including
interfering with the smooth routines of daily work in the household.
Message sent . . . Message received . . . All is now well between you and
your husband. Confidence is restored.

   Another scenario: you are a stevedore at the main port facilities in
Muqdisho.[2] Marketing in Somalia does not operate on fixed prices but
on bargaining, and labour negotiations are no exception to this rule.
As is the custom, negotiations for work are made each morning by
competing crews of men who make up the labour-force at the port.

You have brought several of your kinsmen to the docks in order to make up a work crew large enough to load and unload materials on and off ocean-going ships now berthed in the port. And since you are the elder, you are the organiser of the crew; you conduct the negotiations concerning the pay for the day's work. An agreement is reached, and your crew begins its work. One of your kinsmen is not doing his fair share, and the other workers are becoming more and more disgruntled about his laziness. In fact, they are beginning to slack off themselves, and this fact is becoming apparent to the dock bosses at the port authority. Your crew's chances of being rehired for similar work the next day are threatened. But the slacking worker is a kinsman of yours, and since you must show loyalty and courtesy to him publicly, especially in front of other Somalis not in your extended family, you choose not to confront him directly. But what can you do?!

During the work, songs are being sung by you and the other workers. It helps keep up the pace of work and prevent accidents dangerous to the workers. Embedded inside one of the poems you place a veiled message to your lazy kinsman. You disguise the message so that only he and the other members of your crew can understand. You tell him that he is endangering the day's work, and that negotiating tomorrow will become difficult if his poor behaviour continues. You threaten to dismiss him at the end of the day and not to include him in the work crew tomorrow. The man hears the message and picks up his pace. Message sent . . . Message received . . . All is now well between you and your crew, and between you and the dock bosses who will be more likely to hire you and your kinsmen tomorrow.

A third scenario: you are a middle-aged woman and a mother living in the bush with your family, herding animals and seasonally migrating according to the rhythm of the rains.[3] Your youngest daughter has finally reached the age of marriage, taken off her head covering to expose her hair to the public, braiding it in the manner which announces that she is marriageable. In consultation with his elder male kinsmen, your husband has carefully weighed the alternatives involved in choosing a suitable husband for his daughter, and negotiated with a neighbouring family for a fine young man for his daughter and a useful social and perhaps political joining of two noble lineages. But you don't think he is a fine young man at all. In fact you think he is decidedly inappropriate for the match. You are overcome with frustration, anger and resentment! But what can you do?! You are powerless over the collective decision of your husband's male clansmen.

One day, on the way to the wells, you sing a herding song to the dominant ram in your flock of sheep and goats. The song chastises the ram for choosing the wrong mate for his youngest ewe-daughter. You make certain that the husband can hear your song, and you sing it several times within his earshot. You may not have any authority to speak out in this matter, but you are definitely going to have your opinion known in no uncertain terms! Message sent . . . You hope the message has been received.

The final scenario (Johnson 1974: 123–5): you are a junior radio announcer at Radio Muqdisho. You have been assigned the envied task of covering parliamentary elections for President of the Republic, and you are sitting behind your microphone, announcing to an anxious public the goings-on here on the floor of the largest chamber in parliament. From your stall at the very top of the gallery, you can see everything happening on the floor: the Members of Parliament, the electronic voting board, the Speaker, the present President Aadan Cabdulle Cismaan, the contenders, Cabdi-rashiid Cali Shar-Ma-Arke, and others. A vote is taken; it is time consuming, so you play music (the modern song/poem, a genre called *heello* or *hees*), while the MPs caucus and cast their votes. The music and poetry is set up on loud speakers so the parliamentarians, as well as the radio audience, can hear it. The vote is announced: no majority! Another caucus ensues; more music and poetry; another vote; another announcement: no majority. Yet another caucus occurs; more interlude entertainment. This time you pick a cassette tape to play on which is recorded a very popular contemporary poem called 'Leexo'. On the floor of parliament and over the nation's radio waves, the voice of the singer goes out:

Innakoo lammaane ah,	While we were yet together,
Iyo laba naf-qaybsile,	Helping one other in every way,
Talo geed ku laashee,	You cast good counsel away, to the top of a high tree;
Adigaa is lumiyo,	You caused yourself distress,
Isu loogay cadowgoo,	And slaughtered yourself for your enemy,
Libintaadii siiyee,	Giving your victory to him,
Waadigan se liitee,	Now you are so weakened
Leexadu ku sidatee,	That light breezes bear you up,
Had ba laan cuskanayee,	And from time to time you grasp at a branch.
Liibaanteed adduunyada,	For all the pleasures of this earth
Ruux na laasan maayee,	One cannot fully enjoy;
Maxaa luray naftaadii.	Tell me what causes you this distress?
Waa laac adduunyadu,	The world is but a mirage.
Labadii walaalo ah,	And for every two brothers,
Mid ba maalin ladanyoo,	Only one being happy each day,
Ruuxii u liil-galay,	The one who is fortunate

La ma loolo dhereggoo,   Should not abuse his prosperity;
Luggooyada ma geystee,   Should not maltreat his neighbour.
  Waadigan se laabtiyo,   And in your case, however,
  Lugaha is la waayaye,   Your breast and feet were out of accord.
  Meel sare lalanayee,   For you are drifting up, up into the air.
  Liibaanteed adduunyada,   For all the pleasures of this earth
  Ruux na laasan maayee,   One cannot fully enjoy;
  Maxaa luray naftaadii.   Tell me what causes you this distress?

Aniga ba laftiyo jiidh,   Behold my flesh and all my bones
Waakii i laastaan,   Were completely consumed by him.
Liqi waayay oontee,   I cannot even swallow food!
  Adigaa lis caanood,   The abundance of milk,
  Iyo laad xareediyo,   Pure rainwater,
  Laydhiyo hadh diidee,   Fresh air, and rest in the cool shade: you have
                                 rejected.

  Waadigan sidii liig,   It is you, who like the male garanuug,
  Laasimay ugaadhee,   Left the (other) game, and
  Waaclada u leexdee,   Turned to a desolate place.
  Liibaanteed adduunyada,   For all the pleasures of this earth
  Ruux na laasan maayee,   One cannot fully enjoy;
  Maxaa luray naftaadii.   Tell me what causes you this distress?

Dhaaxaad ladnaan rays,   So often in the prosperity of the rains,
Sidaad aar libaax tay,   As though you were a (proud) lion,
Taalaabada ladhaaysoo,   You walked about majestically,
  Anna lahashadaadii,   Whilst I, because of your carousing,
  Ledi waayay ciil oo,   Had sleepless nights from impotent anger,
  Liidnimo i raacdee,   And sometimes behaved like a fool.
  Lallabaa habeenkiyo,   The beacon-fire in the night
  Ma libdhaan jacayl oo,   And love: they never disappear;
  Waa labalegdoodaan,   They roll on after you, unrestrained.
  Liibaanteed adduunyada,   For all the pleasures of this earth
  Ruux na laasan maayee,   One cannot fully enjoy;
  Maxaa luray naftaadii.   Tell me what causes you this distress?

Innakoo lammaane ah,   While we were yet together,
Iyo laba naf-qaybsile,   Helping one other in every way,
Talo geed ku laashee,   You cast good council away, to the top of a high tree;
  Adigaa is lumiyo,   You caused yourself distress,
  Isu loogay cadowgoo,   And slaughtered yourself for your enemy,
  Libintaadii siiyee,   Giving your victory to him.
  Waadigan se liitee,   Now you are so weakened
  Leexadu ku sidatee,   That light breezes bear you up,
  Had ba laan cuskanayee,   And from time to time you grasp at a branch.
  Liibaanteed adduunyada,   For all the pleasures of this earth
  Ruux na laasan maayee,   One cannot fully enjoy;
  Maxaa luray naftaadii.   Tell me what causes you this distress?

Poem over; caucus completed; vote announced: Somalia has a new
president, Dr Cabdi-rashiid Cali Shar-Ma-Arke! The next day you are
arrested by the Criminal Investigation Division and charged with

sedition against the state: influencing parliamentary voting with your choice of poem played over the airwaves. The word goes out far and wide: the poem 'Leexo' has brought down the government of Aadan Cabdulle Cismaan. Later in your trial, your lawyer argues that the poem is a lover's lament. Besides, he claims, it was composed earlier, not at the time of the election. How could it be a political statement? Nothing can be proved against you, so you are acquitted and released. But did you really choose that poem because of the political context of the elections and the symbolism of the poem? Or was it just an entertaining piece of music for the interlude between votes? No one ever finds out. 'Leexo' will forever be known as the poem that brought down a government. And this incident, as well as many others, will ultimately influence government policies concerning what is allowed and what is not allowed to be broadcast over the airwaves in Somalia.

All of these scenarios are true; they are not hypothetical cases. None of them was made up just to make a point. They exhibit a remarkable range of performance of Somali oral poetry employed for social intercourse. This kind of communication is not something that smaller segments of the population are involved in; it is not professional or specialised. It does not even require creative skills only the very talented are capable of, as poetic composition of this kind is open to almost everyone in the country. Somalia has often, and for good reason, been called *a nation of poets*, an epithet surviving from the first Western pre-colonial explorer to visit Somalia in the nineteenth century who noticed this remarkable use of verse. I mean, of course, the renowned explorer and scholar, Sir Richard Burton, the same Burton who joined with other European explorers like John Hanning Speke, David Livingstone and Henry Morton Stanley, in the mad search for the source of the River Nile. Burton visited the far north coast of Somalia in 1855 disguised as an Arab, and was astonished at the extensive use of poetry by so many people in so many situations, describing it in his book about this journey, *First Footsteps in East Africa*, with the following passage:

The country teams with poets, poetasters, poetitos, poetaccios: every man has his recognized position in literature as accurately defined as though he had been reviewed in a century of magazines, the fine ear of his people causing them to take the greatest pleasure in harmonious sounds and poetical expressions, whereas a false quality or a prosaic phrase excites their violent indignation (Burton 1966a: 93).

We must forgive Burton his sexist orientation; in fact I do not know if he even explored women's poetic talents at that time, but what he says of men in this passage could also be said of women as well. Indeed, the situation remains similar to what it was almost a hundred and fifty years ago. Somali poetry is remarkable for many reasons, and has been extensively studied, but the work poetry, as earlier stated, has heretofore been neglected. A book on this topic, by Axmed Cali Abokor (1993) has shed a lot of light on this too long neglected topic. The title of Axmed's book reveals the basic theoretical idea in the work: *Somali Pastoral Work Songs: The Poetic Voice of the Political Powerless*. Let us look more closely at work songs.

The delineation of forms of work in Somali life is culturally defined according to several criteria. Watering animals, for example, is not specific enough. The watering of camels, cattle and caprines (sheep and goats, which are herded together) are considered different forms of work. Even more specific, the watering of adult and juvenile caprines is differentiated as separate units of work in Somali nomadic life. Each of these culturally defined areas of labour is accompanied by its own specific genre of oral poetry. Each of these genres bears a unique name in Somali, and is characterised – as are all Somali genres – by four criteria: a specific scansion pattern, a group of melodies to which it and no other genre may be sung, a narrow range of social functions and a narrow range of topics appropriate for use with it. Work poetry in general helps people keep the proper pace of specified work, and it can even be argued that it aids in the prevention of accidents in the work place with such labour as tossing full water containers to waiting hands from the bottom of deep wells, in timing of the pounding of grain in mortars by more than one woman wielding a pestle, or in the loading of heavy materials at the docks mentioned earlier. A partial list of genres from the pastoral economy alone will illustrate how Somalis divide work in the countryside, and includes the following forms:[4]

hees-geel	camel watering song
hees-lo'	cattle watering song
hees-adhi	adult caprine watering song
hees-maqal	baby caprine watering song
hees-ido	adult sheep watering song
hees-riyaad	adult goat watering song
hees-waxaro	kid goat watering song
hees-naylo	lamb watering song
hees-carruur	lullaby
hees-alool	mat-weaving song

hees-kebed	another mat-weaving song
hees-harar	another mat-weaving song
hees-haan	clarified-butter churning song
hees-mooye	mortar-pounding song

Also of interest is the use of much of this poetry to mediate social tensions in the extended family and its use to debate social and political issues both overtly and through the use of veiled speech. Debate, banter and even mocking verses among nomads in the pastoral workplace is communicated through the words of work songs, ostensibly composed to pass the time of boring, repetitive work. Some of the social interactions involved with this poetry involve issues such as male–female banter and tensions, conflict between different lineages, hostility between city dwellers and country folk and competition between farmers and pastoral nomads.

While some work poetry is situation specific and even person specific, other poems reflect more general tensions and attitudes which sometimes exist between segments of society. Men and women, for example, tease each other in verse, reflecting some of the tensions they share in daily life. This poetic banter can be illustrated in a popular mortar-pounding song in which a soloist is answered by a rhythmic chorus of women who may happen to be in the compound when she is at work. The poem goes as follows:[4]

Gaacalooy, gacalooy,	gacalooy,	Yes, my dear, yes, my dear, my dear,
Gaacalooy, gacalooy,	gacalooy,	Yes, my dear, yes, my dear, my dear,
Gaacantay midigay,	gacalooy,	You are like my right arm, my dear,
Waan ku faaninayaa,	gacalooy,	I am praising your charm, my dear,
Faan u waa kugu yaal,	gacalooy,	You deserve all the praise, my dear,
Faayahaad ku siddaa,	gacalooy,	Your beauty shines on your face, my dear,
Afar kaaga digaa,	gacalooy,	Let me warn you 'gainst four, my dear,
Kaaga dayriyayaa,	gacalooy,	I will make you reject them, my dear,
Gaacalooy, gacalooy,	gacalooy,	Yes, my dear, yes, my dear, my dear,
Kaaga diin dhigayaa,	gacalooy,	An amulet for you I will write, my dear,
Ninka geesi ha gursan,	gacalooy,	Do not marry the brave man, my dear,
Ninka gaaban ha gursan,	gacalooy,	Do not marry the short man, my dear,
Ninka dheer na ha gursan,	gacalooy,	Do not marry a tall man, my dear,
Fuuleygii na ha gursan,	gacalooy,	Do not marry the coward, my dear,
Ninka geesi ha gursan,	gacalooy,	Do not marry the brave man, my dear,
Marka geela la qaado,	gacalooy,	Your camels will be looted, my dear,
Guudubbu ka erdaa,	gacalooy,	He'll run after them first, my dear,

Geeb xun baa la dhigaa,	gacalooy,	The battle will slay him first, my dear,
Geeblan buu ku badaa,	gacalooy,	And he'll make you a widow, my dear,
Gaacalooy, gacalooy,	gacalooy,	Yes, my dear, yes, my dear, my dear,
Ninka gaaban ha gursan,	gacalooy,	Do not marry the short man, my dear,
Marka geelu cadhooboo,	gacalooy,	For when the camels get mange, my dear,
Garba-saarka ma gaadhe,	gacalooy,	The sores will be out of reach, my dear,
Goondhuhuu ka dhayaa,	gacalooy,	He'll cure only camels' hooves, my dear,
Ninka dheer na ha gursan,	gacalooy,	Do not marry the tall man, my dear,
Marka gaajo timaad,	gacalooy,	For, when hunger attacks, my dear,
Guriguu is goglaa,	gacalooy,	He'll be asleep in the house, my dear,
Go'ayeey ku yidhaa,	gacalooy,	He'll say to you, 'I'm dying,' my dear,
Waa na baahi darteed,	gacalooy,	He could be right, and he'll need you, my dear,
Waa na been quwideed,	gacalooy,	But he may be lying to you, my dear,
Fuuleydii na ha gursan,	gacalooy,	Do not marry the coward, my dear,
Meel fa'iis ka teguu,	gacalooy,	Because you'll often find him, my dear,
Fayle-weyn yahayee,	gacalooy,	In a place where his friends have all departed, my dear,
Fool-xumuu la rergaa,	gacalooy.	He'll always bring you shame, my dear.

In conclusion, the people of Somalia have a long history of dealing with their political and social issues through the medium of oral poetic composition. Since the advent of European colonialism in the country, Somali and foreign scholars alike have collected, transcribed, described, analysed, and theorised extensively about this poetry in literary journals, in books and at many an academic conference. Somali oral critics, of which there are many, have made exegeses of their oral art for an even longer period of time, perhaps for as long as this poetry has been employed in the political and social limelight. Some of this poetry is truly breathtaking in its aesthetic beauty and linguistic complexity. Saciid Sheekh Samatar remarks in his book about the Sayid Maxamed Cabdille Xasan (1982) that soldiers in the British military expedition to Somalia in the early part of this century would have been astonished to have known that the man they called the 'Mad Mullah' composed poetry comparable in aesthetic quality to their own William Shakespeare. But these genres, the *gabay*, *jiifto*, *buraambur*, *geeraar*, *guurow*, and *masafo* are very structurally complex forms. Their main functions in society are political and their composition requires great skill and years of training. Their impact enjoys high prestige and their poets and reciters attain fame like Western film stars and novelists. In this essay, I have dealt with forms of poetry which represent the voice of people who are marginal in the Somali power structure. Their poetry may not attain the aesthetic heights of the classical genres, but they are nonetheless valid, and perhaps even more influential in the long run, within the daily flow of Somali social relations. Work poetry and, to some extent, the modern popular song or *heello*, are the voice of the numerous masses of Somalia: the youth, the women, the politically disenfranchised. Their poetry is simpler in its structure, of lower prestige in the overall aesthetic of oral art, and seemingly innocent in its overt function, providing rhythm, among many things, for pounding grain, churning milk, for dancing and watering camels and goats. In reality, its functional innocence lends power to its rhetoric and overall impact, because it catches the powerful off guard. Composed for other reasons, suddenly a work song can catch the authorities unawares by voicing some underlying social tension or attitude by those not permitted or skilled enough to express themselves in the prestigious forms of the political elite. If we are to have a more holistic understanding of Somali society and its use of poetry in the conduct of it social affairs, including politics, we must not neglect the media reserved for the marginal and powerless on the Horn of Africa. To paraphrase Hamlet: 'There are more ways to express poetic opinions in Somalia, Horatio, than are dreamt of in our current literary theories.'

NOTES

1 This poem was collected from Isniino Cartan Maxamed in her home in Muqdisho.
2 This information was collected in an interview with Mohamad Moallim Profume in Muqdisho. Profume has an extensive collection of work poetry he has collected in the city life in Muqdisho and his knowledge is extensive concerning how work poetry from the Somali countryside has been converted to new uses in city life.
3 This information was collected in an interview with the renowned Somali scholar Xaaji Muuse Xaaji Ismaaciil Galaal.
4 This poem was collected by Muuse Galaal in the 1960s (when I was working with him through the auspices of the United States Peace Corps) and translated by Muuse and myself.

CHAPTER 9

The function of oral art in the regulation of social power in Dyula society

Jean Derive

In societies with an oral culture the social circulation of verbal genres is governed by precise rules stipulating which social units may produce them and which consume them. This etiquette is itself an expression of power relationships: certain groups produce genres which others are not allowed to perform; some groups enjoy the exclusive privilege of hearing speeches which others must perform for them. But these power relationships which are bound into the practice of oral art are not independent of other power relationships based upon moral, economic or political criteria.

On one level, power in the realm of institutional orality may seem to be merely consequent on other already-held social power, the former being nothing more than a distinctive sign of the latter (as it may be in the case of dress, for example). However, on another level, orality may also constitute itself an effective tool of power in that speech may have a direct effect through its performative or ideological functions.

In this chapter, I examine the range of relationships between social power and the practice of orality in Dyula society. The Dyula are an ethnic group based around Kong, a large village of 1,500 inhabitants in north-eastern Ivory Coast. Here, it is possible to count some fifty institutional oral genres, authenticated by a local taxonomy. If some, such as folktale (*ntàlen*) or riddle (*ntàlenkɔrɔbɔ*), may, roughly speaking, circulate freely in the society (anyone being allowed to perform them for anyone), this is not the case for most genres. There have been a number of studies of Dyula oral genres, including: (J. Derive 1978, 1980, 1984, 1987a and b, 1990; M. J. Derive 1978; Derive and Diabaté 1977; Derive et al. 1980; Giray-Saul 1989; Nebie 1984; Prouteaux 1985).

In this discussion I begin by investigating the rules by which the Dyula demarcate the social units that have the right or duty to produce or receive various oral genres. We shall then be in a better position to understand the nature of the relationships between the institutional practice of speech and the general system of power, viewed from a range of vantage points. These social units are characterised by several criteria.

Age

Dyula who have not reached maturity are excluded from participating in certain oral genres, either in their performance and/or reception. For example, only persons who have reached maturity are allowed to tell *lámara*, which may be translated by 'proverbs', or *kó kòrɔ*, kinship group chronicles mixing history and legend. In the same way, only those who have passed through the initiation ceremony given on reaching a certain age are allowed to perform, or even hear, certain powerful and dangerous mask songs belonging to the initiation cult.

Gender

Gender is another relevant criterion in the social sharing of oral genres. Thus the *kó kòrɔ*, chronicles, are the speech of men more than of women. Sexual exclusivity is even more marked in other cases. A large proportion of mask songs are hidden from women, who are not allowed to be initiated into the mask cult. They are similarly excluded from war songs (*cúkuri cúkuri*). On the other hand, women have monopoly of some wedding songs and many dance songs; songs for female circumcision (*kɛ̀nɛkɛ̀nɛ dɔnkili*) and *kúrubi* songs, which they sing when they have a grievance to air with their close relations.

Caste

In Kong there are two endogamic castes, free citizens, *hɔ́rɔn*, and domestic slaves, *wóloso*. There is no firm rule stipulating that the *wóloso* are excluded from the production or reception of certain genres of oral art but there are some effective restrictions. For example the *kó kòrɔ* chronicles which recreate the past of Dyula kin groups are seen as not concerning uprooted people such as the *wóloso* who were obtained by purchase or as prisoners of war. In the same way, the *wóloso* do not take a part in performing Islamic songs because their faith is not highly valued.

Nevertheless, except in the above cases, the *hɔ́rɔn* who hold economic and political power, do not forbid the *wóloso* to participate in the different genres of their oral folklore, perhaps because the power conferred by the right to perform such discourses is not of a political nature. It is probably not chance that the single restriction concerns historical chronicles and Islamic songs. These genres are indeed the ones which are political in nature, the first on a temporal level, and the second on a religious one.

Yet although the *wóloso* can associate with the *hɔ́rɔn* in almost all the discourses of oral tradition, they themselves have a monopoly on certain genres. In the first instance, they monopolise *wóloso dɔ́nkili*, slaves' songs, the very genre of the caste, as its name shows. The fact that they are the sole performers of such songs indicates the voicing of a kind of power exclusive to the *wóloso*; they are not highly appreciated, and no one would be likely to contest their right to perform them. Nevertheless, since such songs are often salacious parodies of other genres of Dyula folklore, chiefly aimed at the *hɔ́rɔn*, the performing of these songs is an expression of power that the *hɔ́rɔn*, restrained by decency, cannot allow themselves to participate in or interfere with. We shall further see how the content of these songs provides the *wóloso* with the opportunity of exercising real social power.

A further example of the link between oral genre and social power in the case of the *wóloso* caste is the specialised performance of *bàra*, a sort of showdance which is a medley of other genres. From the *bàra*, performed to order, the *wóloso* gain economic and social benefits, hence showing in a different context the link between genre production and the exercise of a kind of power.

Village district
Kong is divided into several districts (*kàbila*), each of which has its specific discourses, especially in the field of mask songs and dance songs. The distribution of songs through the different districts is itself the sign of a certain hierarchy, since a thorough listing of Dyula genres shows that certain *kàbila* use more genres than others. The ability to produce a great number of cultural speeches, as opposed to mask and dance songs, is generally proportional to the numerical importance of the districts. However, the *kàbila* with most political or religious power perform only a very few songs of this kind. We may assume, therefore, that the performance of such songs indicates a sort of compensation in the balance of powers.

Kinship group
Within the *hɔ́rɔn* caste, each kin group, identified by the same patronymic (*jàmu*) is in charge of the production of certain 'device songs', the function of which is to praise another kin group, according to specific alliances. Each kin group also possesses its own repertoire of chronicles (*kó kɔ̀rɔ*) which are only for personal use.

Social function

Some genres are linked to specific social functions, such as for example, hunter songs (*dàndaga dɔ̀nkili*). In the same way, the genre of *jɔ̀mɛndɛ dɔ̀nkili* is sung by a griot (*jèliba*) who performs it during the month which begins the Koranic year. This type of song commemorates the gratitude of the griot's ancestor to the leading kin group (the Watara) for a gift offered in the past. Lastly, the leaders of the districts (*kàbilatigi*) have the sole right to relate more general chronicles of Dyula history, which go beyond the framework of each kin group.

In general, as we can see from the above instances, there is a social sharing of verbal genres relating to status and function in Dyula society. There are further examples of this which we can point to. For instance, the right to tell *kó kɔ̀rɔ* is determined by the following criteria: age, district affiliation, kin group and gender, since such power is preferentially granted to men. Similarly, mask songs are common to many districts and their performance is governed by criteria of exclusion relating to age and gender, as here too, women are excluded.

Thus the intersecting social units of Dyula society combine to give the individual access to different kinds of power, although the overarching and fundamental divisions remain those of age and gender. Within these grand divisions, though, membership of overlapping categories remains important and governs access to the production of genres of song. Thus verbal production relates to one's membership of a particular kin group. This is itself combined, in a *kàbila*, with a broader membership which gives the individual access to another group of songs belonging distinctively to a particular *kàbila*; membership of a particular caste gives the individual access to yet other songs relating to a sense of hierarchy and consciousness of solidarity based upon common interests.

We can thus conclude that the power of producing verbal art is always bound to a social condition. But we have still to investigate in which cases such power is merely a distinctive sign of this social condition and in which cases it constitutes an effective means of pressure within the general system of power relationships in Dyula society. Answering this question is the task of the second part of this analysis.

Among the Dyula, the practice of institutional orality may offer performers opportunity for positive action against certain social groups, either by means of a sort of implicit pressure on them, or through ideological pressure by the portrayal of cultural stereotypes.

'Implicit pressure' is exerted by those who perform certain speeches, insofar as those at whom these speeches are aimed need them – to reinforce their social position – or are afraid of them, through fear of being a butt for speeches which will cause public shame or ruin.

A good example of the 'implicit pressure' is offered by the performers of *bàra* (*bàrakɛbaga*) who belong to the *wóloso* caste. In the performance of this genre, they praise the *hɔ́rɔn* who has requested the show. Yet this means that this *hɔ́rɔn* is in the hands of the interpreter who can, through his speech, offer him more or less social support. In this way, the *bàrakɛbaga* exerts pressure as a result of which he gains material benefits in the form of gifts or money.

There are other social units which implicitly pressurise others, not by the threat of withholding a laudatory speech, but by the threat of producing a socially damaging speech. This is what the women do with *kúrubi* songs. These songs are small circumstantial epigrams which women perform at the end of Ramadan, according to a Dyula cultural code, to hint at the domestic problems they have had to face during the year, especially with their husbands, their in-laws and their co-wives. Through this genre, which is exclusively theirs, the women can effectively exert pressure. A husband or a son-in-law fears such public criticism – even though the rules of the genre require that the criticism remains allusive rather than direct – and their behaviour towards women may be mitigated by the fear of such an eventuality and such public criticism.

Another social group in Kong, the *wóloso*, exerts a more or less similar pressure though its function is more ambiguous. The members of this caste are the sole owners of songs parodying other genres (most of the time ceremonial songs) in an obscene form. When they perform such songs, the *wóloso* receive money from the *hɔ́rɔn*. The official explanation of this tradition is that, since these songs cause shame among well-educated people, it is necessary to quickly move the singers away by offering them gifts. But the phenomenon may be more complex. Indeed, if the *hɔ́rɔn*, because of their social status are obliged to express shame on hearing such obscene songs, it is clear that, at the same time, they do take pleasure in watching other people doing what decency prohibits them from doing. It may even be asked whether it is not the *hɔ́rɔn* caste which has given such a function to the *wóloso* in order to create a longed-for catharsis? The money the *wóloso* receive on these occasions can be seen, paradoxically, as both an entreaty to stop, and a reward for speaking the hidden desires of those whom they address.

Another form of 'implicit pressure' may be linked to the transcendent power associated with the performance of certain sacred genres. Those with the exclusive right to articulate these will be treated deferentially by those who fear they may be the targets of a particular performance. This is true as well for certain Islamic genres performed by Koranic masters (*kàramɔgɔ*), and on the animist side of Dyula culture, for the mask songs to which only initiates have access.

The second major kind of power exerted by institutional orality is what we have called 'ideological power': a power by means of which a social group imposes upon others cultural concepts according to its self-interest. For example, by keeping the privilege of telling historical chronicles, the oldest men, leaders of kin groups, can impose upon the whole of Dyula society a pattern of control which is both gerontocratic and phallocratic. The heroes of these narrations, depicted as the founders of the present social order, are generally elders – and ancestors – and this double emphasis is another way of justifying the precedence of the older generations. The most aged women, likewise, exert pressure on the young ones by performing certain wedding songs which present models of behaviour for future wives.

Having demonstrated the link between institutional orality and pressure, either 'implied' or ideological, I now turn to the relationship between verbal power and domains such as the political, the economic, the religious and the customary.

In Kong, the political and economic hierarchy functions at three levels: those of caste, district and kin. In such a traditional structure – although this may sometimes be undercut by the influence of modernity – powers reside with men of the *hɔrɔn* caste who are themselves set in a hierarchic order according to kin group, with the Watara (the descendants of Sekou Watara, founder of Kong kingdom), at the top of the hierarchy. In this kin group are the customary territorial chief (corresponding to the former king, nowadays called *jàmantigi*) and the chief of the village (*dùgutigi*). Among the members of the *hɔrɔn* caste, the old men always hold political power, and the roles of kin group chief (*lútigi*) or district chief (*kàbilatigi*) are reserved for the oldest men.

Religious power, which is held by particular kin groups in Kong (Saganogo and Baro for Islam, Diabagate and Watara for the animist mask cult) is also masculine. In both Islam and animism women are without exception subordinate or entirely excluded.

Customary moral power is based above all on the criterion of age, and secondarily on gender, a man being regarded as having more moral authority than a woman of the same age. But in a general way old people, in this moral context, always exert authority in the sphere of what constitutes right behaviour, for instance, over younger ones, no matter what sex, caste or kin group the individuals belong to. So an old *wóloso* woman may exert her moral authority over a young *hɔ́rɔn* boy, even if he belongs to the leading kin group of the Watara.

There is undoubtedly a certain agreement between social power and access to the oral genres at the top of the Dyula hierarchy, namely those known as *kumaba*, 'important talk'; thus the old chiefs of kin groups tell the historical chronicles (*kó kɔ̀rɔ*) which authenticate cultural identity; the Koranic masters have the use of Islamic genres, and initiated men the use of mask songs. Also the oldest generations of each sex keep a certain control over social morals by the use of *lámara*, proverbs. However, in Kong those who possess the largest part of such social powers, the political and religious leaders, more widely the *hɔ́rɔn*, and more widely still the aged men, perform very few genres of the Dyula oral patrimony and do not in any way monopolise the whole field of speech to legitimise their authority.

In a society in which power is autocratic and hereditary, with a vaguely theocratic base (the founding nations of the Kong kingdom portray the leading founders as being chosen by God and their victory as the victory of Islam over animism), a chief does not need to constantly provide ideological justification for his authority. His power is not regarded as a historical accident, but as belonging to the natural order of the world. Similarly gerontocratic and phallocratic powers are seen as so basic that they need only the minimum of ideological support necessary to legitimate their origin.

Nor is it the case among the Dyula that those who have the power are the ones who in some way 'manage' the whole very extensive patrimony of oral genres (around fifty in all). Indeed, among the Dyula, to talk too much is a sign of weakness. The powerful have influential speech but its very strength results from its scarceness. Therefore the powerful individual is not so much the one who talks, as the one who is the recipient of speeches performed for him by others. So the main *hɔ́rɔn* kin groups profit from *wóloso* praises, when, for example, *bàra* or *jɔ̀nmɛndɛ dɔ̀nkili* are performed.

On the other hand – and it is an important aspect of relationships between speech and power – institutional orality gives wide scope for offering compensation to dominated social groups (women, children, slaves), who are indeed holders of the main areas of this field and who take most part in its production.

Sometimes this institutional orality offers them a simulacrum of power which is a sort of pale reflection of what in real social terms they do not have. For example, women who take only a very minor part in the spoken liturgy within the framework of Islamic worship, perform some songs which begin with Koranic verses. In the same way, male children who are too young to be initiated into the secret language of masks, hold, in a ludic field, their own secret language which anticipates initiation language. Sometimes the compensation is material rather than gestural. We already remarked that from the performing of *bàra* or *wóloso dɔnkili*, the slave caste can gain economic profit.

In other cases, some genres offer a cathartic antidote to the experience of social subjection: for instance some wedding songs in which the future wife cries because of her new matrimonial condition; some parodic songs of the *wóloso* probably perform such a function. Lastly, institutional orality offers such groups the opportunity to exert counter-powers as we have observed in the case of the *wóloso* towards the *hɔrɔn*, on the one hand, and in the case of women towards men, on the other. These dominated groups use songs which present them with the opportunity to exercise what I have called 'implicit pressure' against the dominating group and so mitigate and limit the domination.

Orality is therefore not only the field of expression of social powers of a political, economic or moral nature, but also the expression of counter-powers. Nevertheless, in order that such counter-powers do not become so subversive as to overthrow the established order, it is necessary that the Dyula, even if the production of kinds of speech belonging to the category of *kúmaba* (important speeches) is limited, mark out that category as paramount. And so those genres, which function as counter-powers, are called *tólon kúma*, 'ludic speech', 'speech without any importance'.

To conclude, it is impossible to ignore the field of oral art when one studies the power relationships of a society based upon oral tradition. It may indeed be an important vector in the practice of power. In the case of the powerful, the use of speech, of course, is only one way among many to express power. But in the case of the socially dominated, a genre authenticated by tradition is sometimes the only legitimate means of exerting compensatory or counter-powers.

CHAPTER 10

The power of words and the relation between Hausa genres

Graham Furniss

The power of the artist manifest in his or her use of language constitutes the focus of this chapter, and this is then set in a wider framework of the relations between different oral and written genres in Hausa seen as representing dominant and marginal cultural forms. While the bulk of the discussion draws on oral genres, I make no apology for moving into discussion of written genres, where questions of self-definition or perceptions of 'dominant' and 'marginal' require it. I find it difficult to think of 'the written as against the oral' as a useful boundary in Hausa where contrast and parallel repeatedly refer one backwards and forwards between genres across this 'line'.

THE GENRES OF HAUSA LITERATURE/ORATURE

A brief introductory résumé of the genres of Hausa literature/orature[1] is as follows (see also Skinner 1980; Pilaszewicz 1985). A number of prose forms are usually distinguished – among prose narratives *labari* and *tatsuniya* contrast as 'presumed real' and 'fictive' respectively. While the term *tatsuniya* is predominantly therefore 'traditional tale', it is sometimes also used to denote a conundrum or riddle, more often referred to as *ka cinci ka cinci*, 'pick up pick up' which acts both as name conveying the interactive nature of the genre and as introductory formula. *Tatsuniyoyi* (pl.) as 'tales' refer to animal/trickster tales, to narratives of human–human interaction, and of human–supernatural being interaction. Within short-form verbal art *karin magana* distinguishes 'proverbs/sayings' (the Hausa term implies 'folded speech' thereby 'allusive diction', which requires, on the part of the listener, interpretation of imagery or secondary reference). A functional distinction among such short-form expressions identifies *kirari* as 'praise-epithet' and *habaici* as 'innuendo' depending upon the presumed intent of the speaker. Non-prose or rhythmic language is generally represented by the term *waka* which is, in common parlance, a single term covering instrumentally accompanied, solo or 'lead and chorus', oral song and also another genre – written verse/poetry intoned without accompaniment. The relation between these two forms is discussed in a later part of this chapter.

There is a further range of labels for creators of such genres and for other performers. *Mai tatsuniya* simply implies 'story-teller', but the term *maroki* 'one who begs' for 'singer' implies specifically a praise-singer in search of reward for his services; *mawaki* 'one who sings', on the other hand, could be applied to a singer or a poet. There are further terms for public entertainers of various kinds, *'yan kama* 'burlesque players', *'yan gambara* 'rap artists', and a wide variety of types of musician (see Ames 1973), including those musicians and performers associated with the spirit-possession cult, *bori*.

Waka as 'praise-song' is intimately bound up with relations of power in Hausa society, as I discuss below, particularly as regards the establishment of public perceptions of big men, be they from the traditional aristocracy or from the new commercial, military or civil service elites. But beyond the boundaries of praise-singing strictly defined, it is often the case that a freelance singer such as Mamman Shata or Dan Maraya Jos will sing about groups or types within Hausa society, their characteristics and their position in society. Daba (1978), for example, has provided the texts to many of the songs of Dan Maraya Jos and among his most well-known songs is one in praise of the humble labourer, outlining the way in which many other groups in society, commercial, aristocratic and others, rely for their survival upon the sweat of the daily paid labourer. Song helps to identify and characterise other categories and groups in society, such as 'the young', 'the prostitutes', 'the new entrepreneurs' or 'the peasant from the rural areas'.

Many freelance singers have also operated in the service of the various political parties that have held power in Nigeria during the occasional periods of civilian rule since independence, such as the Nigerian People's Congress (NPC) or its successor, the National Party of Nigeria (NPN), on the one hand, or the series of opposition parties that have opposed the northern Nigerian establishment, the Northern Elements Progressive Union (NEPU), its successor the People's Redemption Party (PRP), or the Greater Nigerian People's Party (GNPP), on the other. Political song during such periods has tended to operate, as with praise-poetry, to laud the leadership of the one party and vilify the leadership of the other. Political poetry has played an important part in the political process in northern Nigeria as can be seen in Hiskett (1977), Birniwa (1987), Suru (1980), among others. Typically such poetry presents a characterisation of the leader(s) by which a variety of dimensions of legitimacy and personal quality are outlined along with an affirmation of the loyalty, fervour and quantity of his/their popular following. The strength of the relationship between leader and followers is affirmed as part of the process of creating a following at meetings and in the media. In this respect therefore, song and poetry are integral to the rhetorical processes whereby political support is sought and affirmed.

POWER AND THE USE OF LANGUAGE

There are two aspects of the relation between power and language I would like to discuss here. Orature, and in particular praise-song, is one important factor in the demarcation of status distinctions in Hausa society. But the facility that allows the public establishment of an individual's distinctiveness is essentially ambivalent; an ability to create individuality from the throng does not correlate with immutable allocation to particular positions within society – he who raises up can also cast down. Furthermore, an imposition of, or invitation to, individuality by the praise-singer masks a further ambivalence between assessing an individual and assessing that individual in society. Playing with these areas of ambivalence gives the praise-singer power, as I illustrate below. The second dimension to power and the use of language is the deployment, in a variety of forms of orature, of rhetoric – political language, ethical language and, most particularly, didacticism, all of which involve an attempt to make the listener think or act in a certain way, and this I address in the second part of this section.

Since Smith's important (1957) article there has been a view of Hausa praise-singers distinguishing broadly a number of categories of performer. First, the court musicians with their singer(s) and praise-crier(s) (Gidley 1975) performing on public occasions at the behest of the chief. Second, freelance and itinerant singers 'preying' upon a local constituency of worthies; and, thirdly, a new class of singer, freelance and professional, making a living from both praise and other song broadcast on TV and radio or marketed on disc and cassette. Ames (1973) distinguishes further categories of artist. To some extent these categories do not represent separate groups of artists, more a variety of contexts in which performers may operate. In some cases singers have been closely attached to particular courts,

Jankiɗi with the court of the Sultan of Sokoto Abubakar III, Muhammadu Sarkin Tabshi with the Katsina court, Narambaɗa with the court of Sarkin Gobir na Isa (for discussion of court musicians and singing see, for example, Bello 1976; Zurmi 1981; King 1969, 1981; Besmer 1971; Mack 1981), and these well-known artists would rarely, if ever, perform outside the context of their relationship as clients of the court. It is these artists and their kind of which Smith speaks when he says that, 'the most elaborate developments of *roƙo* [praise] are associated with the highest levels of power and authority, and that periodic ceremonials reassert the relation between the nobility and the values of the social structure' (1957: 41). In his study of Daura, Smith (1978) distinguishes between two sets of state musician, one of higher status only able to play for the chief and another more freely able to address both the chief and other title-holders at their own compounds around the city. In terms of function Smith sees both groups operating to distinguish aristocracy from populace and to exalt the institution of chieftaincy and the state (1978: 104). The terms in which the exaltation of the chief are couched relate in part to values ascribed to the position of the person praised – his lineage, both parental and spiritual, and therefore his connection with deeds and qualities of former titleholders and the greatness of the state itself, while on the other hand the language of praise presents values which may be conventionally applied but which nevertheless are descriptive of personal qualities – bravery, piety, magnanimity, generosity, among others (see also Yahaya 1981). Ames (1973: 159) follows Smith (1957) in asserting the predominance of praise of the office rather than the person in Hausa praise-singing, thereby 'exalting the institution of chieftaincy'. However, the characteristic shared by all categories of praise-singer is mastery of the language of personal praise distinguishing the recipient from singer, audience and all potential rivals. Smith (1978: 140) acknowledges this function in terms of distinguishing 'dynasty' from 'officials and populace', but sees it still only in terms of classes of people and their interrelations. This functional role in relation to the establishment and public acknowledgement of social strata is clearly of great significance. Yet the singer's full role is obscured by an insistence purely on relations between classes of people. The praise-singer homes in upon the individual and in so doing pins the individual to certain positions and roles in society. The ambivalence between assessing the individual and assessing the individual in society is the resource available to court singer, itinerant *maroƙi* and pop star alike. The itinerant *maroƙi*, for example, makes his living from asserting that the individual who is the

subject of his attentions fulfils the expectations and values associated
with his position in society. A particular position in society may be one
which the 'praisee' is claiming for himself, or may be one which the
singer is ascribing to him, but in all cases such positions are objectified
and publicly claimed for the individual in contrast, whether tacitly or
openly, to rivals within the broader community. The power of, and
the danger in, the singer's ability to play between the individual and
his position lies in his control of flattery and also of what Gidado Bello
(1976: 31) has termed 'the co-wife to praise': vilification. In Hausa
there is a perceived gradation in the 'severity' of this second dimension
of language, ranging from *habaici*, 'innuendo', through *zambo*,
'ridicule/satire', to *zagi*, 'insult/abuse'. Smith illustrates the potential
of the praise-singer to vilify in the following extract from a discussion
of problems at the court of Daura between emir and vizier in 1908:

At this point Musa's drummers and court musicians, acting independently,
began to parade about the town in the early morning, before the dawn
prayers (*asubahi*), when the people were still inside their compounds, singing
satirical songs they had composed to honor Na'inkali and his thefts. As
maroka (praise-singers) the musicians thus exercised their privilege or license
as public spokesmen; but they also relied on the power of their patron to
protect them. These taunting songs, rich in innuendo and insinuation, soon
became popular hits and hurt Na'inkali where he was most vulnerable. For
some weeks he bore this mounting tide of ridicule and contempt without
finding a suitable answer. Musa, who could hear these songs, was also
uneasy, foreseeing that he was likely to be held responsible and accused of
slandering the vizier (1978: 328)

and Gidado Bello (1976: 31-4) illustrates the way in which certain
famous court praise-singers have included in their songs vilification of
rivals to their local chiefly incumbent. In both these cases vilification is
openly directed at rivals to the patron. In Furniss (1988a) I illustrated,
with reference to two written texts, the reversals involved in switching
from praise to vilification of the same person, and it is that ability to
switch which has been seen as the dangerous characteristic of the
itinerant *maroki*. Ames (1973), Gidley (1975) and others have commented
upon the occasions when government has intervened to ban the
activities of itinerant *maroka* on the grounds of their 'extortionate'
behaviour. While praise will deploy both attributes of social position
and of the individual himself, vilification tends to concentrate upon
the negative qualities of the individual while maintaining the positive
view of the the structure within which the individual is expected to
operate. The poet does not vilify chieftainship or the values associated

with the role of patron but the individual's failure to live up to the expectations of the role.

The distinction between singers on the basis of their being tied, court musicians, on the one hand, or freelance singers, on the other, is again more fluid than would appear at first sight. It is true that there is a continuing patron–client relationship to be seen between the court of Sokoto, for example, and associated praise-singers, but Jankiɗi himself (a famous praise-singer now dead) travelled through many parts of Nigeria, singing in praise of individuals and chiefs in Zaria, Katsina, Bida, Minna and Daura and many other places, before finally being appointed to a formal position in the court of Sokoto (Pilaszewicz 1984: 273–4). The itinerant group of musicians is a familiar sight in many towns of Nigeria and beyond, and it is only the transition of 'making it' into a courtly position or into the public eye and popularity which distinguishes the one from the other. The last category of 'pop star' referred to earlier is again a non-exclusive characterisation. Famous artists, such as Mamman Shata (see Abdulkadir 1975), Haruna Oji, Ɗan Maraya Jos (Daba 1981: 210) and many others, have sung in praise of temporary and long-standing patrons as well as of themselves. They, however, go beyond the limits of the language of praise and vilification into discussion of many topics of current interest in society at large. Ɗan Maraya Jos, for example, is noted for his songs addressing the problems faced by ordinary people, truck drivers, labourers, peasants (Daba 1978, 1981). With all these categories of singer, then, we see them, temporarily or semi-permanently, in a clientage role *vis-à-vis* an actual or claimed patron, articulating both structural values and personal values. But in so doing these singers are able to single out the individual and ascribe either positive or negative values in assessing the degree to which that individual matches up to expectations of role. They acknowledge and articulate the basis of the patron's power and in so doing can also exercise power over that individual's hold on power.

A second aspect of power in the use of language is the deployment of political language concentrating upon the process of persuasion and the representation of power relations. This is a subject that has long been of interest to anthropologists (see for example the review presented in Parkin 1984). In Hausa I have tried to demonstrate the way in which poetry is a medium in which the characterisation of people and events is overlaid with evaluatively charged language and presented through a variety of tropes (Furniss 1977, 1989; see also the discussion of tropes in rhetoric in Sapir 1977). At the risk of repeating myself I would just like to draw attention to the essentially political nature of the process of characterisation to which I refer. Crocker (1977) talks of the way in which a metaphor or metonymic representation may crystallise and objectify an idea which had hitherto been vaguely felt or diffusely expressed and that an ability to create such knowledge is one of the skills of the orator. In Furniss (1988b) I tried to demonstrate the way in which poetry publicly articulates and 'fixes' views of such things as, for example, landlord–tenant relationships, young people, drug addicts and the problems of under-education. On the one hand, such representations monopolise, for that moment, the space available for the characterisation of such things in such a way that any alternative view is inhibited, on the other, the relationship between speaker and audience is always ambivalent, no one can tell the extent to which the audience accepts that particular characterisation. But it is clear that the rhetorical intent is to persuade the audience of the truth value of that representation. The intent is clear because the overlaid evaluative language is unmistakable. Figurative language may cloud the meaning such that the characterisation of the topic allows a variety of interpretations, but in Hausa poetry rarely does irony muddy the waters as to the evaluative intent of the writer, certainly where the poetry taps into the long tradition of didactic or laudatory writing.[2] The gap between evaluative intent and the 'reception' of persuasion is not simply filled by an 'automatic' matching of components within a shared belief system, political persuasion is 'negotiated' (Parkin 1984: 352–6, quoting Paine 1981). One aspect of this 'negotiation' is the presentation and the subsequent/simultaneous appreciation of artistry and skill. Artistry and skill in Hausa poetry, I would venture to suggest, lie in a variety of dimensions – in the consistency of metre/rhythm; sometimes in the deployment of arcane vocabulary, sometimes in clarity of expression; sometimes in the deployment of imagery and of proverbial reference; sometimes in the symmetries and patterning of parallelism and recursiveness. The 'negotiation' takes place in at least two ways. On the one hand, the perception of artistry in the artefact makes it first a whole and then a valued whole, on the other hand, the features that were 'artistic' were also those which organised and highlighted parts of the content – negotiation of the understanding of the 'text' took place through the contextual clues, or the explicit hints, to the interpretation of metaphor, or through the links, demanding interpretation, created by the parallelism or the repetitiveness. The 'negotiation' is never predetermined, it is in the articulation, the performance that the 'meaning' is (or 'meanings' are) created. Such an activity of creative articulation is, most obviously in the case of didactic Hausa poetry, an intrinsically political act. As Parkin says: 'These many particular uses of tropes point, nevertheless, in one direction: it is people who retain the power to name, entitle, and objectify others, who determine the terms of discourse' (1984: 359). A key issue, therefore, is the way in which the orator creates a particular typification, 'determining the terms of discourse' as Parkin puts it, but goes further to overlay an evaluation that is integral to the process of persuading the listener to accept both the typification and the 'moral' standpoint of the speaker.

RELATIONS BETWEEN GENRES IN HAUSA ORAL AND WRITTEN LITERATURE

Studies of orature generally begin with an outline of genres. On the one hand, there have been attempts, more or less successful, to render the characteristics of particular forms in such a way that cross-cultural equivalents can be drawn, and so we commonly use terms such as 'tales', 'proverbs', 'song', etc. On the other hand, there are those who have directed their attention to the terminologies and distinctions employed within the language and culture under discussion. In looking at the myriad ways in which particular cultures draw their own distinctions it soon becomes clear that any such discussion of genres ranges across a full range of distinctive criteria: performance characteristics, social or ritual occasion, content, form, style of language, performers. Both approaches, however, produce a tendency to regard genres as a catalogue in which each component has its separate and more-or-less equally important niche within an overall classification. This can obscure, on occasion, an alternative view whereby, as Bakhtin (1966) pointed out with medieval European carnival and church liturgy, the one form may define itself specifically in antithesis to another, sometimes simply exemplifying definitional distinctiveness, and in other cases presenting itself as subversive and oppositional. To illustrate these two positions I would like to outline, first, the way in which poets and singers in Hausa define the differences between their two activities to some extent as 'not doing what those others do'; and then, second, to look at the combination of distinctiveness and subversiveness that is to be seen in the art of the burlesque – subversiveness in the sense that there are dominant cultural genres and forms which constitute the basis for the burlesquer's pastiche.

A further dimension to the picture of Hausa genres is the way in which certain genres occupy a position within a dominant and/or urban, male, public culture and others appear to reside within a marginalised and/or rural, female, private world. These are clearly not permanent or unambiguous positions, nor can they be assigned simply to the co-existence of a 'high art' with a popular culture. Revaluation, à la Leavis, has occurred with the passage of time and 'rehabilitation' has been attempted. In the case of Hausa genres it is tale-telling which has seen the most recent and most marked attempt at rehabilitation, and I discuss this in more detail in the second section below.

In Hausa the single term *waka* is used for two forms which people generally acknowledge to be distinct, as mentioned briefly at the beginning of the chapter. Song, whether praise-song or modern popular song, is distinguished from poetry/verse. Muhammad (1979) has set out the distinctions, terming them *waka* I and *waka* II respectively. In drawing the distinction in normal Hausa parlance they would be distinguished as *wakar baka*, 'oral *waka*', and *rubutacciyar waka*, 'written *waka*'. For this discussion I would like to single out characteristics which practitioners themselves identify as distinguishing their art from that of the 'others' in such a way as to imply a cultural superiority of the one form over the other. At the same time, a process is at work by which practitioners cross the cultural boundaries to borrow characteristics of the other, sometimes simply to adopt them into their own form, sometimes to make substitutions or alterations which reflect back in opposition to, or as a subversion of, the source. In discussion with poets (see Furniss 1977: 61–70) belonging to a poetry-writing circle it was clear that the primary criterion put forward by poets for distinguishing their art was that, unlike singers, they did not do it for money or other material reward. This categorical statement implied that the poets were free of the client relation and therefore were not in the business of praise. In reality, the circle maintained senior figures as patrons to the group and relations between the leader, Mudi Sipikin, and younger members were such that he exercised, as patron, even the prerogative of rewriting their poetry if he felt it did not meet expectations of form or content. Furthermore, all the poets in the circle, including the leader, did in fact write praise, but the operative distinction was that to praise famous men was different from praising patrons in the expectation of reward. The statement, however, was intended to establish the social superiority of poetry writing over singing. This was reinforced by a second distinction linking poetry to the expression of Islamic religious thought in contrast to the association of song with a variety of un-Islamic practices. The signs of this distinction were considered to be manifest in the serious and didactic tone of poetry, the admixture of a high proportion of Arabic, the existence of rhyme schemes and Arabic metres and the solo recitation of poetry in contrast to the 'lead and chorus' framework of so much musically accompanied song. From the point of view of the poets these characteristics were positive qualities that were lacking in song and which marked out poetry as a superior cultural form. To some extent such claims related also to a view of the poet as a member of the Islamic cleric class (*malamai*), whose reputation and status derived from their control of religious knowledge; this in contrast to the low social status ascribed to singers (for discussion of the question of status, see Smith 1957; Ames 1973: 155–7). In fact status among singers is a complex question – traditional status distinctions are in any case breaking down to be replaced by new wealth-based distinctions within which the famous singer may be accorded relatively high status. A parallel situation can be seen in J. P. Olivier de Sardan's (1982) discussion of griots in Songhay society where he sees a blurring occurring between ordinary griots (*jesere*) of low status and master griots (*jesere-dunka*), of higher status. Interestingly, Sory Camara (1976) in his masterly study of Malinké griots sets the griots apart from the system of social hierarchy thereby explaining their ability to cross boundaries and act as social mediators between groups.

Returning to the question of the poet's view of what distinguishes his craft from that of the singer, the obverse of that coin is the singer's view of his own qualities in contrast to those of the poet. Mamman Shata, the famous singer, bases one of his claims to excellence on his ability to create and adapt in performance (Abdulkadir 1975), this requiring a level of skill and mental agility not to be found in the fulminations of the poet. The complexities of interplay between lead singer and chorus, with the Hausa terms for such patterns used by singers, are set out in King (1981). The deployment of particular patterns are acknowledged to be part of the conscious skill of the performer when, for example, Dankwairo extols his own ability to make use of them (King 1981: 122). While commentators have teased out the use of Arabic metres in poetry, so also the complexities of rhythmic patterning in song have been the subject of attention from musicologists (Besmer 1971; King 1969) and also linguists (see particularly the important comparative work on scansion in song and poetry by Schuh 1988, 1989, 1988/9). Among both practitioners of song and poetry there is a common assessment that quality of material and performance is most directly manifest in skill in the deployment of language, *azanci* (Gidley 1974), an ability to deploy a rich and expressive vocabulary with wit and point. Shata is renowned for those qualities as a singer and Alhaji Akilu Aliyu similarly in the poetry-writing world (Muhammad 1977). While poets, particularly, define their art in contradistinction to that of the singer they also borrow features of song. It is said that the famous blind poet of Zaria, the late Aliyu na Mangi, in describing the origins of his twelve-canto poem, 'Imfiraji', stated that he used to hear his daughter singing to herself a famous popular song, 'Wakar Caji', by the singer Hamza Caji, and determined that he would write for her a poem using the same *kari* 'rhythm/metre' but which would substitute serious religious thought for the frivolousness of the original. Borrowing the model of the original meant retaining a tune with an embedded rhythm while substituting alternative and often contrasting subject matter. Muhammad (1979) cites eighteen other cases, like that of Aliyu na Mangi, where poetry has borrowed a rhythmic model from song. The precise implications for an analysis of metrical form are traced in Schuh (1988/9) while the tendency to see the process, from the point of view of the poet and commentators, as substituting the serious for the frivolous reinforces the sense of cultural superiority in the practitioners of poetry. A further indication of this cultural imbalance is perhaps provided by the fact that when song strikes back it is sometimes in the form of parody. Muhammad says the following:

Mamman Shata's *Sha ruwa ba laifi ba ne* 'Drinking is no crime' is a parody of the famous admonitory poem *Gangar wa'azu* 'Drum of admonition' by Muhammadu na Birnin Gwari which extols drinking and equates the hard-drinking companions of the oral artist with the upright and saintly Muslim malams of the literate poet, using the same metrical framework, employing a closely similar opening doxology, and indeed echoing several lines of the literate original in caricature. (1979: 88)

Parody as subversion is a theme I would like now to pursue somewhat further in relation to another genre of orature in Hausa, namely burlesque (Gidley 1967), the art of the *dan kama*. Parody/pastiche represents the identification of other cultural forms and the pointing up of their characteristics of form and content. In the performance of Hausa burlesque those 'other cultural forms' can be other genres of orature, but may also be other rhetorical forms and styles of speech, broadly defined. For the purpose of the current discussion however, the significant feature is that burlesque takes on, and plays with, dominant cultural forms, serious business of one kind or another, and reduces the audience to paroxysms of laughter at the travesty. Whether it is possible to go further and to identify burlesque as part of a wider counter-culture defining itself in contradistinction to 'dominant culture' I am not sure. Nevertheless it is clear that, in the same way that medieval carnival parodied the serious language and ritual of the Catholic church (Bakhtin 1966), Hausa burlesque, in the form of the performances of Malam Ashana 'Mister Matches' (Furniss 1991), parodies praise-song and admonitory song, but, interestingly, also parodies the performance of exegesis of religious texts and of other stylised forms of speech such as the parade-ground language of the military. In each case the parody operates by breaking the normally seamless continuity of form and content. The rhetorical techniques that lie behind religious exegesis go normally unnoticed as the listener's attention is directed at an appreciation of the serious nature of the content. Burlesque imitates closely the forms, the use of language, the style of the original but tears it away from its embeddedness in both appropriate context of performance and in appropriate subject matter. Thus extracted, the form of the original is hung out for all to see by the substitution of alternative subject matter and by being shifted from the serious theatre of religious gathering or military parade-ground to the moving, do-it-yourself, theatricality of stall-holder and customer in the market. The alternative subject matter is the distinctive feature of the *ɗan kama* – whatever the context, whichever the model, the *ɗan kama* talks about food, getting it, preparing it, cooking it, wresting control of the cooking of it away from women and finally eating it – the taste, the texture and the pleasure of it. Everybody understands food, so when Malam Ashana slips food into the cloak of Arabicisms, provides exegesis of that which does not require explanation and produces a performance style closely reminiscent of religious exegesis, then the listener has form foregrounded by the parallel. Laughter is engendered in two ways, appreciative laughter at the exactness in the imitation of the original and laughter at incongruity produced by the parallelism – form is constant, content is variant, the parallelism demands an interpretation of the relation between the variant elements. The parallelism draws into relation two subjects intrinsically unrelated, religious thought and food. The expectation that the listener should find an interpretation of the relation between the variant elements produces laughter – recognition that the variant elements are intrinsically unrelated produces a sense of incongruity or absurdity and hence laughter. The only alternative would be a search for some, as yet unnoticed, dimension of similarity or contrast – part of the interpretative side of artistic creativity. In sum, then, burlesque of this kind asserts its own distinctiveness in its content, discussion of food; by translating food into forms that are associated with other subject matter, the oral artist both highlights those forms and creates incongruity. Incongruity is subversive of serious subjects and their more usual presentation. Dominant culture is the world of Islamic learning, of poetry-writing, of praise-song, and of the use of English. Burlesque is part of a popular counter-culture, apparently in decline (Gidley 1967), defining itself in part as having its own subject matter and in part as being in opposition to dominant cultural forms. Genre definition needs, therefore, to take account not only of particularities of social groups and performance contexts but also of the internal cultural dynamics whereby forms define themselves, either consciously through their practitioners, or unconsciously in the nature of their form and content, in contradistinction to each other, or indeed in relations of dominance and subversion *vis-à-vis* each other.

With some genres of orature in Hausa there is a correlation between the genre and, on the one hand, an urban, public, male culture and, on the other, a more rural, private and female world. In the world of song and poetry there have long been women artists who have made their mark on the genre. At the beginning of the nineteenth century the daughter of the Shehu, Nana Asma'u (Boyd 1989), was renowned as a scholar and writer as well as the founder of a women's education movement, the 'Yan Taru movement. More recently, poets such as Hauwa Gwaram and Alhajiya 'Yar Shehu (see Mack 1981; Furniss 1977) have made an impact upon the literary scene. In song there have been famous women praise-singers (*zabiya*) (see Mack 1986 on Maimuna Coge) as well as women singers with a variety of different song groups. Nevertheless, Mack is of the following view:

A significant portion of northern Nigeria's oral and written poetry remains unknown to the world and unrecognized in its own cultural setting because it is created by women. Women's extemporaneous oral verse is not regarded as serious artistry because it is created by those who are not considered respectable; the written works remain hidden with their authors, traditional Hausa women who are secluded in their homes in urban areas. (1986: 181)

In the case of song and poetry there are both men and women practitioners but with differential access to the public arena. In the case of oral narratives however, we see a rather different pattern. In tracing attitudes to oral narratives in Hausa we can see a progressive marginalisation of the whole genre followed by a more recent move to rehabilitate it, and it is this I wish to turn to now. Ahmad (1986) reports an attitude among the Islamic cleric class since the Jihad, and perhaps before, that oral narratives (*tatsuniyoyi*), while not specifically to be condemned, were *hululu*, 'idle chatter', and to be avoided by all good Muslims. This position he credits for the fact that urban, male, public culture frowns upon the telling of such tales. Male heads of household would not consider it seemly to be present at or to participate in any such story-telling sessions. Typically their attitude would be that such activities were only for women and children in the privacy of the compound at the end of the day. In Ahmad's collection women narrators predominate. It is by no means clear, however, that in earlier times, story-telling was more generally current and not limited to the domestic sphere among women and children. What is clear, however, is that there has been a move to bring *tatsuniyoyi* more directly into public culture in recent years. Ahmad reports that, since the 1970s, a cultural revival movement which has been manifest in a variety of ways sought to counter the 'idle chatter' tag attached to tales and to provide an educational justification for bringing tales more directly into formal education and into the celebration of Hausa 'traditional' culture. State Ministries of Arts and Culture in Nigeria have busily been patronising dance troupes, poets, singers and, to a lesser extent, story-tellers through the organisation of festivals and other performance occasions. While the invention of tradition proceeds apace it is also true that some of the best of these artists are able now to subsist on their art in a way which they were not able to do before. Ahmad also reports the institution of a tale-telling programme on Kano State radio, presented by a man, in which the presenter recites tales sent in to him by his listeners. Interestingly, Ahmad indicates that the presenter has clear ideas on the constitution of the 'world of the tale' – he edits out any reference to cars, telephones, radios or Europeans; the tales live in a reconstructed vision of a mid-nineteenth-century Hausa world with aristocracy and peasants, Islamic clerics and other ethnic groups, but nothing of modern Nigeria. The drive to incorporate tales into the formal educational process has been spearheaded by academics within the university. Ibrahim Yaro Yahaya (1979) put the case for 'Hausa folklore as an educational tool' concentrating upon the ability of tales to inculcate moral values. This assessment of tales as fulfilling a valuable educational social role within 'traditional' society constitutes the counter to the condemnation of them as 'idle chatter'. Yahaya himself was the author of a substantial series of primary school books in which he retells a large number of such tales. Such books are intended for use as both reading materials and as models for the children in a classroom situation to tell and write their own versions.[3] The reassessment of the value of tales is part of a wider cultural movement to revive and strengthen the Hausa language and to rediscover the value of cultural 'roots' in opposition to the advance of English and Western culture, whether imported direct through textbooks and television or in the form of an English-based Nigerian culture. Many of the protagonists of this movement are themselves bilingual and 'bicultural', working within, or are products of, the formal education sector. Their aim is to secure the long-term future of Hausa and *al'adun gargajiya*, 'customs inherited from the past' (Ibrahim Yaro Yahaya, interview). In this sense, then, the move to bring in a particular genre from the 'cultural cold' is part of a broader move to prevent the cultural marginalisation of the language and culture as a whole in relation to competing languages and cultural forms within Nigeria. Within the panorama of Hausa literature/orature, however, this recent history demonstrates the way in which positions within a cultural 'pecking order' are renegotiable – a dominant group, the clerics, marginalised tale-telling, or so it would appear, only for a later dominant group, the modern-day intellectuals to rehabilitate it.

NOTES

1 There is a very considerable body of literature on genre theory that considers both the intra-cultural perspective (for example, Ben-Amos 1976) and cross-cultural issues (for example, Bakhtin 1986; Bauman 1986; Honko 1976, 1989; Jason 1986; Ryan 1981). Genre theory encompasses both questions of sets of formal features and the embedded contrasting communicative functions that are linked to particular genres and to changes of genre. The discussion here introduces the terminology and generally accepted distinctions employed in Hausa.

2 Not all poetry is of these two kinds and there is some poetry in which evaluative intent is unclear, often combined with highly elliptical imagery, see for example 'Hawainiya', 'Chameleon' by Tijjani Tukur, and some recent poetry by Bello Alhassan.

3 Oddly, the trickster, Gizo, who, in the imaginary world of the tale, stands upright, has two arms and two legs and is small of stature, is drawn in accompanying illustrations in these books as a real spider; it is true that *gizo-gizo* in Hausa is the name for a spider, but I have yet to hear of a Gizo story where the character has eight legs, spins a web and lives under stones, etc. No doubt the wide currency of such illustrations will create a generation of people who think of Gizo in such terms.

PART IV

Endorsing or subverting the paradigms: women and oral forms

CHAPTER 11

Sexuality and socialisation in Shona praises and lyrics

Herbert Chimhundu

This chapter is a comparative discussion of imagery, meaning and function in Shona traditional praises and modern songs by popular Shona bands, with particular reference to gender politics in the widest possible context of the extended family. Selected examples drawn from three sub-genres of love poetry and from Afropop recordings are used to show that, in many cases, traditional praises and modern lyrics are quite similar in terms of imagery and symbolism, as well as in terms of socialisation for complementary role-relationships. This, of course, has wider implications outside the family and in effect this situation tends to support the status quo in gender politics at the national level.

In a way, Afropop music has taken over from love poetry as one of the strongest conservative influences that psychologically condition the young in particular to conform to traditionally prescribed norms in order to be socially acceptable individuals. Part of the power and impact of both love poems and love songs derives from symbolism and beliefs that are related to sexuality, procreation and the spirit world. Many of the Afropop songs recorded in Shona are in fact love songs, because perhaps 'Love-making, in one form or another, is one of the major interests in life' (Hodza and Fortune 1979: 289). The impact of modern love songs is greatest on the young, for whom personal appearance and erotic expression are relatively more important and for whom courtship is a major preoccupation. Like the oral poets before them, the Afropop composers of today use aesthetically pleasing, sensuous language for social comment, moral persuasion and sentimental expression. Their music finds wide appeal because of the way they blend the beat and the message. Because the message is presented in picturesque form, it 'tends to create a deeper and more lasting impression in the mind' (Gombe 1981: 158).

In Zimbabwe at any rate, the essential difference between indigenous pop music and the pop music that Africa imports from the West is that, although both seem to be preoccupied with love and sex as themes, and although both convey highly intense and personal feelings, the African love songs typically provide a family and/or community context while Western love songs do not. By providing a family context for love, whether this family already exists or is yet to be set up, Afropop actually helps to counteract some of the harmful influences of the relatively more individualistic and explicit Western love songs. This is one reason why, despite continuing and pervasive cultural imperialism, Shona society is likely to remain heavily family oriented. In effect, Shona popular musicians are quite a powerful conservative force, in spite of the unconventional and sometimes outrageous public image individual recording stars may project, as they may want to emulate Western pop stars. Like the traditional declaimers of courtship praises (*madetembedzo okupfimbana*) and praises for love-making (*zvirevereve zvomugudza* by men and *madanha omugudza* by women) (Hodza and Fortune 1979, esp. 289–338), and like most Shona writers, the modern singers have continued to project the idealistic image of the woman as the symbol of beauty, family stability and the moral fibre of the whole nation (Chimhundu 1987, 1995). Indirectly, therefore, oral literature, written literature and popular music all combine as a force to maintain double standards of behaviour for men and women in Shona society. Where socially prescribed norms and expectations are not met by women in particular (Gaidzanwa 1985: 11, 1987: 6), the poets, novelists, playwrights and singers alike all portray those women characters who do not conform to sex stereotypes as deviant and then punish them by ridicule, marginalisation, ostracism and sometimes even death (Chimhundu 1995: 13–14; Zinyemba 1986: 75).

The typical examples used in this essay will show that most of the key images used to perpetuate traditional perceptions of women (and men) relate to sexuality and procreation, the only traditionally legitimate reason for love-making in Shona society in which marriage is the most important institution and family, in the widest possible sense, remains the basic and only permanent unit of organisation for most practical purposes. Because of this, love poems and love songs give family as background while erotic expressions and images are thrown in both for symbolism and for spice. The family context provides a direct link with the dead ancestors in the spirit world, whose approval and encouragement are sought and provided. In *Shona Praise Poetry*, for example, Hodza and Fortune give praises for love-making (*madanha* and *zvirevereve*) in the sections for the clan praises of different totem groups. This link between sex, marriage and religion is fundamental in traditional Shona philosophy and it is vitally important for maintenance of the status quo in gender politics. However, modern love songs do not make the link as explicit as love poems, for the simple reason that love poems are intended to be performed or read privately while love songs are performed publicly, mainly in recreation halls and on the radio, and are therefore more liable to both public and self censorship.

LANGUAGE AND GENDER

I have shown elsewhere (1987) that even everyday language has built-in sex differentials. Names and complex nominals for kinship titles, for instance, are reflective of basic assumptions about status, roles, responsibilities and even capabilities sometimes. Conventionally established patterns of transitivity restrict the use of some verbs to collocation with nouns indicating males only. For instance, all the actions of the transitive verbs indicating courting (*kunyenga, kupfimba, kutsvetsva*) or marrying (*kuroora, kuwana*) or making love (*kusvira, kuisa*) can only be performed by male subjects. Referents for females are slotted in object position, as in the sentence frame:

Male DOES female.

Alternatively, the female is made the passive subject and the male becomes the agent as in the sentence frame:

Female IS DONE by male.

It is doubtful whether any social revolution can do away with such entrenched sex differentials in language, which in fact are not peculiar to Shona. Add to this a host of terms which give all important positions in society to father figures. *Baba* (father) is head of the *mhuri* (family) and *Mwari* (God) or *Musikavanhu* (the Creator) is also *Baba*. Hierarchies of family and clan leaders, rulers, ancestors and spirit mediums (*madzibaba, madzisekuru, madzishe, midzimu*) are invariably male. So are all other prominent or successful persons such seers, healers, hunters, ironsmiths and fighters (*n'anga, vanachiremba, hombarume, mhizha, magamba*). These terms have always been assumed to refer to men recognised to have power because Shona society is patriarchal, although the Shona language is, in actual fact, less sexist than English or French in that there are no male/female forms for, say, nouns or pronouns. This male power and superior rank are reflected in numerous expressions and images which were used traditionally in personal praises and which have survived in one form or another from orature to popular music. In a sentence, the total effect is to put the male above the female, both physically as during sex and symbolically as in virtually all positions of leadership and authority.

Particularly in relation to the sex act, some of the images used in idioms with male subjects are very strong or, some would argue, quite violent, e.g. *kugara mbabvu* (to sit on the ribs) and *kutyora gumbo* (to break someone's leg). Current slang expressions coined by today's youth have even stronger or more violent images and are created in the same tradition which makes the female the passive recipient or victim of the male's action, e.g. *kudhinda* (to stamp) and *kutsika mapapiro* (to pin down by stepping on a chicken's wings, i.e. when you slaughter it). Even the most euphemistic references to pregnancy, such as *kuitisa pamuviri* (literally to make someone grow a belly), make the woman an object or victim of the man's action. The same logic is found in riddles such as

> Hari inovira norukuni rumwe.
> Lit: The pot that boils from the fire of one stick.

where reference is to the female organ (*hari*, pot), the male organ (*rukuni*, piece of firewood) and pregnancy (*kuvira*, boiling). Not infrequently, the male organ is referred to as an instrument of discipline in traditional love poems. Equality between the sexes seems to be achieved only during intimacy:

> Navari kumhepo vonyenamira
> Uyu mutambo wavakatisiyira
> Mutambo wakadzora nebhinhya
> Usina mukuru woumwe.

> Even the ancestors in the spirit world must be smiling
> For this is a game they left for us
> The exciting game that humbled even the savage murderer
> The game that makes people equal.
>   (R. Mashoko, 'Zvaonekwa Chikandamina',
>   in Haasbroek 1988: 311–12)

Still, however, even in the most intimate love poems, the man is portrayed as having the power to inflict both pain and pleasure, and to make the woman happy or unhappy. In *madanha* (praises by women) in particular, it is the man's physical power that gives him sexual prowess. The same physical power also makes him the provider, e.g.

as a successful farmer (*hurudza*), hunter (*homabarume* ‹ *gomba*: lover + *–rume*: man). Both these abilities are reflected in the hyperbole used in the opening lines of a wife's praises for a husband of the Soko Murehwa totem set out below. These lines contain an extended image of the man's power:

> Zvaitwa, Murehwa:
> Mukonde wangu yuyu
> Hekani Mbereka
> VaMurova-pasi-pachitinhira
> VaChiokochisingatunhwi
>
> A service has been rendered, Murehwa
> My dear one, close as a bead belt to me
> Thank you, You who bear up those you love
> Who strike the ground and it resounds
> Whose hand disdains no service.
>> ('Madanha emugudza evekwaChinamhora',
>> 'Endearments uttered by wives to husbands
>>   of the Chinamhora, clan') (Hodza and
>>   Fortune 1979: 201–2).

At the same time, fatherhood assures him of admittance to the spirit world (*nyikadzimu*) in the after-life, while in the living world it makes him the leader of the household (*musoro wemba*) and *roora* (lobola/bride wealth) gives him paternity/legal custody of the children.

Apart from sexual prowess, in *zvirevereve* by men, the women are praised for a completely different set of qualities: beauty, fertility, dignity, kindness, generosity, loyalty and hard work. The implications of this for the socialisation process will become more obvious in the next section when key images in praises and lyrics are discussed. Suffice it to say at this stage that the difference between the qualities for which men and women are praised are reflective of a complex system of complementary role-allocation based on gender and which today is probably still regarded by most as being more important than equality (Chimhundu 1987: 9). All forms of Shona literature accord the highest status and esteem to married mothers (*madzimai*) who are contrasted with the despised prostitutes and loose women (both *mahure*, a term used very loosely in Shona), particularly in the context of the city (cf. Little 1974, 1980), which writers portray as 'the death-bed of the Shona people's morals and decency' (Kahari 1986: 108).

The Shona language lends itself very well to usage of this type. Therefore, it is not enough merely to look at the meanings or messages in verses and lyrics composed in the language without looking at relevant linguistic aspects, for the language itself must also be seen as a tool for lifelong sociological conditioning of the sexes.

FOLKLORE AND SOCIALISATION

In their function as tools for socialisation, Shona praises and lyrics are augmented and reinforced by figures of speech that are drawn from folklore. Collectively, the figures of speech themselves are a summation of observation, tradition and experience which is expressed through the analogical imagination, which then takes a variety of ancient and fairly rigid forms in the proverbial lore, as well as in other figurative expressions such as idioms, metaphors, similes and ideophones (Pongweni 1989: 1–46). The symbolism used in all of them, which is now also exploited in written poetry and in popular music, is recurrent and fairly standard. Their total effect, in the various situations in which they are performed, is to reinforce the traditional ethos, norms and practices. In all this, sexuality and gender politics have probably become more important now than in the past when numerous assumptions about the sexes, power, status and role-relationships were taken for granted.

Much in the same way, but not to the same extent, as the proverbs which are typically viewed as distilled words of wisdom (Hamutyinei and Plangger 1974: 7) and whose correct and appropriate use may be viewed as a measure of the declaimer's or protagonist's identity and cultural immersion (Chimhundu 1980: 44; Nyembezi 1989: 41), the lyrics of Afropop music also advance 'the communal view of the world based on first hand experience' (Pongweni 1989: 1). Although, unlike proverbs, the songs do not remain popular forever, some of the key images and recurrent lines in their lyrics continue to be used as popular sayings. A good example is the Bhundu Boys' song title 'Chokudya chese, tanga waravira' ('Whatever food you are offered, taste it before you decline the offer').

These sayings have the same multivalence that accords proverbs potency of meaning and their use and significance is also closely linked to both the historical and the immediate situational contexts (Pongweni 1989: 3). Because they are often intended as summaries of stories and experiences, both proverbs and songs have multi-level meanings within the literal, micro and macro contexts (R. A. Parker cited in Pongweni 1989: 5).

Proverbs have both a juridical and a reference function in that they are used to resolve situations in which plans for behaviour are ambiguous and, therefore, they help to facilitate the smooth flow of social interaction. Because the socialisation of the individual puts a premium on being accepted by 'the generalized other' (Sprott 1958: 25) as the individual's 'reference group' (Bell 1976: 105), the common purposiveness of the wider, secondary group is clearly towards a golden mean which is achieved by discouraging extremes and excesses (Kriel 1971). Not infrequently, this is indicated by contradictory pairs of proverbs, such as:

> Mbeva zhinji hadzina marise.
> Too many cooks spoil the broth.
> Rume rimwe harikombi churu.
> One man cannot surround an anthill.

also,

> Zano pangwa uine rako.
> Have your own ideas before you seek advice.
> Zanondega akaonekwa nembonje pahuma.
> Know-it-all ended up with a scar on the forehead.

The total effect is to persuade people to conform and to cherish such traditional ideals as peace, tolerance and mutual co-operation (Chimhundu 1980: 44).

Although proverbs are not abundant in modern Shona lyrics, the philosophy they express is. Occasionally whole proverbs are used in modern songs and, even less frequently, a whole song may be a string of proverbs as in Mashura and the Okavango Boys' song 'Chembere mukazdi' ('An old woman is still a woman'). Sometimes song titles are popularly used as pithy sayings akin to proverbs, as in the case of 'Zvinonaka zvinodhura' ('All nice things are expensive') by Patrick Mukwamba and 'Chokudya chese, tanga waravira' ('Taste before you say no') by the Bhundu Boys. Alternatively, compounds that indicate a whole social problem are coined, as in the song title 'Tangawandida' ('Jobs for sex/Sex for jobs') by Paul Matavire and the Jairos Jiri Band. These sayings and expressions have gained general currency and acceptance, and are comparable to the traditionally accepted canonical proverbs that are restricted in their imagery to the pre-industrial surroundings of the Shona past. Proverb coining by singers may also be compared with what happens in slang when young people substitute lexical items in older proverbs with new ones to incorporate new imagery reflecting a new environment and changed circumstances, as in:

Kumisa hure hunge une mari.
    If you stop a prostitute, you must have money.
cf. Kubata mwana wengwe senga pfuti.
    If you must hold a leopard's cub, then carry a gun.

In this way, a symbiosis is established between lexis and ecology, as 'Figurative language of all types and from all communities derives its imagery from the environment in which the speakers of the language live' (Pongweni 1989: 13–14). As Kriel has observed, with particular reference to Shona, 'oral literature is not all that traditional and static but living and changing all the time' (1971: 18). A further suggestion now being made here is that the life and change that make orature dynamic are not only in content and form, but also in situation, performance and vehicle or medium of transmission. In other words, today's popular and mass cultures are creating and transmitting oral literature through print and electronic media, with much the same purpose, although perhaps not quite the same effect, as the traditional declaimers or performers.

Just as we can say that our forefathers provided us with a proverb for every situation (Chimhundu 1980: 40), the music industry today is providing us with a song for every situation, and, in this way, we are continuing the tradition of summarising past experience for the benefit of posterity. Not infrequently, the key images and expressions used to achieve this are derived from oral traditional literature, and thus indirectly also verbalise customary law and enunciate rules of conduct in life (Hamutyinei and Plangger 1974: 19). Although their juridical function has diminished because the traditional judicial system has been largely abandoned or suppressed, the continued expression of the traditional ethos through modern media helps to ensure that a new, transformed oral literature will remain a powerful socialising influence for many years to come.

KEY IMAGES IN LOVE POEMS AND LOVE SONGS

In traditional Shona society, it was not unusual for children who selected each other as partners at *mahumbwe*, 'playing house', and during matching games such as *sarura wako kadeyadeya*, 'Select your own dearest', to become man and wife in adult life (see, for example, Hodza 1984: 51). As Hodza and Fortune explain, 'courtship among the Shona may begin very young and continue into old age', and the poems of courtship which a man has worked at from youth upwards may become poems in praise of a wife (1979: 289–90).

Consider, for example, the striking similarities between the key images in the two poems 'Amai vaZvichauya' ('Mother of what-is-yet-to-be') and 'Zvirevereve zvomurume kumukazi mugudza' ('Words of love from a husband to his wife in bed'), both examples of oral poetry written down (Hodza and Fortune 1979: 292–4 and 278–9 respectively). The verses in the former are praises to a girl recited at the courtship stage while those in the latter are praises for a wife during/after love-making. The first six out of the eight key images of desirable qualities and attributes listed below are found in both poems, although the elaboration or extension may vary:

Key image	Elaboration
1 Kindness	Cares for the young and helpless
	Feeds them and provides for them
2 Generosity	Gives freely
	Gives to all
3 (Married) motherhood	Fertile
	Nurses children
	Nurses husband
4 (Physical) beauty	Neck: long and slender
	Skin: smooth and shiny
	Nose: straight
	Teeth: white with gap
	Eyes: bright with life
	Legs: smooth, shiny shins
5 Fitness	Gait: graceful
	Pace: brisk
	Buttocks: large, firm
6 Personality	Dignified
	Pleasant
	Softly spoken
	Respectful
	Patient
	Loving
	Lovable
7 (Known) ancestry	Clan
	History: places, people
	Praise names
8 Family (background)	Good family
	Well brought up
	Cultured.

Not infrequently, the imagery revolves around a traditional praise name such as *VaChireranherera*, Guardian of Orphans, as in excerpts 1(a) from 'Amai vaZvichauya' and (b) from 'Zvirevereve' below, both referring to kindness (key image 1):

1(a) Maita zvenyu, VaChireranherera.
      Mune mwoyochena unenge wetsoro
      Inoriritira vana vasi vayo.

      Thank you, Guardian of Orphans
      You have a generous heart as that of the honey-guide
      Which cares for children other than its own.

  (b) Maita, VaChireranherera
       Munodai kurera nedzisi dzenyu

       You are kind, You who cares for Orphans
       You go as far as to treat even those who are not your own.
       (Original translations by Hodza and Fortune (1979)).

Sometimes complex nominal constructions that are not praise names
are used to summarise a specific attribute and then the imagery they
contain is expanded upon in subsequent lines. Examples from the
same two poems are *nhongoramutsipa* and *redzvamutsipa*, both
referring to a beautiful, long and slender neck, as in excerpts 2 (a) from
'Amai vaZvichauya' and (b) from 'Zvireverere' below:

2(a) Nhongoramutsipa yangu yiyiyi.
      Mune mutsipa unokwira nda ikazorora.

      My dear one of the long and graceful neck.
      You have a neck that a louse may not climb without a rest.

  (b) Redzvamutsipa rangu riri,
       ziendanetyaka;
       Nhongora yangu yiyi,
       ine muviri unotsvedzerera sewetsinza.

       My dear one of the long and slender neck,
       going in grace as the sound of your knee-joints reveals;
       My dear one of the long and swaying neck,
       whose body is smooth as the oribi.

Key images referring to family background and ancestry are restricted
to use by spouses. Because they refer to ancestors and family, they
cannot be used at the courtship stage. Further, it must be noted that
references to the sex organs and to the physical act of love-making are
mostly subtle, and prominence is given to the wider significance of the
sex act in a total family context. It should also be noted that the man
continues to love, cherish, praise and thank the wife for her beauty and
good deeds throughout their married life. Traditional custom makes
mutual praises of this type obligatory. Their usefulness for the spouses
is rather obvious.

The following excerpts, 3(a) and (b), taken from the poems 'Changu Chikomba' ('My lover') by A. Muyaya and 'Zvaonekwa Chikandamina' ('Thank you, porcupine') by R. Mashoko are examples of love poems by women composed and written for publication in a modern anthology (Haasbroek et al. 1978: 145; Haasbroek 1988: 311–12 respectively), but in the old tradition of *madetembedzo okupfimbana*, 'courtship praises', and *madanha omugudza*, 'praises by the wife during love-making':

3(a) Changu chikomba ndibaba vavana, baba vaZvichauya
      Murume murefu mutema muuya
      Ndakatomupiwa naNyadenga nokuhope
      Bva kubvira musiwo handichazivi hope

      My lover is father of my children, father of what-is-yet-to-be
      He is tall, dark and handsome
      He was given me by God in a dream
      But since that day sleep has deserted me

(b) Maita masvingo aGovere
      Navari kumhepo vonyenamira
      Uyu mutambo wavakatisiyira
      Mutambo wakadzora nebhinya
      Usina mukuru woumwe

      Thank you, the great monument of Govere
      Even the ancestors in the spirit world must be smiling
      For this is a game they left for us
      The exciting game that humbled even the savage murderer
      The game that makes people equal.

The imagery is similar to but not as dense as in the older, orally transmitted poems. In 3(a) the girl is already eager to get married and to raise a family with her beloved boyfriend, already a father figure. She says she is lucky to have had such a wonderful and handsome man indicated to her by her ancestral spirits. Their love is bigger and stronger than everything. In expressing the intensity of their love and how close they are to each other, there are more traditional images used (the drum beat, the mountain, the pot and the stirring stick, the upper and lower grinding stones, gravy and *sadza*) than modern images (the patch and the trousers, the belt and the trousers). This mix is clear evidence of originality, improvisation and dynamism of the oral literary tradition in modern day Shona society.

The dominant imagery earlier in 3(b) relates to the totem group. The totem animal is the porcupine, which is notorious for throwing its quills around. This is likened to sowing of seed by the man during the sex act while the woman symbolically sprays manure so that the couple can grow a healthy crop, i.e. children. These extended and complementary images of virility and fertility are linked to the spirit world. In other words, their ancestral or guardian spirits are happy because both parties are not only being good to each other but, more importantly, they are making their contribution to ensure the continuance of the race.

Similar sentiments and images are contained in the lyrics of the songs 'Vimbai' ('Faith') recorded by Marshal Munhumumwe and the Four Brothers and 'Rudo Ndimandivhaidza' ('Love it is that makes me proud') recorded by Yellowman Big Zhanje and the Spiders. In 'Vimbai', singer Marshal Munhumumwe is the suitor who is singing praises for his girlfriend Vimbai. She is very beautiful and very kind:

> 4(a) Vimbai mwana akanaka
> Mwanasikana chichekererwa seshereni
> Chitoramwoyo pakaperera shungu dzaMwari
>
> Vimbai the beautiful one
> A girl moulded and cut to perfection like a shilling
> One who steals the heart, God's ultimate handicraft
>
> (b) Meso akapfekedzwa tsitsi nengoni
> Mwoyo wake igumbeze rechando
>
> Her eyes radiate sympathy and kindness
> Her heart is a blanket for the winter.

Both attributes are emphasised by repetition of images for the perfect shape of an exquisite creature, and of the synonyms *tsitsi* and *ngoni* for kindness. Vimbai is a well-brought-up girl who has good manners, and she is admired and praised by all:

> 4(c) Vimbai mwana ane tsika
> Ndiye akatora mwoyo kwete wangu ndega
> Tiri vazhinji vanomurumbidza
>
> Vimbai the well-mannered girl
> She is the one who took not only my heart but others' as well
> There are many of us who praise her.

She is loving, tender and warm as a winter blanket. It is interesting to note how modern images have been incorporated for traditionally acclaimed virtues. Vimbai's long and slender neck is likened to that of the king's, i.e. settler magistrate's, horse which now replaces the images *nhongoramutsipa*, 'long and slender neck', and *mutsipa unokwira inda ikazorora*, 'the neck that a louse may not climb without a rest', which are used in 2(a) and (b). Her kind heart is now metaphorically called *gumbeze*, i.e. a modern blanket, rather than *gudza*, 'traditional blanket'.

In 'Rudo Ndimandivhaidza', singer Yellowman Big Zhanje is the proud husband who is boasting about his good wife, much in the same vein as a traditional *sahwira*, 'ritual friend', would at a beer party. To the singer, his wife is the most beautiful woman in the world, although everybody else may say that she is ugly or too dark or crippled:

> Rudo ndimandivhaidza
> Rudo rwechokwadi . . .
> Vanhu vanonditaurira
> Mukadzi wako akanyangara
> Ini handizvione
> Nekuti ndinomuda . . .
> Pane vamwe ndinovhaira naye

> Love it is that makes me poud
> Love true love . . .
> People say to me
> Your wife is ugly
> I do not see that myself
> Because I love her . . .
> Among the crowd I boast about her.

As the saying goes, beauty is in the eye of the beholder. In a culture without commercial modelling, and in a culture where every woman found a husband, every woman had special praises composed for her and, therefore, every woman was beautiful to someone.

Thus, we find that the key images in traditional praises are repeated in modern, written love poems and in the lyrics of modern love songs, although the language used in the more modern compositions may not be as imageful or as intimate. Obviously, it is not socially acceptable among the Shona to be sexually explicit in public fora (i.e. through music for public consumption), although this may be perfectly all right in love poems, because these are supposed to be personal and private anyway.

ORALITY IN WRITTEN POETRY AND POPULAR MUSIC

Today, as in the 'traditional' past, poetry and song are used to criticise and ridicule people whose behaviour is unacceptable in terms of societal norms and expectations. A typical such character in the extended family is the *vamwene*, 'mother-in-law', who is making life unnecessarily difficult for her *muroora*, 'daughter-in-law'. The *vamwene* –*muroora* conflict has always been a popular theme in oral poetry, usually with the daughter-in-law expressing her anguish and frustration, as in the traditional poem 'Nhuna dzomuroora' ('A daughter-in-law's complaints') in Hodza's collection (1984: 64), which is very similar to M. A. Hamutyinei's poem 'Muri Parumananzombe Varoora' ('You are in deep trouble, daughters-in-law') in the more modern anthology *Mabvumira Enhetembo* (Literature Bureau 1969: 21). The same sentiments are expressed in very similar verses and images by Marshal Munhumumwe in the song 'Vamwene Vanoshusha' ('My mother-in-law is a problem'), which was recorded a few years ago and was very popular.

In the poem 'Nhuna dzomuroora', the *muroora* narrates her complaints in verses typical of the traditional *jikinyira*, 'complaints', and *nheketerwa*, 'rhythmic utterance of complaints' genres. Such complaints could be uttered by the *muroora*, daughter-in-law, while she was grinding flour. In the written poem 'Muri Parumananzombe Varoora', Hamutyinei expresses his sympathy and support for *varoora*, 'daughters-in-law' in general, while he narrates the same complaints as in 'Nhuna dzomuroora' in more or less the same terms. In the song 'Vamwene Vanoshusha', the singer Marshal Munhumumwe repeats the same complaints as in the two poems 'Nhuna dzomuroora' and 'Muri Paramanzombe Varoora'. Actually he simplifies Hamutyinei's poem and adapts it into a song while he plays the role of the *muroora*.

Together, these three compositions are a good example of how modern written poetry adopts and adapts from traditional oral poetry, and how Afropop songs then adopt and adapt from the written poetry.

PRAISE, REBUKE AND CONFORMITY

This chapter has focused on the transition from traditional courtship praises through modern love poems to modern love songs, but the last set of three examples shows that this transition process and change are not restricted to courtship and love-making. Neither are they restricted to praises. Examples from virtually all areas of life can be found in Shona oral literature showing the same pattern. Whether through praise or through rebuke, whether through poetry or proverbial lore or song, the effect remains socialisation for conformity. Many writers, poets and singers portray women characters who are independent and/or enterprising in a negative manner. There is a contradiction nowadays between the rhetoric about equality of the sexes and advancement of women on the one hand, and, on the other, *mabhatani*, 'patronage', and *tangawandida*, 'sexual harassment' or 'bottom power', at the workplace.

One finds a very similar contradiction between rhetoric about liberation, democracy and civil rights while free intellectual debate and political choice are not permitted as, directly or indirectly, everyone is forced to conform. Conformity is relatively easy to achieve in a culture that generally does not challenge authority. Quite often, justification for undemocratic tendencies by the rulers is sought by reinterpreting the traditional culture. In Shona, for example, the contrast between *madzimai*, 'married mothers', and *mahure*, 'prostitutes and concubines', may be used to silence women in public life, while authoritarian interpretations of the behaviour of individual members of the community is always possible, because the whole socialisation process tends towards conformity, as, traditionally, it was designed to meet expected norms of behaviour in specified role-relationships.

I have compiled the lyrics of many Afropop songs other than love songs, and, although it would be premature to make any categorical statements at this stage of the research, the preliminary indications are that Shona oral art forms encourage conformity in everything from politics and ideology to individual social behaviour. One hopes that, in time, it will become possible to come up with detailed studies such as the ones on South African black music and literature (Coplan 1985; February 1988). Modern African nation-states may well be using crooked interpretations of traditional culture for selfish purposes in order to legitimise the policies, programmes and actions of the rulers by making comparisons with traditional rulership (*ushe*) which was permanent. At the same time, continual references to the nation (*nyika*) as one family (*mhuri*) may well be used to justify a one-party state. Quite often one hears statements such as:

> Muchikwere chimwe chete hamugari machongwe maviri
> There is no room for two cocks in the same chicken coop.

The *jongwe*, 'cock' is the symbol of Zimbabwe's ruling ZANU (PF) party.

· CHAPTER 12 ·

Nontsizi Mgqwetho: stranger in town

Jeff Opland

In the years following the First World War, black South Africans publicly defied white systems of control both in urban centres like Johannesburg, to which many migrated to work on the mines, and in the rural areas. Throughout the country, blacks boycotted stores, mounted strikes, and demonstrated against the pass system. This post-war political activity culminated in the mineworkers' strike of 1920, 'an event of major significance. Of a total of thirty-five mines, twenty-one had been affected, and not far off a half of the black workforce had participated at some stage' (Bonner 1979: 274). One of the consequences of the strike was the establishment of a weekly newspaper by the Chamber of Mines (Willan 1984: 251–3): the first issue of *Umteteli wa Bantu* appeared in May 1920. *Umteteli's* contribution to Xhosa literature was considerable until 1956, when it became *Umteteli wa Bantu e Goli*, changed its policy and adopted a magazine format: its pages were filled with creative writing of the highest order. Two poets were particularly prominent in its early decades. After 1927, a steady stream of historical and cultural articles, gossip and poems flowed from the articulate pen of Nzululwazi, 'Deep knowledge', one of a number of pseudonyms employed by S. E. K. Mqhayi, the dominant figure in the history of Xhosa literature.[1] And from 1920 to 1929 over ninety poems were contributed by Nontsizi Mgqwetho. The recovery of Mgqwetho's sizeable corpus is particularly significant if only because, although women were prominent in the early development of the Xhosa novel, no published volume of poetry in Xhosa has ever been written by a woman.[2]

This gender discrepancy in generic output is almost surely attributable to the fact that women are prominent participants in the tradition of *intsomi*, the Xhosa folktale, but, although women are as active as men as composers and transmitters of personal and clan praises, the *imbongi*, the court poet, is always a male. Indeed, Mgqwetho addresses this very issue in the first of her poems, submitted from

Crown Mines in Johannesburg and directed to the editor, which commences with the following lines:[3]

Nkosi, mHleli wo*Mthetheli* wethu,
  Wanga ungaphila ubomi obude,
Mzukulwana wamadoda afela kwaHoho;
Tarhu, Gatyeni! Hamba sokulandela.

  Hom! Zajika!
Amadoda afela izwe lawo,
Afa kunye nenkosi yawo uSandile.

  Hom! bo!!
Thina sokulandela,
Kuba singabantwana boGaga,
UGag' oluhamba lugongqoza lukhwez' iXesi,
UNdanda koVece uXesi maGqagala,
Umthunzi wabantu bonke bengakanje
Nditsho kuSandile mna.

  Hamba sokulandela,
Kuba akuzange kuphume
Ntamnani kowenu.

  Hamba sokulandela,
Kuba thina simadoda nje
Asizange siyibone kowethu iMbongikazi yenkazana,
Kuba imbongi inyuka nenkundla Ithuke inkosi.

  Hamba sokulandela,
Nezi mbongikazi thina sizibona
Apha kweli lolayita nebhekile.
                    (*Umteteli* 23 October 1923)

  Sir, Editor of our *Mteteli*,
    May you flourish a long life through,
  Child of heroes who fell at Hoho; [4]
  Peace, Gatyeni! Go, we'll follow you.

  Whoa! Rein in!
  Those Hoho heroes fell for their country,
  Died alongside Sandile their king.

  Whoa there!
  We'll follow you:
  We're children of royalty,
  'Who rumbles along Xesi's banks,
  Flutters at Vece, settles at Xesi,
    Shade for all, whatever their number.'
    These are Sandile's praises I cite.[5]

> Go, we'll follow:
> Your house has produced
> No traitors.
>
> Go, we'll follow:
> As for us, our house has produced
> No female poet:
> The poet who rouses the court
> And censures the king's always male.
>
> Go, we'll follow!
> Female poets first appeared
> In this land of thug and booze.

Mqgwetho here contrasts the cohesive heroic code of allegiance to chiefs with the lawlessness of life in the urban townships, where traditional practices have been supplanted, permitting a female to contribute poetry to a newspaper in which she claims the role of an *imbongi*: Mgqwetho laments the loss of rural values in the cities, but at the same time welcomes the opportunities it offers her. In various roles she adopts in her poetry, Mgqwetho flutters like an iron filing between two magnetic forces, adopting self-contradictory and irreconcilable positions. In the rapidly evolving, alienating urban world to which blacks had recently migrated, Mgqwetho seems to have experienced what Robert Park terms a 'sense of moral dichotomy and conflict' that 'is probably characteristic of every immigrant during the period of transition, when old habits are being discarded and new ones are not yet formed. It is inevitably a period of inner turmoil and intense self-consciousness' (1928: 893). Park finds that in the autobiographies of European immigrants in America 'the conflict of cultures, as it takes place in the mind of the immigrant, is just the conflict of "the divided self", the old self and the new. And frequently there is no satisfying issue of this conflict, which often terminates in a profound disillusionment' (p. 892). The poetry of Nontsizi Mgqwetho – powerful, outspoken, urgent and engaged – reflects just such a deeply torn marginal personality.[6]

THE LITERATE *IMBONGI*

Nontsizi Mgqwetho identifies herself with a new breed of poets. In greeting the New Year, she praises 1923 for its settled calm:

> Siya kuncoma noko 1923
> Khayakhulu lilumlel' abantwana

Tu! Naziphithi-phithi unyaka wonke
Tarhu ke! Ndlovu eyadla igoduka
       (*Umteteli* 5 January 1924, 5)

We praise you, 1923,
Great fosterhome for babies.
Quiet! No troubles all year!
Peace then, Elephant browsing homewards

but immediately passes on to threaten 1924:

Uze uqonde mhlophe 1924
Thina maAfrika sihamba ngentswazi
Thina asivarhi zimbongi zangoku
Apho sikhona – wotyiwa nazizinja.

Make no mistake, 1924,
We Africans travel well armed,
We modern poets don't lounge about:
On our turf dogs will devour you.[7]

She is one of these modern poets in the front line exhorting resistance
to oppression through the medium of a newspaper just as the *imbongi*
did orally. Her poetry is redolent with the diction of traditional
izibongo (see Opland 1983, 1989), as in her metaphorical reference to
1923 as a great elephant, and in the concluding lines of the same poem:

Tyaphile! Ufike 1924,
Iimbongi azingebongi lungakanani;
Mazitsale iifolosi, zide ziguqe,
Khona kuyo'ba mnandi kumaAfrika.

Awu! Yatsho iDrummond Castle
Yakwa'Chizama'
Inkomo enobugqi benyamakazi.
   Camagu!

You're welcome, 1924;
New poets, reputations untried,
Must strut their stuff today
And tickle African fancies.

Oh! Hear the *Drummond Castle*
Of the house of Chizama,
Beast with an antelope's guile.[8]
   Mercy!

In a style typical of the *imbongi*, Mgqwetho's first poem to be
published in *Umteteli* appropriates the voice of the *imbongi*, invokes

the warriors who fell at Hoho, and quotes from the *izibongo* of Sandile. Her poetry is dense with traditional clan names and praise references.

The diction and ethic of oral *izibongo* is evident too in the poem that follows this New Year poem in the sequence, a poem about Mgqwetho herself, which vaunts her outspoken poetry, poetry that benefits the African people and brings her fame, but which is also unpopular among envious poets and among those who fault her for invading a traditional male preserve:

Tarhu! Nontsizi dumezweni ngentsholo
Nto ezibongo ziyintlaninge yezwe
Indlovu ke ayisindwa ngumboko wayo
Awu! Tarhu! Sikhukukazi phiko eAfrika.

Esikusela amathole aze angemki
Emke nezinye iintaka eziwadlayo
Uyaziwa lilizwe nambakazi yezulu
Enqenwe nazimbongi zada zaxelelana.

Wugqwethele Mgqwetho lo mhlaba kaPhalo
Betha izizwe ngesithunzi zidangale
Ulirhamncwa akuvelwa ngasemva
Nabakwaziyo babetha besothuka.

Tarhu! Mdakakazi omabal' aziziba
Ovumba linuka okwenyoka yomlambo
Camagu! Nawe Ndlovu edla phezulu
Uzibhalile noko iinkomo zakwaMgqwetho . . .

Tarhu! Nontsizi bulembu eAfrika
Ozihluba izibongo ekuhleni
Zitsho neentaba zelizwe zikhangelane
Xa waphuka imbambo macala omabini . . .

Tarhu Mbongikazi Flamingo kaVaaibom
Esunduza iinyawo xa isukayo
Esunduza inyawo xa ihlalayo
Ziphume izilo zonke zigcakamele.

Tarhu! Dadakazi lendaba zeAfrika
Ubhibhinxa lwentombi esinqe sibi
Awu! Nontsizi bulembu eAfrika
Akusoze wende nezitho zigoso.

Tarhu! Mbongikazi phiko leAfrika
Sudukani bo arha ndabonelelwa
Tarhu! Somikazi lomthi wekhiwane
Ubonga noko side siphel' isoya . . .

Tarhu! Nontsizi ntsasa enemizila
Egqibe izinga zonke iprofethesha
Awu! Tarhu! Sanusekazi sezibongo
Nalo nerhamncwa liwabhul' amaphiko . . .

Awu! Tarhu! Nontsizi bulembu eAfrika
Ntokazi etsho ngentlombe ezimnandi
Zitsho zidume neendonga zeAfrika
Arha hayi abhitye onke amadodana.

Mhlana wafa Nontsizi losibekela
Hashe lenkumanda loba lilahlekile
Awu! Tarhu! Nangaye uNtsikana
Owayegqibe zonke izinga eprofethesha.
(*Umteteli* 12 January 1924)

Peace, Nontsizi, renowned for your chanting,
Your poems the nation's bounty.
No elephant finds its trunk clumsy.
Peace, mother hen, Africa's sheltering wing!

Hen shepherding chicks
Safe from the talons of birds of prey,
The nation knows you, lofty she-python,
The poets' clique avoids you.

Upset Phalo's land, Mgqwetho,[9]
Loom over nations and sap their strength.
Wild beast too vicious to take from behind,
Your associates tremble in tackling you.

Peace, dusky woman, treasure-house of stories,
Your stench reeks like the river snake.
Mercy! Elephant browsing the tops,
You've made a name for Mgqwetho . . .

Peace, Nontsizi, African rivermoss,
Your poetry goes to the core
And the peaks of the nation swivel
As you sway from side to side . . .

Peace, poetess, Vaaibom's flamingo,
Who tucks up her feet for take-off
Untucking them to land:
Animals emerge to bask in the sun.

Peace, newsy duck of Africa,
Ungainly woman with ill-shaped frame.
Oh, Nontsizi, African rivermoss,
With bow-legs like yours you'll never marry!

Peace, poetess, Africa's sheltering wing,
Make way, they're hot on my heels.
Peace, starling perched in a fig tree,
Your poetry puts paid to pleasantries . . .

Peace, Nontsizi, match-stick legs all scratched
From prophesying in clumps of thorn;
Oh, peace, poetic sybil,
Watch out, the wild bird's flapping its wings . . .

Oh peace, Nontsizi, African rivermoss,
Woman, the winsome song of your voice
Sets Africa's walls vibrating,
Utterly shaming all the lads.

We'll hear of the day of your death, Nontsizi,
The commando's horse has lost its way.
Oh, peace! And to you, Ntsikana,[10]
Who prophesied in clumps of thorn.

Typical of *izibongo* (and traditions of praise poetry throughout Africa and elsewhere) is the litany of nominally based praises referring to the subject of the poem, phrases such as lofty she-python, African rivermoss, Vaaibom's flamingo, newsy duck of Africa. The stanzaic structure may be Western, but there is little to distinguish the diction of this poem from an oral *izibongo* anyone would utter about himself or herself. Although she is communicating through the printed word, Mgqwetho uses kinetic and aural images of her poetry: her torso sways, she chants poetry and her voice arouses Africa.

In the very next poem (*Umteteli* 19 January 1924, 6), however, this illusion of oral performance is dropped as Mgqwetho twice invites her readers to consult the Bible (she cites specific chapters and verses), and admonishes her readers directly, 'Phawula mleseshi', ('Reader, take note!') a phrase that recurs in her poetry. At times, even though her earlier poems are couched in four-line stanzas, Mgqwetho speaks in the voice of the *imbongi*; at other times, she drops this pose and writes as a literate poet for readers. She distances herself still further from the illusion of oral *izibongo* with the appearance of a poem on 2 August 1924, the thirty-second of the sequence, in which she adopts rhyme. Thereafter, rhyme is a regular feature of her poetry. This is an unfortunate development, not only because rhyme is quite absent from Xhosa tradition – and thus represents a significant departure from the poetic diction of the *imbongi* – but also because rhyme is a feature of the European culture she is elsewhere at pains to denigrate.

At times Mgqwetho's poetry speaks from within Xhosa tradition, but
gradually it comes to belong self-consciously to the literate world of an
alien tradition.

THE DESPAIRING ACTIVIST

The martial tone assumed from the diction and style of the poetry of
the *imbongi* suits Mgqwetho's purpose, for she is outspoken in
rallying blacks to organise against their oppressors and exploiters. She
consistently asserts that blacks must find common ground and seek a
link to a new dispensation for themselves independently of whites. In
her second poem, for example, she says

> Izibuko kuqala lobonwa
> Ngamakhaya –
> Aze noKing George
> Abeke nesitampu.
>> (*Umteteli* 13 November 1920, 7)

> First we'll find
> A ford alone –
> Then King George
> Can set his seal.

White oppression bears down on blacks: early in 1921 she reflects on
the past year:

> Hanewu, 1920,
>> Nyaka wendaniso!
>> Safuna inkululeko;
>> Wathoba iimbumbulu.
>>> Qho ke khona; Qho.
>> (*Umteteli* 15 January 1921, 7)

> But wait, 1920
>> Year of frustration!
>> We sought independence:
>> You cowered from gunfire.
>>> Pow! And Pow! again.

The black is vanquished, a victim in his own land:

> Unazo neempawu zibuz' imvelaphi
> Seyinguwe na? Ngoku ongumfiki apha?
> Andikuphinda nditshilo nje nditshilo
> Baza amehlo kade ndandibona.

Unjengondwendwe namhlanje eAfrika
Sowuhamba ubutha amabibi
Hluba ikhakha lilo izwe loyihlo
Lusi sivivinya sayo imishologu.

Gquba kube mdaka, mDaka weAfrika
NjengoMoses ephuma eJiphethe
Khawuyek' ukubuza nantso iAfrika
Isi sivivinya sayo imishologu.

Xa ndilapho intliziyo ibuhlungu
Siyileli yokukhwela izizwe
Namhlanje sesothuka kukudala
Saginywayo!
                    (*Umteteli* 14 June 1924, 11)

Ubiquitous signs inquire your origins:
Are *you* the latecomer here?
I won't rehash what I've often said.
Open your eyes: I've long foreseen it.

Today you're a stranger in Africa,
You go about clutching at straws:
Repair your shield, the land of your fathers
Is now the playground of strangers.

Bellow the challenge, black man of Africa,
As Moses did quitting Egypt.
Stop asking questions. Clearly Africa
Is now the playground of strangers.

It pains my heart to say these things,
We're a ladder others ascend.
Only lately we're starting to stir
Long after we've been consumed.

She sees no hope in the change of government in 1924 (*Umteteli* 12 July 1924, 5), concluding that it makes little difference to blacks whether Smuts or Hertzog is in power.

But if whites are the enemy, blacks are the problem. If Mgqwetho is critical of white domination, she is even more scathing of ineffectual black opposition to oppression. Early in the sequence she derides Congress and its organ, *Abantu-Batho*. In her third poem she castigates the dissension within the ranks of Congress and among blacks in general:

YiCape Native Congress!
   Bantu Union!
   Zulu osebenzela ekhaya!
   Nezibuko esingazi ngomso.

Yiyiphi na ke kuzo
Eginyisa amathe
Nenika abantu ithemba
Lokubuyiswa kweAfrika?. . .

Kuba ooFunz' eweni
Bashumayela
Abangakwamkeli kuCongress
Bakwenze indaba zesizwe.

Imkile iNatal Congress
Ngenxa yabo
Imkile kwaneFree State
Nantsiya neKoloni izintlantlu ngentlantlu.
          (*Umteteli* 27 November 1920, 6)

Cape Native Congress
And Bantu Union!
Zulu takes care of his own!
And a ford leading nowhere!

Which one of these
Makes the mouth water,
Raises hopes
Of Africa's return?. . .

For rabble rousers,
Without leave from Congress
Sermonise
And hit the headlines.

And as a result
Natal's Congress walks out,
The Free State's walks out,
The Cape's splinters splinter.

She assails the pass system (*Umteteli* 17 January 1925, 8), but also black leaders, as in a graphic prose account of an earlier anti-pass demonstration:

Kuthe ngo1919 kwehla isiphithi-phithi esikhulu kakhulu apha eRhawutini, sophawu lukaKayin (Passport). Baza ke bafa nabantu kanobom. Phula-phulani ke! Ndiza kuthetha endakubonayo ngamehlo ingekuko endakuva ngoVazidlule.
  Kuthe ngomhla wesithathu kuApril 1919, sanduluka thina nkokeli zesizwe, kunye nesizwe ngokubanzi, saya eGantolo, apho sasiye kulinda khona ukuphuma kwe'kwezi le Afrika', kwanokuwiswa komthwalo lo wePasi usemagxeni. Esa sinethemba ke elikhulu ngenyani, siqonda mhlophe ukuba wona lomthwalo uyakuwa sakuba siyinyukile 'Induli kaXakeka'. Kuthe siselapho, sisaqwalesele eyona nto kode kube yiyo. Asibonanga ngani? Kwathi thu 'Nduli' yimbi 'kaXakeka', eyatsho saxakeka ngenyani. Amahashi ooNongqayi esiza kuthi kanye, engasaphali, etsiba izihogo. Zabaleka iinkokeli

zona engekafiki nokufika loo mahashi apho eGantolo. Zathi ziyoyika ngokumhlophe azafihla, kuba ziluvile utyikityo olwenziwe ngooNongqayi eFidasidolophu ngezolo. Zasishiya ke bethu kololudaka zaziluxovile. Inene, makowethu, sakhutshwa kolodaka ngamandla ezulu kuphela.

(*Umteteli* 13 December 1924, 6)

In 1919, here in Johannesburg, an unspeakable horror made its appearance: the mark of Cain (that is, the pass). People died by the thousands. Now just listen. I'm going to tell you what I saw with my very own eyes, not what I heard from some passer-by.

On 3 April 1919, we the leaders of the nation marched with a mass of people to the Fort, where we were going to wait for 'the dawn of Africa', the lifting of the burden of the pass from our shoulders. We had high hopes, truly believing that this burden would fall once we'd scaled the Hill of Struggle. We got there and stood around, wondering what to do next. What did we see? Another Hill of Struggle suddenly confronted us, scattering confusion. Cops on horseback charged us down, at full tilt, like bats out of hell. Our leaders took to their heels before those horses reached the Fort. They made no bones about their fear, saying they'd been pounded by the cops at Fordsburg the day before. They just left us there in the mess they'd invited us to. I tell you truly, my people, it's only through the power of God that we survived that mess.

Blacks are afflicted by poor leaders ('Where are the leaders like Daniel?' she asks in *Umteteli* 5 April 1924, 10). As traditional and political leaders abdicate their responsibilities, she appeals for unity time and time again:

> Ke le nto izinkosi
> Ifuna umanyano
> Kuba zingonyama ezijonga
> Ngeliso elibomvu.

> UThixo udinge
> Ukuba wosinceda
> Kodwa kungengaphandle
> Kweyethu imigudu.
> (*Umteteli* 15 January 1921, 7)

> We must have unity
> To face the bosses,
> Lions that stalk us
> With bloody eyes.

> God won't deign
> To grant us help
> Unless we strive
> To help ourselves.

But the people, like their leaders, are too self-absorbed (the title of her poem in *Umteteli* on 19 July 1924, is 'Strangers strip people selfishly squabbling').

Time and again in her poetry, Mgqwetho adopts the position that before blacks can rightfully appeal for Africa to come home, they must set their own homes in order. Having abandoned their traditions to the bottle, continually squabbling among themselves, blacks themselves constitute the greatest impediment to victory in their struggle for freedom. Blacks are thus the victims of white oppression, which Mgqwetho opposes in stirring martial imagery, seeking to rally her people against their common enemies, but at the same time she is painfully sensitive to the dissension amongst blacks and the failure of black leaders that constitute major obstacles to the attainment of black freedom. In frustration, she rails against white oppression before a riven community, caught between callous whites and self-seeking, indifferent blacks.

THE TORN CHRISTIAN

Mgqwetho's political convictions are inseparable from her powerful religious commitment. She regularly writes pious poems for Easter and Christmas, she sees earthquakes as divine punishment for her people's iniquity, she speaks as a member of the temperance movement and of a woman's prayer union. In seeking to draw a distinction between true and false prophets, she refers her readers to Revelation and Deuteronomy, holds Jonah up as a true prophet, but inveighs against the false prophets misleading black people:

> Ndihleli nje andisoze ndilibale
> Ukutsho noko andimntu wakugxeka
> Nto abayityhilelweyo yethini na
> Le nto ngathi idukela esiswini.
>
> Le nto ingumprofethi yinto ni! Nje bo
> Makavele noseKapa neqhinga
> Umprofethi ngumbola isezulwini
> Umngxolisi wezulu lididuma . . .
>
> Bakhona abenyani – nabobuxoki
> Phawula mleseshi wobakhetha ngokwakho
> Abobuxoki mabafe ndaweninye
> Izindlu zamagqwirha ke zimelane . . .
>
> Ngumangaliso mni na lo e Afrika
> Akuba porofethi yindiba-ndiba
> Iphambene imidaka iyaprofetha
> Tyho! Yonganyelwe bubuhle nobuciko.

Satshabalala ke thina ngokungazi
Besiswele isanuse na sivumise
Kuba nomprofethi oyakuza ngenyani
Camagwini bo! Asisenakukholwa.
            (*Umteteli* 19 January 1924, 6)

I'm not one for scorn,
Yet I can't forget
Their revelations served
To line their pockets.

But what *is* a prophet?
Let's hear a plan from those in the Cape.
A prophet's mark is made in heaven,
He scolds the thundering skies . . .

There are prophets both true and false
And – Reader, take note – you can tell
      them apart.
Let the false ones die on the spot
They live next door to witches . . .

What wonders occur in Africa!
Prophets in every nook and cranny,
Each so fine and silver-tongued
The blacks are rent asunder.

We're crushed because we're out of
      touch
There's no diviner to consult
To tell if a prophet is true.
Oh mercy! Who can we turn to?

At times Mgqwetho is able to reconcile her Christianity with her politics. Yet at other times, contradictions lurk just below the surface, for the gospel was introduced by whites. In criticising whites as colonial oppressors she decries the Bible as an agent of oppression ('Silence implies consent'):

Lo vangeli yabo yokusikhohlisa
Mina ingangam ndigaqe ngedolo.

Lingasiphosa nezulu siyimamela
Kub' inomkhonto obuye usihlabe
Iyahana-hanisa kumntu ontsundu
Iwugqwethile ke lo mhlaba kaPhalo.
            (*Umteteli* 28 June 1924, 6)

This gospel of theirs, designed to deceive us,
Stands as tall as I do down on my knees.

Heed its word and heaven's lost,
It's a spear that wheels and stabs us:
The land of Phalo's upset
By the hypocritical cant of the white man's
    gospel.

Mgqwetho speaks as a committed Christian, her faith deeply rooted in the Bible, yet she rejects the culture which brought Christianity. As in her political dilemma, Mgqwetho is also caught between white Christians and black. Incensed at the godless ways of urban sophisticates, her admonitions frequently urge a return to traditional values. In one passionate poem, for example, Mgqwetho addresses urban Christians in the voice of that bane of the missionaries, the red-blanketed traditionalist[11] who disdains conversion:

Ingxoxo yomGinwa kumaGqobhoka!

Ziph' iintombi zenu? Izwi liyinto ni?
    Zigqibe lo mhlaba, zifuna ukwenda
Ziqeshe zindlwana; zishweshwe uthuli
    Zibeth' onomtatsi kwaThulandivile!

Oonina balila amehlo azidudu
    Kushiywa lusapho; lumka bekhangele
Beyala belila bengenakuviwa
    Zintombi zemfundo noonyana bemfundo!

Kuzel' iintolongo kwaphuk' iiHovizi
    Ngala matshivela asezikolweni.
IiSatifikethi zaseSimnareni
    Ziyinto yentsini ebukwa ziJaji.

Onk' amabhedengu asezikolweni
    Onke namasela asezikolweni
Onke namagqwirha asezikolweni
    Ninga bokusikwa ndifung' uNontsizi.

Nikho ngakuThixo nasebuqabeni
    Nigqobhok' emini kuhlwe nizingcuka
Udlul' uMfundisi angakubulisi
    Kodwa ngumalusi weemvu zikaThixo.

Sothini na thina xa bese njenjalo
    Sibambe liphi na kulo mpamba-mpamba
Nerhatshi likuni nina magqobhoka
    Nambathis' uThixo ngengubo yengwenya.

Nina magqobhoka ningodludla nazo
  Nayek' izikhakha nanxib' ezomlungu.
Nithe nzwi nendlebe butywala bomlungu
  Kodwa yen umlungu akabudl' obenu.

Ngemini zecawe nihamba ezindle
  Nikhaba ibhola kunye netenese
Nigqishel' ububi ngezwi likaThixo
  Nixak' uSathana usinkwabalala.

Aninaluthando aninayo nani
  Kodwa nizibiza ngoThixo wothando
Lo nkolwana yenu yokusikhohlisa
  Mina ingangam ndiguqe ngedolo.

Nakufika kuthi thina bo maqaba
  Thina sakunoja sithi niyinyama.
Anditsho ukuthi izwi likaThixo
  Ukuthetha kwalo akunanyaniso.
    Camagu!
(*Umteteli* 24 November 1923, 4)

'*A red blanket addresses Christians*'

Where are your daughters? Cat got your tongue?
  They roamed the countryside searching for
marriage,
Shamelessly shacked up with live-in lovers,
  Cut capers in New Clare till all hours of the night.

With eyes of porridge their mothers bewail
  Their absent family, who left them standing,
Advising the air and pleading in vain
  With sons and daughters who've all been to school.

Jails crammed to capacity, courts jam-packed
  With the learned products of school education;
The judges in charge just hoot in derision
  At college certificates brandished by bums.

Our every crook can be found in the schools,
  Our every thief can be found in the schools,
Our every rogue can be found in the schools:
  I swear by Nontsizi,[12] you should all be kicked out!

You still wear red blankets in God's very house,
  You're Christians by day, hyenas by night;
The pastor's the shepherd of God's own flock,
  Yet he scurries past you without a nod.

What do we make of this curious behaviour?
Which voice do we choose from their babble?
You Christians harbour pride in your midst,
    Cloaking God in crocodile hide.

You Christians are suckers for every fad,
    You discarded skin garments and dressed up like whites.
Your ears ring for white man's booze,
    But whites won't touch a drop of yours.[13]

Every Sunday you romp on the veld
    Kicking a football, whacking a racquet,
Clothing your shame in the name of God:
    Satan's struck dumb in amazement.

You have no love, you have nothing at all,
    And yet you proclaim a God of love:
That faith of yours stands just as tall
    As I do down on my knees.

If you should ever approach us again,
    We red blankets will roast you like meat.
But of course I don't wish to imply
    That the word of God's devoid of truth.
        Mercy!

The concluding couplet reflects Mgqwetho's dilemma. As a Christian she is sickened by urban godlessness: red blanketed rurals lead more Christian lives than do the converts. She is fully comfortable in neither community.

THE MILITANT FEMALE

Mgqwetho is involved in women's affairs, and often leaps to the defence of women. Her early poems express high regard for the activist Charlotte Maxeke. She is also a member of a prayer union (*manyano*), and vigorously defends women against the charge that they are neglecting their duty at home by attending prayer meetings.[14] She constantly laments the sorry state that women have descended to in the cities, a condition she likens to slavery:

> Wazinyathela na iintombi zezwe lakho
> Zangamakhoboka na ezweni lakho
> Baza amehlo kade ndandibona
> Kulapho namhla wotshabalala khona . . .

Iintombi zezwe lakho sisivatho sakho
Ooguda-zilingeke ezweni lakho.
Zitsho kamnandi ekhumbini lentaba
Ndingazicinga kuthi gongqe nenkaba.
            (*Umteteli* 31 January 1925, 8)

Are you trampling the nation's daughters,
Enslaving them in your own land?
Open your eyes: I've often foreseen
That here, today, we faced destruction ...

Your nation's daughters are ornaments,
Their beauty a pride to your land,
Their voices ring sweet from the mountaintops.
I catch my breath at the thought.

And she is an ardent supporter of the rural movement that started with
women boycotting stores in Herschel, the members of which became
known as *amaFelandawonye* (*Umteteli* 6 July 1924, 5; see Beinart
1987). But Mgqwetho's outspoken claims for women's rights are
somewhat undercut by her adopted stance as an *imbongi*: a number of
formulaic phrases and poetic disclaimers are dressed in masculine
garb. Expressing the erosion of tradition, for example, Mgqwetho
often says 'I'll even take a Hottentot wife'; a recurrent opening stanza
is built on lines such as these:

Tarhu, mHleli ngesithuba sezimbongi!
Ndisahleli ndingumfana andimbongi
Ndingumphathi-thunga lezinxiba-mxhaka
Into elwa ngezulu iinduku zihleli.
            (*Umteteli* 28 June 1924, 6)

Thanks, Editor, for the space for poets.
I'm still here, a young man and no poet;
I carry the milk-pail to arm-ringed dignitaries,
I fight armed with thunder alone.

Outspoken as a woman, Mgqwetho assumes a masculine voice in
speaking as an *imbongi*.

Mgqwetho's poetry is clearly the expression of a woman frustrated
at male hegemony, yet in decrying an aspect of white exploitation and
urging a return to traditional values, she is caught in another
self-contradictory stance. In one of her prose pieces, she opposes easy
divorces which, effected through the judicial system, only enrich
whites; but the alternative to judicial divorce is hardly favourable to
women:

Akukho mthetho kaThixo nakanye, onokumanywa yindlu yetyalike, uze uyo kuqhawulwa yindlu yamatyala. Naphakade! Umfazi owendileyo ngomthetho kaThixo, ubotshiwe ngulo mthetho kwindoda yakhe bade bahlulwe kukufa. Isahluko sesixhenxe kwabaseRoma ivesi yesibini.
San' ukusoloko natyebisa abelungu, madoda. Anisenazo na nina ezakowenu iinkundla zamatyala? Indlu inokuchithwa ngokukrexeza komfazi; akhe agxothwe agoduke, kuba uyingozi endodeni yakhe ngokweloxesha. Unokuthi ke lo mfazi ugxothiweyo, emva kwexesha elikhulu ukuba usayithanda indoda yakhe, abuye azokucela uxolo, ngokuzithoba okukhulu nokunyaniseka. Yandule ke indoda yakhe imxolele xa yayimthanda ngenyani. Kuba ke akakho umntu onokuma phakathi kothando lwabantu ababini. Uthando lubalulekile emazulwini ngaphezu kweento zonke.
Ma ungachitheki konke umzi ngokukrexeza kwendoda. Indoda ivumelekile ukuthatha izithembu. Kodwa ke mayibahlonele abo bafazi ibathabathileyo ngokulinganayo, ukuze izinto zihambe ngolungelelaniso.

(*Umteteli* 28 Febuary 1925, 6)

No single law of God laid down by the church can then be repealed by a court of law. Never! A woman married under the laws of God is bound to her husband, until death do them part – Romans chapter 7, verse 2.

Gentlemen, please cease this habit of always enriching whites. What's wrong with your traditional law courts? A marriage can be dissolved because the wife has committed adultery. In such cases, the woman is sent back to her people since she is for the moment a danger to her husband. And yet, after a period of time, if she still loves her husband, such a woman can in all humility and sincerity return to beg her husband to forgive her. And if the husband really loves her, he will forgive her; for truly no one can stand in the way of two people who love each other. In heaven love is more important than anything else.

No marriage need break up because the husband has committed adultery. A man may take another wife. But he must give equal respect to the women he marries, for only then will the home be harmonious.

The protests of the outraged woman are here swamped by the voice of the anti-white traditionalist.

STRANGER IN TOWN

Thus in all four of these areas of concern – poetry, politics, religion and gender – contradictions emerge in the positions Mgqwetho assumes, and the tensions seem to mount as the sequence of poems progresses. She calls for more dynamic leadership in the political struggle, but in the social struggle she laments the erosion of traditional values: she would wish her people to enjoy closer ties with their chiefs, but acknowledges that the chiefs are a sorry lot. As a

Christian, she reveres Ntsikana, but she opposes the annual celebrations
in his honour because they fire ethnic animosities and contribute to
political disunity (*Umteteli* 7 March 1925, 8). As a Christian apologist,
she views the traditional past as a time of religious darkness (*Umteteli*
13 December 1924, 6); yet the Christianity blacks adopted was the
religion of the white oppressor, and adoption of a new religion meant
a break with that traditional past whose values she yearns for:

> Makabhange amasiko ezolo
> Izithixo zawo zikhupa umxhelo
> Ngenxa yawo asizazi nenkqu zethu
> Kwaneenkosi zethu konke kwathi quthu
>   Siyavuma!
>
> Namhlanje ubuninzi babantsundu
> Bahlukana namasiko abantsundu
> Bagalel' emzini atshona awabo
> Mhla kwakushushu ilanga lehlobo
>   Siyavuma!
>   (*Umteteli* 21 February 1925, 8)

> Let yesterday's customs perish:
> Those gods ripped out our hearts,
> And so we don't know who we are
> And our chiefs have all disappeared.
>   Yes, it's so!!
>
> Today a vast throng of blacks
> Have long turned their backs on tradition,
> In the broad light of day they embraced the stranger's,
> And their traditions sank from sight.
>   Yes, it's so!!

There can be no easy resolution to these contradictions. The only
conclusion is equivocation: the truth must be sought both in Christianity
and in traditional religion:

> Yabonani makowethu sibadala
> Nenyaniso yasiphosa kwakudala
> Inyaniso iqulethwe zizibhalo
> Naphantsi ke kweyakho imibhalo.
>   (*Umteteli* 13 December 1924, 6)

> You see, my people, we're growing old,
> The truth has left us long ago,
> The truth is bound in the Bible's covers –
> And also swathed in custom's blankets.

Mgqwetho is caught between two worlds; there is no solution to her dilemma. As the sequence progresses, the poetry becomes more and more repetitive, less specific politically, more pious and didactic. It sounds more and more tired, weary, defeated; on 14 August 1926, she writes 'I understand those who have already lost hope' (9). After September 1926 there is a two-year silence. Then a Christmas poem appears on 22 December 1928, followed by a salute to the new year, a celebratory poem she has often contributed. But in this poem the diction has lapsed into tired cliche, there is no fire, just a whimper, no threatening the new year with a spirited black resistance to white oppression, as there was in 1924:

> Wadlula umnyaka sewusishiyile
> Naango namabala athi sewumkile
> Nendanduluko zokubuka omtsha
> Oza ngentwentsha

> Umnyaka omdala ngoku uyaphela
> Nzulu-zo-Bubele, kuWe sibulela
> Ezingozini osigcine sonke
> Umnyaka wonke

> Ezobunzima obusemhlabeni
> Iimbandezelo ezisebantwini
> Imfithi-mfithi eziphazamisa
> Nokudumisa . . .

> Mnini-nto-zonke namhla siyacela
> Thina, maAfrika kuWe; sikhangela
> Ungawuthathi kwanomhlaba wethu
> Ngokona kwethu.

> Kwintshabalalo nokuswel' ukutya
> Kwimbandezelo, sibhinqa imitya
> Kwimpathwano-mbi nezibulalwano
> Fika ngombono.
>   (*Umteteli* 5 January 1929, 7)

> The year has gone and left us,
> All signs point to its passage,
> Even the joys of saluting the new,
> Arriving in its own fashion.

> The old year has come to an end.
> Deep Fountain of Kindness, we thank you
> For shielding us all from dangers
> Throughout the course of the year,

> From the world's hardships,
> The people's want,
> Calamities that disrupt
> Our worship of God . . .
>
> We implore you today, Owner-of-all –
> We Africans look up to you –
> Don't take away our land
> Because of our sins.
>
> Wretched and starving,
> Deprived, in rags,
> As we cruelly slaughter each other,
> Come with a miracle.

For Mgqwetho, urban life is too godless, too lacking in cohesion; urban blacks are too absorbed in the problems of survival in an economic system dominated by whites, too eager to court assimilation to unite effectively in opposition to their oppressors. As Park put it, 'The effect of mobility and migration is to secularize relations which were formerly sacred. One may describe the process, in its dual aspect, perhaps, as the secularization of society and the individuation of the person' (1928: 888).

Mgqwetho's poetry is the anguished outcry of an alienated stranger: in Georg Simmel's classic formulation, 'The stranger is an element of the group itself . . . an element whose membership within the group involves both being outside it and confronting it' (1971: 144). The confrontation defeats her. Her later poetry lacks fire, her protest is couched in generalisations; she yearns increasingly for the gates of heaven. At the end of the decade's first year, Mgqwetho's reaction to the afflictions her people suffer is to rally all blacks to unite to reclaim heroically their lost patrimony; here, in the last year of the decade, she laments their afflictions because they disrupt prayer. The second stanza of this poem, the ninety-third and last in the sequence, is almost identical to the first stanza of her first new year poem, which appeared on 15 January 1921, the fifth in the sequence, only here the third line reads 'Even the joys of saluting the new' where the earlier poem had 'Even the trials of saluting the new': it seems the Hill of Struggle has proved too steep for Mgqwetho. Mqhayi the rural *imbongi* spoke and wrote integral poetry that has defined and continues to define the mainstream of Xhosa oral and written literature. Mgqwetho the urban woman wrote as a divided self spiralling downward into disillusionment; her unspoken poetry has lain these past sixty years shrouded in profound silence.

NOTES

1 From January 1922 Mqhayi contributed poetry to *Umteteli* under his more familiar pseudonym of Imbongi yesizwe jikelele 'Imbongi of the whole nation'. I offered grounds for my identification of Nzululwazi as Mqhayi to Ncedile Saule in 1985; my file of contributions by Nzululwazi to *Umteteli* formed the basis of Saule's MA dissertation (1989). Subsequently, I noticed that Peires (1981, 204 n. 29; 1989, 322 n. 4) had previously correctly identified Nzululwazi.

2 Letitia Kakaza's two novels *Intyatyambo yomzi* (1913) and *UTandiwe wakwaGcaleka* (1914) are preceded in the history of the genre in Xhosa only by H. M. Ndawo's *Uhambo lukaGqoboka* (1909); two other early novels by women were Victoria Swaartbooi's *UMandisa* (1934) and Zora Futshane's *UJujuju* (1939).

3 All translations from the poetry of Nontsizi Mgqwetho are based on initial translations prepared for me by Phyllis Ntantala (Mrs A. C. Jordan). I am indebted to the Research Committee of Vassar College for a grant to subvent Mrs Jordan's assistance. I bear responsibility for the final translations that appear here; the Xhosa texts have been edited in accordance with modern orthographic practices. It is clear from Mgqwetho's poetry that the first editor of *Umteteli wa Bantu* was Rev. Marshal Maxeke: Skota (1965; 64) notes that he was 'at one time' editor of *Umteteli*; Willan (1984) records the unsuccessful attempts of the Chamber to secure the services of Sol Plaatje as first editor.

4 Hoho, the forest facing the plain of Amalinde, was the site of the internecine battle between the Xhosa forces of Ndlambe and his nephew Ngqika in October 1818.

5 The preceding lines are an extract from the praises of the Xhosa king Sandile (born 1820), who was killed in the last frontier war, the War of Ngcayechibi (1878–79): see Rubusana (1911: 247).

6 However marginal it might be, Mgqwetho's poetry is not oral, although it does draw on the oral poetic tradition. However, I draw some justification for this consideration of Mgqwetho's poetry in the present context from the work of Renwick, who admits contemporary local working-class poetry 'for recitation or reading, not singing' (1980: 4) as English folk poetry.

7 The poets of today are active in their criticism: the whole stanza warns the new year to beware a spirited black resistance.

8 Mgqwetho assigns to herself – or associates have assigned to her – the qualities of an ocean-going liner; Chizama is her clan name.

9 Here, and elsewhere, Mgqwetho evidences verbal dexterity as she juxtaposes her name and the verb *ukugqwetha*, to turn something upside down, to transform it. Paronomasia is a marked feature of *izibongo*. Phalo is an ancestor of the Xhosa chiefs; the land of Phalo is Xhosa territory, and by extension the whole country.

10 Ntsikana (d. 1820) is the revered Xhosa prophet of Christianity; see Bokwe (1914) and Hodgson (1980) and Holt (1954: 105–27).

11 The title refers to a discussion (*ingxoxo*) between one who retains

traditional beliefs and a convert to Christianity, but the poem is a monologue; perhaps Mgqwetho is alluding to W. W. Gqoba's two serial poems, 'Ingxoxo enkulu ngemfundo' ('The great debate about education'), and 'Ingxoxo enkulu yomGinwa nomKristu' ('The great debate between Red Blanket and Christian'), originally published in *Isigidimi sama Xosa* in 1885 and 1887–8 respectively and reprinted in Rubusana's anthology *Zemk'inkomo magwalandini* in 1906 and 1911; on these two pioneering poems, see Jordan (1973; 64–7). *Amaqaba* are those who continued to smear with red ochre, and *amakholwa* are those who converted to Christianity: see Dubb (1966) and Pauw (1975).

12 Oaths are taken in the names of relatives: in swearing by Nontsizi, Mgqwetho establishes that her red-blanketed spokesperson is not Mgqwetho herself but someone close to her.

13 Callinicos refers to liquor as a form of control on the mines (1981: 46); on urban brewing, see Callinicos (1987: 206–9) and La Hausse (1988).

14 The prayer union, *manyano*, was especially concerned with the loss of sexual control over young girls in the cities: this is a recurrent concern in Mgqwetho's poetry. According to Gaitskell, 'the *manyano* . . . should be seen in part as the attempt by African women converts to internalise new domestic norms or perhaps lament the difficulty of doing so under the destructive influence of South Africa's industrial revolution. The demands of both God and gold removed key supports from the married woman, while pressing her to accept new responsibilities. Thus, as new economic and social forces increasingly conflicted with new religious prescriptions, certain features of the Christian culture which female Africans were being urged to adopt, struggled to take root in urban working-class society' (1982: 338). The *manyanos* also encouraged female solidarity, reinforcing a code quite at variance with that of men: see Gaitskell (p. 343).

CHAPTER 13

Clashes of interest: gender, status and power in Zulu praise poetry

Liz Gunner

Often in the discussion of forms of culture certain art forms and certain manifestations of culture are privileged while others tend to be pushed out and marginalised. This process is invariably related to power: the forms that are the expression of those who are in a position of dominance are foregrounded. They, in turn, tend to be selected and discussed by those both inside and outside the culture. In the process there is often a further distortion and the art forms that express the dominant discourse of power envelop, muffle or disguise the other expressive forms. These in some cases become so marginalised in the focus of interest and debate that they become almost silent, almost invisible. The dominant forms become at one level the only forms. The others may continue to flourish within the culture itself but in the scholarly or academic discourse that has seen only the dominant forms they are reduced to whispers and footnotes.

This model which relates to selection and distortion, and forms that flourish unrecognised and undebated outside what becomes seen as 'official culture', can be used for an analysis of the relation between high culture and popular culture, or what Bakhtin (1984) calls 'unofficial culture' (see also Barber 1986). In this sense it relates to the divisions of status and power within a single genre, and also a single gender – namely men. It can, though, also refer to divisions on gender lines particularly when gender and power are related in the expressive art forms of a culture. I intend to discuss the power divisions both within and between genders in the single genre of praise poetry. To say that there is a simple division of power and marginality between male and female expressions within the genre is too simple; there is a further division between the praises of men of status, power and authority and those men who are outside this group but who utilise the genre in its unofficial rather than its official guise.

Zulu praise poetry is a form that is in many ways closely related

185

both to power and to patriarchy. It is also a good example of an art form that has often been distorted in the way in which it has been recorded and discussed.[1] If we think of praise poetry as a continuum, at one end is the poetry of kings and chiefs and sometimes, now, also the praises of contemporary politicians. Thus both the one-time ANC leader Chief Albert Luthuli, and the present leader of the right-wing Zulu-focused Inkatha organisation, Chief Buthelezi, have praise poems. This is because both leaders need (or needed) to exploit the rhetoric of power contained within the praises. Likewise, in 1984, the black trade union FOSATU (Federation of South African Trade Unions) was given its own praise poem: one of its members conscious of the potential extension of power to the relatively new and powerful trade union wished to use the rhetoric to which a praise poem has access, to express and give substance to this shift (Gunner 1986; Qabula et al. 1986). It is this poetry, very much in the public domain, intimately part of the discourse of power, that is also tied in with patriarchy. The values it enunciates are those of the rightness of war and conquest, and of wars fought necessarily by men. In the royal praise poems – even in the path-breaking praise poem to FOSATU which Alfred Qabula performed for the first time at Curries Fountain in Durban in 1984 – women appear very little, and when they do it is usually as items of conquest, occasionally as schemers and plotters. There is an example of the latter in the *izibongo* of the chief, Dingiswayo Mthethwa, patron of the young Shaka in the early nineteenth century. One of Dingiswayo's mothers in the royal household was suspected of having helped in an attempt to assassinate him:

> INkomo yanganene; yasendlunkulu
> mayithengwa nayiphi enye yasendlunkulu
> mayithengwa noNombangambi
> yena owaz' izindaba.

> The Cow of the great house, of the royal household
> which other of the royal house will it be bartered for?
> Let it be bartered for by Nombangambi
> she who has knowledge of the affair.
>   (Gunner and Gwala 1991: 164–5)

Izibongo are therefore in some of their manifestations not only cultural power brokers, they also place women on the margins and ascribe very limited categories to them. They are invisible or visible only on the composer's terms. Moreover, the pervasive tropes of the poetry, contained for the most part in the praise names, align the poetry as male and martial: the shield spattered with blood (*isihlangu esinamagqabhagqahha, igazi lamadoda*) the assegai red with blood even at the haft (*ugaq 'elibomvu ngasekuphathweni*); the bull with the gored flank (*inkunzi yakithi abagwaze* ...), the river flowing red with blood (*kubomvu inxeba abakugwaze lona*) – all these recur either as praise names or as statements marking climactic moments of fighting. This is the arena where struggles for succession, struggles for territory, struggles for power or influence, aggressive stances against the enemy are chronicled. The cardinal qualities of courage are displayed through physical action and endurance. The virtues are those of heroic struggle and these virtues and the metaphors which give them expression are reiterated constantly. Although these *izibongo* are sensitive to historical context, and indeed draw on and exploit this context in their specific references, it is largely the same pool of metaphors and store of motifs which is drawn on. Take for instance some of the *izibongo* of the present Zulu king Goodwill Zwelithini: the motif of struggle and, more finely, the struggle for succession, dominate the opening of *izibongo* that have been performed over the last nineteen years on a variety of public occasions:

> INdlondlo enophaph' ekhanda kaMenzi
> Ndaba awulalele lomuntu omemezayo
> sengathi uyakhala uyalila uthi-i,
> 'Igula likaJama lichithekile
> lichithwa yingqwel' endala yakithi kaMalandela'
> Unesibindi Buthelezi ngokukkhuthazela
> UmntakaNdaba bemthuka bemgcokofula,
> bethi, 'UZwelithini kayikubusa kayokuba inkosi',
> kanti bamgcoba ngamafuth' emphepho.
> Eyakithi kwaMalandela uSodidase,
> INkonyane encane kaNdaba edid' im'bala.
> UMphikeleli wensizwa
> ngoba ephikelela amadod' akwaZulu esephelelwa ngamandla
> UMaphokophela obengayinsizwa esinikinikana
> engabubende bezingwe nezingonyama,
> ogijime ngandlela-nde ngaluvivi eyakwadadewabo uNonhlanhla.
> Nani maNdebele seniyoguga nidelile
> enike nabona izinyane leSilo sikaNdaba
> ohlambe izandla amakhanda amadoda ethi yiwona ayokuhlabanela,
> kwaye kwagcwal i'mfunda zemfula ezinye zoMkhuze ezinye zoThukela.
> Nani magundwane ahlala eyikhotheni kwaNongoma
> gijimani nge'ndlela zonkana niyobikela abangake-e-ZW-A!

Nithi, 'Lukhulu luyeza luyanyelela,
silufanisa nendlovu emnyama yasoBhalule
luzoshis' i'khotha zakwaNongoma.'

The Viper with the Feathered Head, descendant of Menzi,
Ndaba listen to the person shouting,
it is as if he is weeping and mourning, saying,
'The gourd of Jama is spilt,
it is spilt by our very own elderly chief herdboy of the land of
Malandela.
Buthelezi was brave in his encouragement.
They insulted the child of Ndaba, they pecked at him
saying, 'Zwelithini will never rule, will never be king.'
whereas he was anointed with the sacred oil of kings.
Our own Father of Confusion of Zululand,
Small Calf of Ndba who hides his intentions.
Persistent young man
because he persisted with the men of Zululand when his strength
was gone.
Determined One who was like a young man in rags
One who was like the clotted blood of leopards and lions,
who ran down the long road at dawn to his sister Nonhlanhla.
And you, Ndebeles, may you end your days contented,
you who have caught sight of the leopard cub of Ndaba
who cleansed his hands on the heads of men claiming they would
fight for him,
flooding to the brim the banks of the Mkhuze and the Thukela rivers.
And as for you, you rats skulking in the long grass at Nongoma,
run along all the paths, announce to all who have not HE-A-ARD!
Say, 'There is great, that is coming, that is gliding along.
As great as the Black Elephant of Bhalule,
raging to burn the long grass at Nongoma.'

> (Gunner and Gwala 1991: 54–5)

It is this praise poetry of the public domain which scholars have tended
to overemphasise and the social importance of which they have
distorted.[2] The *izibongo* of the public domain, the praises of (largely)
male status and power articulate closely with the less specialised form
of praise poetry which is performed by both men and women. This
form has its own performance mode in which the praises of the great
can also sometimes operate. It relies on the constant interaction of the
individual and the group and is so widely practised that it can be seen
as a popular art form. It has no clear connection with power, status or
authority in the way that the praise poetry of leaders and chiefs has.
Yet the landscape of the poetry, its grammar, is in some ways very
similar. The *izibongo* of ordinary men are still couched in the language

of patriarchy; and as in *izibongo* of those of status and power, the heroic ethic is to the fore. Yet what is obvious is the way this heroic ethic is diluted, the way in which, at times, it is almost mocked and inverted; it is sometimes used for humorous effect as in this self-praise:

> Ngimnene, ngiyingwenya,
> angidl' umuntu ngidl' udaka.

> I am gentle, I am a crocodile,
> I don't eat a person, I eat mud.
> (From the *izibongo* of Somandla Hlabisa,
> Gunner and Gwala 1991: 194–5)

The heroic ethic can thus be used humorously, bathetically, a praise name resonant with royal echoes can be undercut. The battlefield in these praises is sometimes one of small interpersonal conflicts, and often of conflict between the sexes. Moreover, in these less status conscious praises even the hierarchy of gender is less secure. Thus women are far more visible in these praises, although their appearances still tend to fall into certain categories: the mother-in-law; the courted woman; the good woman; the bad or tempting woman. These *izibongo* often combine the grand, heroic metaphors, with worries about marriage or about courtship, and they sometimes capture anxieties over socio-economic and class differences. The *izibongo* of uNodlalisa Mzimela show some of the interests tugging at male composers of popular praises. Some of these praises which together form the loose complex of his praise poem would have been composed by himself and some would have come from those who knew him well:

> Yimi uNodalis ingane ngokuthand' unina.
> UNomuzwezwe mntakaNomzwayiba kazihlabi ziyabhovula,
> ngoba zizwa ukuvunda.
> Umfana uyahloma uyahlasela unjengoShaka,
> ngoba uhlasela kwabezizwe uMkhont' ogwaz' amambuka . . .
> Untombi kayishingi ushing' abakhwekazi.
> Umama uyayinyunda uyisa kwaneksdo,
> ngoba wayinyunda way' yisa emaKhaledeni.

> It is I, Cuddler of the young child through loving the mother.
> You have fighting spurs, child of Nomzwayiba, the cattle don't only
> gore they tear the mound apart
> because they smell the moist rot of the dungheap
> The Boy storms, he attacks – he is like Shaka
> because he attacks those of strange lands. Spear that stabs traitors . . .
> The girl doesn't play up, it's the in-laws who play up.
> The mother match-makes and fixes her up next door

because she got her fixed up, sent her across to a Coloured family.
(Gunner and Gwala 1991: 184–5)

UNodlalisa, in this cluster of self-images is a courter of women, a fighter in the old heroic mould, comparing himself with the emblematic warrior king Shaka. He uses the image of fighting cattle and then brings in cattle a second time, this time linking it to race differentials and status, and to the role of the manipulative mother-in-law; she prefers her daughter to marry a man of mixed race because of the higher social status and the wider socio-economic opportunities this brings in the racially classified society of the time (this was recorded in 1976) where black is at the bottom.

Frequently in the popular praises of men (and, as the later examples show, of women too) the multi-vocalic character of the art form is asserting itself against the monologic, rigid, heroic mould of the big praises.[3] There is in the following example a sense of many voices jostling within the text and a sense, too, of the speaker himself addressing a number of different constituencies. The military ethic, the discourse of war is present in the language but it has to struggle for dominance. Shishiliza Dube's *izibongo* show a mix of the heroic, comic-heroic and the managing or attempting to manage relations with women. Also, as in the praises of uNodlalisa Mzimela there is inclusion of socio-economic factors – here, a reference to selling liquor without a licence:

> Ng'uShishiliza kwelimaholo limshaye limbhedule,
> limphose phezulu abuye sekumhlophe kuthe wa!
> Amhloph' amahawu amahloph' amagabela,
> 'Ayife sisik' amahawu!'
> Ubhucu 'kagezanga kwelenhlangano
> ngoba wesaba umlando awenza.
> UHaza kamshipiliza ayidl' umuntu idl' amathopisi.
> Siumba 'mgodi yonk' indawo, abomvu amagede.
> UDumo lwamasosha ebhek' Engilandi.
> Umkhovu wesifetshana.
> Hawu mkhwekazi wami wazewashisa kangaka?
> Uzokhwela umkhuhlane yini?
> UMjah'az'akhathale, iMfene yasoNgoye.

> I am the Buttock-scraper over ditchy ground opening up gaping wounds
> It tossed him up and when he came down he was scraped dead white!
> White are the shields, white the shield laces,
> 'Let that bull die we want his hide for our shields!'
> The Naked One couldn't bathe at the meeting place

fearing his past deeds.
The Hot-tempered Swiper doesn't eat a person but eats sugar cane tops.
The Liquor-totter all over the place and the hiding places are tawny brown.
The Big Rush of the soldiers who head for England.
The consumptive little tart,
Ha! Mother-in-law, you are so saucy and hot!
Are you being ridden by a fever?
Young wife ploughing here, what harvest do you expect to get?
Hurrying-One until he peters out, Baboon of Ngoye Forest.
                                        (Gunner and Gwala 1991: 188–9)

Men's *izibongo* often, therefore, show this ambivalence, this irreverence to the grander, more heroic gestures of the *izibongo* of the great, and show a preference for chronicling, in novelistic fashion, the events and voices that go into their own lives. On the other hand, however, the dance songs and chants known as *izigiyo* (items for doing the war dance to), although they have great fluidity and sometimes steal from a number of song genres, are on the whole without this ambivalence. The *izigiyo* which overlay and encompass the performance of *izibongo* are set firmly in the nexus of conflict on the one hand and sexual power relations on the other. Some of the *izigiyo* go like this:

Rhythmic statements

Yash' induku kubafazi!	The stick hit out amongst the women!
DANCER: Ngibatshiwe!	I got stung!
Ngibatshiwe esifebeni!	I got stung at a whore's!
OTHERS: Ubatshiwe!	You got stung!
Ubatshiwe esifebeni!	You got stung at a whore's!
DANCER: Ngithathile!	I snatched!
Ngithath' unondindwa!	I snatched a prostitute!
OTHERS: Uthathile!	You snatched!
Uthath' unondindwa!	You snatched a prostitute!
Isinqawunqawu	The Quick-tempered One
Umfaz ohlul' indo-oda!	Woman who gets the better of a man!

War chants and war cries

DANCER: Igaz lethu!	Our blood!
OTHERS: Jibilibilibi!	It qui-ui-uivered!

DANCER: Dedel' endleleni!	Get out of our path!
OTHERS: Wathinta thina!	You've provoked us!
Singamaphikankani!	We are the courageous ones!
I'nhliziyo yethu zibomvu	Our hearts are angry – red as blood!
igazi!	

(Gunner and Gwala 1991: 226–31)

Although men's popular praises are far from the centre of power they remain, nevertheless, part of the public domain in a way that women's *izibongo* are not. Men's *izibongo* are part of the flamboyant dancing and praising which draw large audiences of men and women, and are the central performance pieces of weddings and other occasions such as engagement and coming-of-age celebrations. Women's popular praises, on the other hand, are rarely performed publicly in a large arena as part of a public occasion. They are usually performed only for other women, during a rest from work in the fields, or in certain houses of the homestead during a wedding where there will only be women present. In a way this privacy, this distance from the overt centres of patriarchy, sometimes gives it a cutting edge, a subverting thrust which it might otherwise lack. More than that, it gives women a chance to fill out for themselves a completely different identity, an answer, even a challenge which undercuts the dominant discourse relating to images of power and the status of men and women.

Although women's praises have their own clichéd topics such as jealousy among co-wives, they are able to move beyond these. Possibly too, as Lila Abu-Lughod (1986) has shown in the working of some Bedouin poetry, the praises contain sentiments and emotions, a certain inwardness, inexpressible in formal, public relations and in outward showings within the culture. Women's *izibongo* in their compressed, autobiographical way can recall courtships, boys with whom they fell out, and men they have outlasted. They too, like men's popular praises deal with sexual power relations but from a different angle. Sometimes, too, they talk of romantic love. Mcasule Dube's *izibongo* show some of these features; they also take a martial praise and extend it to provide a riposte to liars and gossips who ruin reputations with whispers:

Ng'uSidlukuya-dlwedlwe besihlukuza abafazi namadoda.
Bathi bamphe ngaphansi bamphe ngaphezulu.
Dlula bedlana o'nto zawonina.
Abayosala emhlabeni bayosala bedla amakhanda e'nyoni.
Wombuza uthanathana kanyoko
ngoba ngiyesab' amazondo.

Ngeke ngidlul' esangweni kini.
Nawe wena nsizwa
obuthi uyakhuluma ukhuluma nami;
akukhonto angasuyenze kwami ...
Kusho mina nguSidlukuyadlwedlwe
insizwa yendawo yasesigodini
kulesisigodi sakhona laph' eduzane,
kangilali emgwaqwni ngilala ngapha kwendlela.
Kusho mina NgiwumaKati adla imifino,
Nkuku zishaya ihlombe khona emzini
lapha ngiqome khona.
Ngaguqa, ngathandaza
ngathi, 'Suka mfana ngiyakuthanda,
ngeke luphele olwami uthando nami nawe.'

I am the Wild Staff-Shaker shaken by women and men.
They say, 'They've given it to her down below they've given it to her up above.'
She passes as they're having sex, those lousy private parts of their mothers.
Those who remain on the earth will live long and be wealthy.
You go and ask that wretched little private parts of her mother because I myself am afraid of the ill-feeling.
I will never pass in front of your gates.
And as for you, young man
if you're talking to me to make us intimate; there's nothing you can do to me ...
So say I, the Wild Staff-Shaker
the youth of this district,
of this little part right close by.
I don't sleep on the high road, I sleep there on the little path
So say I, I am the-Chickens flapping their wings in applause within the homestead
where I chose my love.
I knelt, I pleaded,
I said, 'Truly boy, I love you,
may the love between you and me never end.'

(Gunner and Gwala 1991: 206–7)

Other women's praises speak of desertion or neglect in married life:

> Abanye omame balala namadoda abo
> ngilala phandle odongeni.

> Some women sleep with their husbands
> I sleep against the wall outside.
>
> (From the *izibongo* of Madlinyoka
> Hlabisa in Gunner 1984)

They can also be scornful of men's promiscuity, and, for instance, compose a cutting line for an old 'bull' who is randy abroad but can't perform his duties when he is in his own kraal. The praises of MaMhlalise Mkhwanazi state the condensed details of her life and personality. They comment on the suffocating constraints of a polygamous household and make their own sharp comments on misused sexual energy:

UXam-phaph-alele kwadadewabo uNomchitheka.
Ng'uMbambo zangiminya
ngangiyoba intombi enkuyu.
UMajub' avuk adl' uthayela.
UNduyana eziyuhlazana
bayoke bezeq' omaqalashu.
UGagane lokubathiya
om'sunu yawonina!
Ng'uXhafaza bath' unyiye,
ingani akunye yena kunya uzakwabo.
USishayi sabamsisa oKwamabhodwe,
ngusiShayi sabavaya ngeyinkethe.
NgiNkunz' enjani
ezeka ngaphandle
ekhaya beyilele.
Awu! Uthini Khandempemvu!

The Basking Lizard lying in wayward abandon at her sister's Nomchitheka.
I am Ribs-Pressed-Me-In
I would have been a well-built girl.
(I am)-Doves-that-woke-and-pecked-at-the-roof.
The High Greenish Grass tufts
that will one day be jumped by the clever ones.
The Mimosa Bush with thorns for keeping out
those wretched vaginas of their mothers!
I am squish on something and they say, 'She's crapped!'
But she hasn't crapped, it's her co-wife that's crapped!
The Beater of those who stand, legs apart, lazy and stiff-legged like cooking pots.
I am The Beater of those who stand, legs apart, lazy and stiff-legged like cooking pots.
I am The Beater of those who use corrugated iron for doors
I am what kind of Bull is it
that mounts outside its own kraal
but is useless at home!
Hah! What do you say to that you old Khandempemvu fellow!

(From the *izibongo* of MaMhlalise Mkhwanazi
(MaMbambo) in Gunner and Gwala 1991: 204–5)

Sometimes women's *izibongo* take over images of vitality from men's *izibongo* such as 'the smouldering log that does not burn out quickly'; they also seek out new images of strength: 'I'll act like a man / I'll lie on my back like a man' 'Angila!' ohlangothi / Ngila!' emhlane njeng' indoda'. Sometimes they take an image from a woman in a position of authority such as 'I am the Sister Superior / I carry my bag under my arm' (instead of sleeping on one's side as women are supposed to do).[4]

Women's *izibongo*, like men's praises, have the dialogic, multivocalic quality that marks them off from the large praises of authority and status. Yet they rarely exploit or undercut the rhetoric of war and the martially related images of courage. When they do use them, as Mcasule does in her *izibongo*, they convert them into a different discourse. Moreover they are not tied into the war ethic with the songs that accompany the dancing and praising. They lose the sometimes rich ambivalence of the men's *izibongo*. Often, though, in the songs for dancing which weave in with the praising, it means that they can more easily fit into the mood of the times. Thus the song of Dayi Mhlongo was simply one that commented on money, the need for it and the lack of it:

DAYI:	Uyimalini lo?	How much is this?
	Uyimalini lokhu?	How much is that?
OTHERS:	Amasente!	Cents!

Another song referred to husbands or boyfriends working away from home and caught up in the maze-like laws of apartheid:

Wagcina nini isoka lakho?
LiseGoli eNumba 4/ eNumba 10.

When did you last see your man?
He's in Jo'burg in Number 4 jail [The Fort] Number 10.

It seems that both men's and women's popular praises stand at some distance from the heroic and status-filled specialist form of chiefly praises and praises of leaders. To this extent they have in common a richer sense of the many voices of the community, and of the intimate social and economic context of their lives. Nevertheless, men's *izibongo* are still confined within an ethos of macho virility, a two-way bind of fighting and sexual conquest. Women on the other hand, being on the margins, have a greater choice and more chance to subvert and question the limitations of the art form and the interests of patriarchy which define it in its specialist form.

NOTES

1 Take for instance Trevor Cope's (1968) *Izibongo: Zulu Praise Poems*, which, fine and seminal though it is, nevertheless focuses on figures of authority and continues a distortion of the genre as a whole and its role in the culture. This, unwittingly perhaps, continues the royalist and non-dynamic emphasis of James Stuart in his recording and collection of *izibongo*, now housed in the Killie Cambell Africana Library in Durban.
2 In addition to the distortion in Stuart's printed and manuscript collections, the same focus on the royal and chiefly part of *izibongo* is clear in Bryant (1929) and Samuelson (1929).
3 Mikhail Bakhtin sets out the distinctions between the two terms in *The Dialogic Imagination* (1981), where he applies it mainly to the novel. His claim that poetry in general is more monologic is not borne out by popular praise poetry.
4 Gunner tapes.

CHAPTER 14

Jelimusow: *the superwomen of Malian music*

Lucy Durán

Juddies [jeliw] . . . have a perfect resemblance to the Irish Rimer . . .
[they sing] the auncient stocke of the King, exalting his antientry,
and recounting over all the worthy and famous acts by him . . .
singing likewise extempore upon any occasion is offered . . . whereby
the principal may bee pleased . . . If at any time the Kings or
principall persons come unto us trading in the River, they will have
their musicke playing before them.   (Jobson 1968: 133–4)

Three hundred and fifty years have passed since Richard Jobson's
vivid encounter with the *jeliw*, the hereditary professional musicians
of the Manding peoples of West Africa. Though the kings have long
since gone, the *jeliw* are still a conspicuous part of Manding culture,
and their behaviour has not changed significantly. Their flamboyant
performance style, their fine music and their ambivalent social status
have been the subject of much comment from the fourteenth century
onwards. Travellers, explorers, scholars and journalists have
documented the multi-faceted roles of *jeliw* as praise singers, dancers,
public orators, interpreters, historians, genealogists, mediators, and
political and social advisers. What remains largely unwritten, however,
is the story of female *jeliw* – the *jelimuso* (pl: *jelimusow*).

The *jeliw* are part of the *nyamakala*, a caste of hereditary
endogamous craftsmen, which includes smiths, leatherworkers and
Koranic reciters and praisers. They are found among all the Manding
peoples, spread across a wide area of West Africa (Mali, Guinea,
Burkina Faso, Ivory Coast, Senegal, Gambia, Guinea Bissau). There
are three main Manding styles, reflecting the three main Manding
languages: Mandinka, Maninka (Malinké) and Bamana (Bambara),
differentiated according to use of instruments, melodies and tunings,
and repertoire. There is however a core repertoire of songs known to
all Manding *jeliw* such as *Sunjata* (recounting the deeds of Sunjata
Keita) and *Lambang* (a song in praise of music and the art of the *jeliw*).

With their special knowledge of Manding history and lineage, the *jeliw* represent an important element in the continuing sense of common heritage and identity between Manding peoples across a broad geographical area.

Simultaneous with the rise of scholarship on Manding music and oral epic, which has burgeoned since the early 1970s, there has also been a steadily increasing flow of recordings onto the international market, opening up this rich musical tradition to a wider audience. Since the mid 1980s, artists such as Mory Kanté from Guinea and Salif Keita from Mali have achieved substantial commercial 'hits' with songs such as 'Yekeyeke' (from the album, 'Akwaba Beach') and 'Soro', which have brought Manding music onto the dancefloors of night clubs around the world. Though their music may sound westernised, with all the 'hi-tech' of modern recording studios, their songs and lyrics derive basically from the repertoire of the Manding *jeliw*.

One of the most striking developments of post-independence Manding music is the phenomenal rise in popularity of the female *jeliw*, the *jelimusow*.

Women singers, especially among the Maninka, Bamana and Jula in Mali, Guinea and the Ivory Coast, are the unrivalled stars of the local music scene, particularly in urban centres. Unlike their male counterparts, who dominate the club and restaurant scene, these women function mainly within traditional contexts. No wedding or baptism is complete without a *jelimuso*, backed by a (male) ensemble consisting of a variety of instruments including electric guitar, *ngoni* (3–8 string lute), *kora* (harp-lute), *balafon* (xylophone) and most recently, drum machine. Women singers dominate the airwaves and the local cassette market; they are the creators of many of the new musical trends in Manding music. For a younger generation of women, the *jelimusow* have become an important role model for the blending of old cultural values with new social norms. Male musicians complain that they are overshadowed by these fabulous *cantatrices*, and have even formed an association (Association Amicale des Artistes) to ensure that they receive their proper share of the sometimes substantial sums of money bestowed on these women by their adoring audiences (Durán 1994).

The special appreciation of women's voices in Manding culture is not, however, recent. Evidence for this may be pieced together from several sources, oral and written: the testimony of senior *jeliw*; a reappraisal of historical documents; and clues provided in the lyrics of songs and epics, as well as in the *jeliw*'s own discourse on aesthetics.

Yet their role is virtually ignored in contemporary scholarship.

Where, in the now substantial literature on Manding oral tradition, is the *jelimuso*? Many scholars do not specifically mention women at all, placing their descriptions of *jeliw* activities in the masculine gender (for example, Innes 1974; Johnson 1986). The informants for the published versions of epics such as *Sunjata* have without exception been men, but no comment is made as to why this should be, reflecting, no doubt, the male perspective of the writers.

Even Camara, in his extensive anthropological study of *jeliw*, barely talks of women, though his passing remarks are telling. For example (with regard to women at the court of Almamy Samory Touré): 'elles chantent pendant que leurs maris font de la musique . . . elles ont des activités spécifiques: elles surveillent les femmes toujours nombreuses du roi' (1976: 220). Camara also cites a Maninka phrase used to praise an appealing female voice: *jelimuso ni ka nawañané*, 'this *jelimuso*'s voice is rough'. 'Cette image [difficile à traduire] signifie . . . que la griotte a quelque chose de rugueux dans le timbre de sa voi, ce que les Malinkés apprécient beaucoup' (1976: 250), but this tantalising glimpse of a Maninka aesthetic concerning women's voices is not further pursued.

Those who have concentrated their studies on the Manding instruments, particularly the Mandinka *kora* (Knight 1984a, 1984b; Charry 1992) have a better excuse for placing little emphasis on the role of women. The Mandinka (Gambia, Senegal, Guinea Bissau) musical tradition – possibly because of the *kora* itself – is male dominated, except in the 'upper-river' (*tilibo*) tradition, of Gambia, which claims direct descent from the old heartland of Manding, and where women are the preferred singers. Only one of Knight's informants was a Mandinka *jelimuso*, from the upper-river area. She supplies the only woman's song in his study, the praise song 'Suolu kili' ('calling the horses') which he describes as 'typically sung unaccompanied, and by women' (1984b: 35).

In the historical sources the presence of women in Manding music is also noted in passing, even as early as 1354, when Ibn Battuta visited the court of Mali:

The interpreter Dugha brings in his four wives and his concubines, who are about a hundred in number . . . a chair is set there for Dugha and he beats an instrument which is made of reeds with tiny calabashes below it, praising the sultan, recalling in his song his expeditions and deeds. The wives and the concubines sing with him and they play with bows.

(Ibn Battuta, cited in Charry 1992: 315)

The 'instrument made of reeds' is the *balafon*, still one of the main instruments of the *jeli*. What is significant here is that this massive choir of women are apparently playing a string instrument. No further references to this have come to light; Manding women do not play any melody instruments, but may have at one time. In nearby Mauritania, for example, the female griots play a harp, the *ardin*, whose name is reflected in one of the *kora* tunings, *hardino*.

The extrovert character of women in music is also mentioned by early travellers. The British seventeenth-century traveller Jobson was struck by their role as dancers and animators:

The most desirous of dancing are the women, who dance without men, and but one alone, with crooked knees and bended bodies they foot it nimbly . . . when the men dance they do it with their swords naked in their hands . . . both men and women when they have ended their first dance, do give somewhat unto the player: whereby they are held and esteemed amongst them to be rich; and their wives have more Cristall blew stones and beades about them, than the Kings wives: but if there be any licentious libertie, it is unto these women, whose outward carriage is such we may well conceit it. (Jobson 1968: 136–7)

These remarks could well apply to the present day: wives of instrumentalists, lavishly bedecked with ornaments, and displaying a proud and charismatic bearing, attracting the lion's share of attention, would still be an appropriate description of the *jelimuso* in the 1990s.

Though the informants of the published *Sunjata* epics have been men, and though Sunjata's main *jeli*, Bala Fasigi Kouyaté, was a man, the *jelimuso* does nevertheless make a few notable appearances. To mention but two: in the Niane version, during Maghan Kon Fatta's wedding to Sogolon, 'poetesses who belonged to the king's sisters chanted the name of the young bride' (Niane 1984: 10). This points to the special role of women at weddings, and their attachment to the court. In the Johnson version as recited by Fa-Digi Sissoko, it is the Kouyaté matriarch, Tumu Maniya, who announces the birth of Sunjata (Johnson 1986: 49), clearly a key moment in the story.

The gendered division of musical tasks portrayed in these early sources does not differ in essence from that of the present day. The *jelike* (male *jeli*) has two main musical functions. He is the instrumentalist, playing one of the three traditional melody instruments (*bala, balafon* – xylophone, *ngoni* – lute, or *kora* – harp-lute) as well as (since approximately the 1940s) the guitar. He also plays the Manding drums: *djembe, doundoung* and *tama* (talking drum). He is the story-teller, using three performance modes: a sung chorus (*donkili*), a sung recitational mode, (*sataro, teremeli*), and straightforward speech (*tarikou*, from Arabic, 'history').

The *jelimusow*, by contrast, specialise in singing. The only instrument they play is the *karinyang*, an iron slit-tube which is struck with a heavy iron needle, producing a loud ringing tone which contributes to the flamboyant nature of women's performance. Both men and women dance. The team of husband/instrumentalist plus wife (wives)/singer(s), is still the most common.

Despite popular belief to the contrary, it is not uncommon to hear women perform versions of *Sunjata* and other epics. Women are more associated with praise singing (*jammundiro, fassa da*), – a genre that uses the melodies of the great epics (*Sunjata, Tutu Jara, Janjung, Duga,* among others) without necessarily narrating the story. The lyrics of praise song are, in some ways, the opposite of an epic. They consist of various elements strung together in formulaic and improvised fashion – praise, proverb, moral/social comment, and isolated references to the heroes of the epic song whose melody is being played. These references, often highly obscure, are a vital factor in the popularity of praise song. They create a sense of history and tradition without excluding members of the audience who do not belong to noble lineages. They suggest that whoever is being praised now in the song is of an equally important lineage. Wealthy businessmen and other prominent members of society commission *jelimusow* to record private cassettes for them in praise of their families, using the favourite classic tunes (Durán 1989: 38). This is the genre *par excellence* of today's weddings and baptisms; these are the songs that predominate on recorded cassettes.

Thus a major musical distinction between the sexes becomes evident: men specialise in history conveyed through the spoken word (*tarikou*), women specialise in praise through song (*fassa da, donkili da*). Women are denied categorically the right to 'speak' their lyrics. This is of central concern here for two reasons: (a) the *tarikou* is considered to be the optimum mode for the conveying of historical information; and (b) *tarikou* may only be performed by senior *jeliw* who have achieved the category of 'greatness' (*ngaaraya*).

Ngaaraya, the art of the *ngaara* 'great musician, master of the word', is a term of great respect that crops up frequently in *jeli* discourse and songs. It is the basic yardstick by which their ability and achievement are measured. All *jeliw* ultimately aspire to become *ngaaraw*, although there are various interpretations of its meaning.

The term *ngaara* does not appear in the Bambara–French dictionaries, but may derive from *ngana*, meaning 'skilled, able'. Only those already deemed *ngaaraw* have the authority to confer the title on others, generally singers who have reached a certain age; it has more to do with ability with words than with beauty of voice.

Women singers are described as either a *kumala*, 'someone whose use of words is competent', or a *ngaara*, 'a great singer, someone who touches your heart'. Almost any *jelimuso* can be a *kumala*, for this merely involves a knowledge of stock proverbs and genealogies. There are, however, few *ngaaraw*. This is acknowledged in a standard proverb often heard in women's songs: *Ngaaraya ye kuu ba ye . . . kumala ning ngaara te kiling ye*, 'The art of the *ngaara* is a thing of great wonder . . . mere use of words and mastery of the word are not the same'.

Only a male *ngaara* may perform the *tarikou* spoken recitation, and the ability to perform *tarikou* is the ultimate test of *ngaaraya*. Nevertheless many women have been accorded the title. Of the four musicians invited by Jamana (an editorial house in Bamako specialising in cultural publications) to participate in a discussion entitled 'Jeli bee ye ngaara ye wa?' ('Are all *jeliw ngaaraw*?'), two were women. They were among Mali's most famous women singers from the 1960s and 1970s: the late Sira Mory Diabaté from Kela, and Fanta Damba from Ségou, both widely acknowledged as *ngaaraw*. Sira Mory says:

> *Ngaaraya* is very difficult . . . it's not about praising someone or expecting money . . . the *ngaara* advised the king on following the right direction to conquer villages . . . Since my eyes were opened I have known many women *ngaaraw* – like my mother, Sere Damba from Segela. She used to mount horses, it's true I saw it! She used to take guns and follow her patron.
>
> (Jamana, cassette recording)

The musicians say that *ngaaraya* is neither taught nor inherited; it is believed to be a gift from God, a state almost of possession that overtakes the singer, often induced by the inspired playing of the accompanists. It is not uncommon for a woman singer, in the midst of an improvisation, to ask the accompanists to 'cool down' their instruments, which might otherwise draw her into the deep art of *ngaaraya* (*kana mbila ngaaraya la*). *Ngaaraya* is considered powerful – draining for the singer, and dangerous for the listeners, not the least because they too may go out of control and commit exaggerated acts of generosity.

The famed singer Fanta Damba, noted for her beauty as well as her clear, classic voice, was the first *jelimuso* to tour Europe in the mid

1970s, and one of the star attractions of the Mali National Ensemble's performance at Festac in Lagos, 1977. After her pilgrimage to Mecca in the mid 1980s she retired from public performance (Durán 1989: 35). She says:

I have known some *ngaara*, like Bintou Fama [Diabaté, from Kela]. Once one of her patrons [*jatigui*], a bad person, knew she was coming, so he told his family to say he wasn't in. When she got there, they told her the patron had travelled. His wives stood in front of the door, blocking it, but she talked to the door and it split open in two. After that, he gave her many gifts, gold and silver. (Jamana, cassette recording)

According to Jeli Baba Sissoko, probably Mali's best-known senior musician, who specialises in story-telling:

A *ngaara* must have a good memory. If a *ngaara* talks, someone will be offended, because the *ngaara* speaks his/her mind, and the truth. The *ngaara* is not afraid of anything . . . Ngaara are few . . . the first *ngaara* I ever heard of was very old, she was from Ségou – Musu Kura Diabaté, she was in the royal court, a king-follower . . . secondly there was Kele Monson from Kita, and third my own brother, Jeli Magan Sissoko who died aged 95. Fourth was Bintou Fama from Kela. I never saw her, but I heard of her.

(Jamana, cassette recording)

In the Gambia among the Mandinka *jeliw* in the upper-river tradition – which, as already stated, claims direct descent from Mali – the term *ngaara* is generally only applied to women who have a whole series of musical and moral attributes (see Knight 1984a: 74). Ami Koita, one of Mali's most famous and popular women singers from the mid 1980s onwards, states:

Women have always been the stars of Malian music in the Manding tradition . . . Women were authorised to sing, men had another role: to speak and to play an instrument. Here in Mande, it's mostly the women who are popular, there are some men but few, you can count them on one hand.

Ngaaraya is like a diploma. You have to reach a certain level to be considered a *ngaara*, by the entire [musical] community. It's the elder griots, the elder people who know history well, who can make that judgement. What happens is that an elder will see a singer, at a baptism for example, and get together with other elders, then all agree to confer this title on the singer. It's not the beauty of the voice, it's the use of words.

When you learn to sing, you also have to learn true versions, for instance of Sunjata. Women know the story of Sunjata as well as men, but men can speak the story, women can only sing it. Usually what happens is that a man will tell the story, and the woman will sing the corresponding song at the right moment. If a man is present a woman will never take the platform from him.

(Personal communication)

Men, therefore, convey the basic historical information, women embellish it. The speech : song gendered division in Manding music is reflected in the common practice whereby a man starts off the performance with a spoken introduction, followed by a woman singing. Women, therefore, are free to introduce lighter genres and to concentrate on the beauty of the art itself.

In Mali today, the female *ngaara* has gained considerable prominence. On television, on the radio, in the market stalls, at live concerts, the stars of Malian music are all women. The cassette shops are a good indicator of their success. While Mory Kanté and Salif Keita may be represented with two or three cassettes, each shop stocks literally hundreds of cassettes representing different women singers. Most of these are *jeliw* from western Mali – some well known and established, others up-and-coming women who may be mediocre singers, but who look and dress the part, in an attempt to match the success of the former.

Those women singers of Mali who have become successful lead their lives with singular independence. In the context of a country which is otherwise largely male-dominated, and where women's liberation movements have made little if any impact, their behaviour could well be described as showing 'unlimited licence'. These women are often the recipients of fabulous gifts from patrons (both men and women): some have been given cars, fully furnished houses, gold, large amounts of money and even in one case a small aeroplane so that the singer could visit her patron in a remote corner of.Mali. Male singers also receive gifts, but rarely on such a scale. Women's resulting economic independence allows them unprecedented freedom. Many drive their own cars, run their own businesses, and are rumoured to prefer the company of women. They set the fashion for dress and hairstyles; they frequently bleach their skins. In performance – whether at a wedding party or at the Stade des Ominisports in Bamako – they prowl like panthers, 'homing in' on the object of their praises. They clutch the microphone, and swoop and swivel, to the delight of their audiences, especially young women who kiss them and shower them with jewellery and money. The divorce rate among *jelimuso* stars is high.

'To be a successful *jelimuso* brings lots of problems because of jealousy, and spells put on you through marabouts [Muslim clerics]', explains Ami Koita, whose status as a *ngaara* is disputed by some, though none will deny her success. Her dramatic performance technique, striking looks, powerful voice and authoritative stage presence have won her a devoted following, and lavish gifts from patrons:

But . . . if someone is predestined to do something, be it man or woman, no one should get in the way . . . with my first husband, my divorce was as a result of that . . . If a woman is very popular, everyone likes her, men and women, but that means nothing, but still you have to have the luck to meet up with someone who will understand the situation and be tolerant. With many of our women stars, they are divorced and unable to find happiness in marriage, except in the case where the husband is their guitarist – and even then – men are too egotistical to allow their women to be more famous. When women attain a certain level of achievement, we don't like that in our society.

(Personal communication)

Malibaliya, shamelessness, is how the older generation of male musicians describes the behaviour of these women. 'You cannot be a *ngaara* if you bleach your skin', claims one of Bamako's most respected instrumentalists, the *kora* player Sidiki Diabaté (interview). The recent ventures of artists such as Ami Koita and other women singers into a more electric idiom is also criticised by some male musicians, who feel that women's proper role is in the traditional domain (Durán 1993: 44).

With changing social and political circumstances, the emphasis in the *jeli*'s music has shifted increasingly away from historical narrative towards praise and entertainment. In this women have had a crucial role to play. While the men are usually seated playing an instrument, women are mobile, singing directly to the object of their praises, often with dramatic theatrical gestures or outstretched arms. This has placed a new emphasis on performance style, remaining, nevertheless, within a more obviously traditional framework than for example the male-dominated dance orchestras (who also draw on traditional repertoires).

As is always the case with art forms, the influence of particular individuals can be seen. Sira Mori Diabaté, who died in about 1990, was an important role model for young *jelimusow* in the days before Independence. She reached the height of her fame under Modibo Keita, Mali's first president (1960–8), though she was not favoured by the subsequent leader General Moussa Traoré (1968–91). An undisputed *ngaara*, her best-known song, 'Sara', must be one of the first Manding songs with an essentially feminist message: it tells the story of a young woman who succeeds in avoiding an arranged marriage by remaining true to her real love.

The era of idolisation of women singers seems to coincide with independence. One of the first of these 'stars' who set the pattern for the younger generation was the Kita singer Fanta Sacko (born about 1930). As a child she travelled extensively between Guinea and Mali with her father, the *kora* player Amadu Sacko. At this time a new style of music was emerging in Mali, accompanied on guitars instead of traditional instruments, but more importantly, the lyrics were not about praise or history, but about the passion of love (*jarabi*). Fanta Sacko's haunting song 'Jarabi', first recorded in 1970, has since become a classic in the Manding repertoire, though she notes bitterly that she has never received any royalties for it (Durán 1989: 35). Her inspiration came from a well-known Guinean song, 'Nina', by Keita Fodeba's Ballets Africains, a hit throughout francophone West Africa in the 1950s. While 'Nina' was dedicated to a girl of that name, and sung by a male singer (Sory Kandia Kouyaté), Fanta Sacko's composition was 'dedicated to the power of love and its predominance over all other feelings'. Her passionate lyrics caused a sensation:

All illnesses can be treated by the doctors, but love is an illness no doctor can cure. Wait for me, wait for me, my beloved! For I cannot live without you . . . the old women do not know the power of love; the old men do not know the power of love. For if they really knew it, they would have understood my passion. For love knows no father, love knows no mother . . . love is deaf to all this. What counts alone is what you have said to me. And never forget, my beloved, what you have promised me, for treason is worse than anything, especially in love. (Fanta Sacko 1970, recording sleeve notes)

The danger of such a message was self-evident. For the older, more conservative musicians, the phrase *Jarabi jarabi*, 'Love love', became their derisive term for the new repertoire that followed. Fanta Sacko, with her love songs, her powerful voice and beauty, soon became Mali's most in demand artist. Following the success of her (only) album, she was called upon regularly to perform for the president, and at official functions of all kinds. Sadly her career ended when she overbleached her skin with chemical products in the early 1980s – a reflection of the increasing pressure on the *jelimuso* to conform to a physical stereotype. 'Jarabi' has nevertheless remained one of the most enduring and popular songs of Mali, reworked in countless 'cover' versions by different singers, male and female, including Ami Koita on her hit album, 'Tata Sira', recorded in Abidjan in 1989.

Fanta Damba, Mogontafé Sacko, Tata Bambo Kouyaté, Kandia Kouyaté, Nahini Diabaté are just some of the other singers who, in the last thirty years, have set the trends for a new breed of 'superwomen' stars in Malian music. As a consequence of their success, women singers have begun to emerge in other, previously male-dominated, genres of music. Of these, one in particular must be mentioned – the music of Wassoulou, a region in southern Mali.

Wassoulou is a Bamana-speaking region with a mixed Fulbe–Bamana heritage and a very different musical tradition from that of the *jeliw*. Their main kind of music is traditionally that of the hunters' societies – played and sung by men only, for a strictly male audience. The youths have their own version of this music, called *Didadi* – dance music accompanied on *kamalengoni*, the six-string 'youth's harp' and *djembe* drum. Lyrics consist mainly of moral sayings and proverbs; praise is not a feature of this music, and there is no specialised caste or group that performs it.

Since independence, this quintessentially masculine genre from Wassoulou has, however, become appropriated by women singers such as Kagbe Sidibé, Coumba Sidibé, Sali Sidibé (on 'Women of Wassoulou') and most recently Oumou Sangaré, whose first cassette 'Moussolou' ('Women'), sold over 100,000 copies in West Africa alone. In her music and public appearances Oumou Sangaré is outspoken about her role in addressing the problems that young women in Mali today face when reconciling respect for their elders with a desire for personal freedom (Durán 1993: 44). Her popularity both at home and abroad is considerable, even though her music is predominantly acoustic and 'traditional'.

From this brief survey it can be seen that women singers in Mali are debating social conventions through their music and are involved in maintaining a sense of tradition within musical innovation.

RECORDINGS

Fodeba, Keita. c.1958. 'Keita Fodeba et les Ballets africains', Vogue VA 160115, long-play disc.

Jamana (publishing house). c.1987. 'Jamana Sorofé: "Jamana" Faamuya yiriwa ton' (recorded interviews with Jeli Baba Sissoko, Fanta Damba, Bazoumana Sissoko, and Sira Mori Diabaté), Jamana K. 2043, Bamako, audio cassette.

Kanté, Mory. 1987. 'Akwaba Beach', Barclay 833 119–2, compact disc.

Keita, Salif. 1987. 'Soro', Stern's African Records ST 1020, compact disc.

Koita, Ami. 1990. 'Tata Sira', Bolibana, compact disc.

Sacko, Fanta. 1970. 'Anthologie de la musique malienne, vol. I: Fanta Sacko', Barenreiter Musicaphon BM 30L 2551, long-play disc.

Sangaré, Oumou. 1991. 'Moussolou', World Circuit WCD 021, compact disc.

Various performers. 1992. 'Women of Wassoulou', Stern's African Records STCD 1035, compact disc.

PART V

Mediators and communicative strategies

CHAPTER 15

Power and the circuit of formal talk

Kwesi Yankah

Scholars have time and again emphasised the rhetorical power of verbal art, its potential as a source of power and knowledge (Abrahams 1972). The very enactment of verbal art is, indeed, an attention ploy, foregrounding the persona of the performer and giving him or her access to certain privileges and power over an audience. Thus for as long as he or she performs, the performer can be said to have assumed an authoritative role: he or she is a potential source of power.

But if verbal art is a source of power, the converse cannot be ruled out: *power as a source of verbal art*, or rather power as a controlling force influencing the form and content of verbal art. In this domain, one could subsume all verbal art forms enacted in the service of power play, or consciously cultivated to depict, project and enhance personal charisma. It is, perhaps, in the exercise of royal power that this is best exemplified:

At the political center of any complexly organized society, there is both a governing elite and a set of symbolic forms expressing the fact that it is in truth governing. No matter how democratically the members of the elite are chosen or how deeply divided among themselves they may be, they justify their existence and order their actions in terms of a collection of stories, ceremonies, insignia, formalities and appurtenances that they have either inherited or, in more revolutionary situations invented. It is these that mark the center and gives what goes on its aura. (Geertz 1983: 124)

Royal power may be asserted in the corpus of panegyrics, legends and history. Another outlet is appellation and aphorisms. According to the Akan of Ghana, who are the source of the data in this essay, *Otumfuor woro nkawa a oworo fa ne bati*, 'When the Almighty King removes his ring, he does so from his shoulders.' This depicts the unlimited scope of the capabilities of the king; he exerts his power in accordance with his wishes. It is also said, *Otumfuor kyekyere boa a yennsane mu*,

This chapter was originally published in the *Journal of Folklore Research*, 28:1 (1991), 1–22.

'When the Almighty King wraps a parcel, it is not unwrapped for scrutiny.' This implies that the king is above reproach; he is to be trusted. The Akan also refer to their kings as *Okasapreko*, 'One who says the last word'. His word is final. Besides all this, the chief is sacred, since he sits on the stool of the venerable ancestors.

One way by which royal power is preserved and enacted is in the conduct of formal talk, where certain norms of communication are observed in part to acknowledge the sacredness of the royal sphere, and partly to enrich the poetics of oratory. In formal situations, a chief or king, in several cultures, does not speak directly to an audience in his presence. He speaks through an intermediary, known in several parts of Ghana as *okyeame* (pl: *akyeame*), who relays or reports his words to the audience present, whose words to the chief must also be channelled through the intermediary.

Communication in the royal realm, or within formal interaction, is thus mediated by a political functionary who co-ordinates the interaction to ward off face-threatening acts.

The use of an intermediary, through whom formal talk is routed, is the social dimension of the general practice of indirection that permeates the speech of several cultures in Africa. The verbal component of this involves manipulation of the linguistic code, such as in the use of metaphor, proverb and circumlocution, where literal or delicate talk is routed through a linguistic vehicle partly for artistic effect and sometimes as a face-saving strategy in the conduct of culturally delicate business. Verbal and social indirection are two sides of the same coin, and it is not surprising that cultures that deploy social intermediaries in communication also indulge profusely in ambiguous discourse.

In predominantly non-literate cultures, the practice of using speech intermediaries attains an added significance due to the socio-political significance of oratory (Bloch 1975), but also because of the potency of the spoken word.

LOSING AND SAVING FACE

An important corollary of the power of speech is the basic risk involved in all face-to-face communication, where there is an instant evaluation of each other's communicative competence, and a test of the ability of discourse participants to deal spontaneously with emergent unforeseen structures (Yankah 1985). The stakes in oral communication become higher in public speaking where discourse participants have a bigger audience to contend with.

This situation makes it necessary for cultures to adopt strategies to overcome or minimise the inherent risks to face-to-face interaction. To ward off face-threatening acts, redressive strategies, including the use of intermediaries have to be adopted by both the speaker and the addressee.

But it is not only oratory in the royal realm that is structured to minimise face threat. In some parts of Africa and the Diaspora folktale, libation, and epic performances adopt various modes of mediation, such as integrated responses, that are intended to minimise the hazards of performance. These verbal genres, by their very norms of performance, are thus partly conditioned to save face.

In the royal domain, where political power needs to be constantly reinforced to give the subjects a measure of security, the most cherished modes of performance are those which pose a minimum threat to royal face (see also Brenneis and Myers 1984).

In several parts of West Africa, modes of royal communication similar to the Akan, have been observed by scholars, particularly historians (Alagoa 1976, Talbot 1926: 59, Burton 1966a: 150). In situations where there is more than one intermediary, and cultural mores demand that the message goes through them all, communication becomes even more circuitous. Tarr reports of the Mossi of Burkina Faso:

The message to be communicated originates with the source. He whispers it up to his friend, who in turn whispers it to a lesser chief, who in turn whispers it to a lesser chief's spokesman, who then finally brings the message in an audible voice to the chief's hearing. (Tarr 1979: 204)

It is significant that this mode of communication does not characterise royal discourse only, but all formal oratory within or outside the realm of a high social personage. Ruth Finnegan observed a similar practice among the Limba of Sierra Leone:

The most elaborate and lengthy of all speeches are the long funeral harangues given on the occasion of memorial rites for some important man several years after his death ... One of the principal highlights is the speech made by the leading men; they speak in turn often going on for several hours, and their words are relayed, half intoned sentence by sentence, by a herald who is specially engaged for the occasion. (1970: 454)

COMMUNICATION MODELS

Such patterns of discourse demonstrate the inadequacy of the Jakobsonian (1960) and de Saussarian (1977: 13) models of communication. They alert us to the simplicity of the notions of sender–receiver, addresser–addressee, as the primary categories of reference, and to the existence of more complex structures of communication.

In a communicative situation of such complexity, where an agent speaks on another's behalf, fine distinctions have to be made between source of the message and sender, and goal of the message and receiver. In recent times, ethnographers of speaking (Hymes 1975), students of pragmatics (Levinson 1983; Hanks 1989b), and others (for example, Goffman 1974) have widened the constituents of communication to encapsulate this complexity: 'The speaker or spokesman can be distinct from the source of an utterance, the recipient distinct from the target, and the hearers or bystanders distinct from the addressees or targets' (Levinson 1983: 68).

Goffman, on the basis of framings within theatrical productions, distinguishes *principal* or *originator* of discourse (the one held responsible for the utterance) from the *animator*, the actual sounding box, the emitter whose voice is heard. An individual engaging in ordinary talk often combines the two roles; he originates as well as animates the discourse (1974: 516–23).

Where the two roles are separated as in the situation of *okyeame*, the question of responsibility for display becomes significant. Who takes the responsibility for performance flaws, and who takes the praise?

A related angle from which the mediated communication here can be viewed is through what Dell Hymes, and later Richard Bauman, call *metaphrasis* in performance, 'a reframing of what is conventionally a performance genre into another mode' (Bauman 1977: 34). Bauman laments, however, that this is a poorly documented aspect of performance systems, but one richly deserving of study, as a key to the 'creative vitality and flexibility of performance in a community' (p. 35).

If this aspect of performance is poorly documented, the same cannot be said of its reflexes in everyday use of language, as seen in the scholarship on pragmatics, philosophy of language, and metalinguistics, the study of speech about speech. Scholars in the philosophy of language (Bakhtin 1981; Goffman 1974; Volosinov 1973) refer to the permeation of everyday speech with other people's words. In other words, the concept of metaphrasis has reflexes in everyday speech.

Reported speech is, perhaps, the commonest reflex of this (Volosinov 1973: 115). Since human speech is generally filled with other people's words, which are transmitted with varying degrees of accuracy, one could investigate the dynamic interrelationships in talk about talk, the extent to which social context and norms condition the dynamics of reported speech.

From yet another perspective, one could consider the nature of the framing rules at work, on the basis of the motive behind the reframing. Is it faithfully to protect the original speaker's image and words, or is it with the intent of parodic distortion for the sake of mockery? In situations and cultural contexts where political power and authority are closely intertwined with speech, there is little room for parodying and mockery by an intermediary reframing or reporting the royal word.

AVOIDANCE

In Africa, formalisation of communication also involves physical distancing and avoidance, of which the situation prevailing in the domain of the king of Benin is a typical example. In the sixteenth century, his noblemen were not expected to have eye contact with him:

> When his noblemen are in his presence, they never look him in the face, but sit cowering upon their buttocks with their elbows on their knees, and their hands before their faces not looking up until the king commands them. When they depart from him, they turn not their backs towards him, but go creeping backwards with reverence. (Talbot 1926: 580)

Among the Akan, similar avoidances prevail. It is prohibited to engage the chief in a direct interaction in public. Exceptions to this are artists such as poets, singers, dancers, in artistic communication with royalty, his personal confidants and counsellors whispering or passing on messages to him, or a subordinate chief or functionary swearing an oath of allegiance. All these exceptional situations convey little or no uncertainty and permit limited fact interaction with the chief.

In formal assemblies, the chief's orators are seated beside him, and those addressing him should obey the relevant proxemic and visual norms of communication. The speaker should not be in direct bodily or visual confrontation with the chief. Indeed, the significance of gaze in the norms of communication is further demonstrated in the lore of certain craftsmen. Wives of certain craftsmen may not speak directly to their husbands when they have their periods. Even in situations where both are present, such wives must communicate with their spouses only through a child, whose innocence is immunity in itself. The condition of menstruation is believed capable of breaking down the spiritual immunity of direct addressees. Where such addressees, by the very nature of their vocation, are in constant interaction with spiritually potent animals and trees, a collapse in their spiritual immunity may lead to fatalities.

The Akan further ensure the sanctity of royal space through lexical avoidance: the use of euphemisms for certain words and concepts considered indecent in collocation with the chief, for example, death, sickness or misdemeanour. In all such cases, the *okyeame*'s name may be substituted for the chief's, or a different euphemism altogether is used.

The above modes of avoidance find their utmost fulfilment in public speaking where the threat to royal face is more immediate, and must be contained through the use of an intermediary.

The threat to royal face, on the other hand, may entail putting him in a situation where his competence in oratory may be publicly called in to question. The chief must not be seen to be rhetorically incompetent. Rerouting his speech enables the orator to edit the content and style of the royal message.

ROYAL SPEECH ACT

A royal speech act requires at least two role participants at the production end. First is the chief, who is the addresser and source of the message, one from whom the message officially originates. On the other hand, the chief's audible voice in a royal speech act is not obligatory. He has the option to exercise his part of the transmission by being present and speaking, or declare it null. In this case, he may be present but not speak, or be completely absent from the scene of interaction, and make his views represented. Where he speaks his speech is still considered incomplete without the *okyeame*'s voice.

As the chief speaks, the *okyeame*, with his staff of authority in his hand, rises to his feet as a mark of respect and also to signal his attentiveness. Ordinarily, he sits close to the chief, either facing the same direction, or facing his side view. The chief and the *okyeame* thus redirect their focus in a mutual gaze as the chief speaks. The two engage temporarily in an internal dialogue, even though they are allied role participants in the macro communication model. In the source of the royal speech, the *okyeame* answers with token confirmatives (*sio*, 'yes'), in solidarity with the chief's word.

The responses to the chief's word lend support or vitality to the royal speech, enhance its rhythm, and set the pace for the *okyeame*'s solo turn that follows. After the chief's word comes the second part of the royal speech act, executed by the *okyeame*.

Akyeame depict their own speech role as *nsoso*, as in *Meso Nana kasa so*, 'I supplement the chief's speech'. The phrase *so so* literally means continue, supplement, add to, or make complete. There is thus the implication of supplementation, suggesting that the chief's speech is intrinsically incomplete. *Nsoso* lends wholeness to an incomplete act of speech. In the absence of *nsoso*, a royal speech act is incomplete. The two are, by definition, parts of one whole.

MODES OF RELAY

Holding his staff of office, the *okyeame* may complete the royal speech act in one of three ways, by (a) verbatim repetition, (b) analytic relay and (c) token relay formula.

In verbatim repetition, the chief's message is relayed almost word for word, as he speaks one sentence after another, a type of simultaneous interpretation.

Analytic relay, on the other hand, appears to characterise most of what *akyeame* do. By this, I refer to discretionary paraphrasing, elaboration or proverbial embellishment of the principal's message without altering its logical focus. In this case, the principal makes an entire speech, which is then analytically reported or animated by the *okyeame*. This type of animation often presents a dynamic tension between the reporting and reported contexts. Embellishing the words spoken by the chief is the *okyeame*'s prerogative, and he is considered to have been faithful so long as its logic has not been altered. *Akyeame* are very sensitive to the aesthetics of discourse animation, the fact that the relayed message must be sweet. To many of them, this is the most delightful aspect of their public duties.

On the other hand, the *okyeame* needs not repeat or edit his patron's message. If he considers it audible, well articulated enough, or rather lengthy, he may simply draw the audience's attention to it by a token relay formula – in local parlance, *oma nsempa*. He pronounces to the party for whom the message is meant, *mo nsempa*, 'the message is yours', or *mo asomu a*, 'it reached your ears, or rather, you heard it all'. It is presumed that the message was clear enough, and does not require a meticulous relay.

RECEPTION

The receiving end of royal communication may also have two constituents. If the listening party is a group, or contains a dignitary, it is likely to have an *okyeame* of its own, or else an *ad hoc* one is appointed for the purpose. In this case, the second *okyeame* is the receiver of the message, and has to be distinguished from the addressee or goal, for whom the message is meant.

The speaking *okyeame* thus directs the message he relays to his receiving counterpart, who in turn passes it on to the principal or group he represents. A message from the addresser to the addressee then has the potential of going through three phases: from the chief (A1, source of the message), to his *okyeame* (a2), to the *okyeame* of the other party (b2), to the eventual addressee (B2). If there is a reply, it must trickle back in a reverse order, also a three-part relay.

The phenomenon of formal communication may thus be schematised as follows:

A1 (Chief, Principal, Source of message, Addresser) → a2 (*Okyeame*, Intermediary, Animator, Speaker) →/ b2 (*Okyeame*, Intermediary, Receiver) → B2 (Audience, Principal, Addressee, Goal of message)

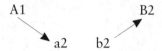

In this diagram, the upper-case alphabets represent the principals and the lower case stands for the *akyeame* who relay the messages of their principals. A1 is the principal (here, the chief), source of the message, the one from whom the message emanates. His message could be in an *undertone*, a whisper, or may be loudly spoken. In any case, his word is meant for immediate deliberation within his party (A), and is subject to a strategic recasting by his orator, before it crosses the boundary to the other party (B). In cases where party A has two or more functioning *akyeame*, the message from the source is received serially and relayed among them before it crosses the boundary. The lower case letters (a and b) representing the intermediaries are therefore subject to recursion:

$$→ a2 → a3 → a4/b4 → b3 → b2→$$

In any case, the message circulating among the allied participants in A may have been unofficially overheard by participants in party B, or other bystanders. So long as the message has not been officially tabled by the orator, however, it is not considered complete.

Receiving the message from his principal, the *okyeame* (orator and strategist), officially presents it to the official receiver, his counterpart in the other party, who also directs it to the ears of his principal, who is the intended goal of the message.

Conversely, B1's reply trickles back in a reverse order until it reaches A1.

Under no circumstances then must the message move directly from

A1 to B1, or vice versa, without going through the intervening stages, regardless of the spatial proximity between the two principals.

In cases where the other party has no orator, the chief's spokesman becomes the sole focus of the interaction. He relays his principal's message as well as the other party's, even though he is not bound to imbue the relay of the two messages with the same finesse. The following diagram depicts this:

A1	B1
Chief	Audience
Principal	Principal
Source of message	Goal of Message

Okyeame
(Mutual/Intermediary)

METACOMMUNICATIVE SIGNALS

The nature of the royal speech act becomes clearer when one takes into consideration the metalinguistic component of the *okyeame*'s speech; for the entire duties of the *okyeame* may be subsumed under metalanguage, he mostly treats language as an object of reference or comment. In compliance with this, the *okyeame*'s speech has a greater metalinguistic component than other speeches.

Since formal speeches are invariably routed through the *okyeame*, they are preceded by addressives referring to him. Thus one making a formal speech alerts the *okyeame* by an addressive, then starts the message. The introductory formula often suggests the intended route of the message's transmission, and the party for whom the speech is meant. The speech may simply begin with, *Okyeame wo ho?*, 'Is *okyeame* alert?', where the speaker checks the channels of transmission and the perception readiness of his immediate target. Here the *okyeame*'s role as the potential receiver of the message is highlighted.

To this, he may signal his readiness, *Mewo ho*, 'I am alert', or rather, 'The lines of transmission are open'. One would then continue with the relay formula, *Okyeame tie ma ento Nana* '*Okyeame*, listen so Nana, the chief, may hear.' The speaker here overtly distances himself from the chief or dignitary; he clearly distinguishes two participant roles at the receiving end of his message: *okyeame* and the party for whom the message is meant (the chief). Indeed, the speaker maps out an operational model of communication; he verbalises the pragmatic model of formal talk. Even though the speaker may not be physically distant from the chief, he has no verbal access to him. He acknowledges the political distance between them by addressing the chief through the latter's surrogate.

In cases where the expected points of the message relay are more than one, the speaker provides an exhaustive list of the intermediaries along the relay path, and then names the eventual goal of the message, such as, *Okyeame W tie ma ento A na Y aso nte se* . . . 'Okyeame W, listen and pass it on to X, that Y may hear and in turn relay it to Z that . . .' Here the speaker encodes in his pragmatic model the multiple frames of reporting expected.

This type of multiple relay may be exercised where more than two different parties, all having *akyeame*, are represented in a formal forum, and a message delivered is relevant to them all. In this case, the message may be picked up serially by the various *akyeame* and passed on to the parties. The multiple relay formula may also be used where a chief's two or more *akyeame* are present at a forum of considerable importance. In this case, the message to the chief may proceed from the lowest- to the highest-ranked (who often sits closest to the chief), and messages from the chief may be channelled in a reverse order, the lowest-ranked being the final medium of relay.

Ending speech directed at an *okyeame*, a speaker may use the formula, *Okyeame, mepaa wo a na amannee ne no*, 'Okyeame, if I called you, that's the message.' After a message from the chief or another has been received by an *okyeame*, he animates it and may end his speech with another metacommunicative formula: *Sedee Nana see ne no*, 'So says the chief'. Here, the source of the message, the principal, is named.

Instead of animating his principal's speech, the *okyeame* may, on the other hand, opt for the token relay formula, *Wo nsempa* or *Mo nsempa*, 'The message is yours – sg. or pl.', or *Wo asomu a/Mo asomu a*, 'It reached your ears, you heard it all – sg./pl.' which directs the message to its goal. The use of the token relay formula, 'You heard it all' does not find favour with the Akan: it denotes an ineloquent *okyeame*, who lacks the skills to paraphrase, embellish or fully ornament his patron's words. To the Akan, *Okyeame a onnim asemka na ose Nana w'asomu a*, 'It's the ineloquent *okyeame* that says, "Chief, you heard it all." '

The Akan have a passion for eloquent rhetoric, and often exploit situations to demonstrate their verbal wit (see Yankah 1991). Similarly, audiences are often on the look-out for witty public speakers who ornament their public oratory with metaphor, aphorisms and proverbs. Since *akyeame* are selected on the basis of their forensic skills, they often justify their positions through witty manipulation of their patron's message, and attract such favourable comments as *N'ano awo*, 'His lips are dried up, he is eloquent'.

ILLUSTRATION

Below I illustrate the various ways in which messages are relayed by the *okyeame*, particularly the verbatim and analytic modes of relay.

Verbatim relay

The occasion was a judicial sitting in 1988 by the Kumasi Traditional Council of the Ashanti state, chaired by the king of Ashanti, Otumfuor Opoku Ware II.

A subchief, among others, had been charged with failure to attend the wake of one of the king's *akyeame*, who had died a few months before. This negligence on the chief's part had been greatly lamented by the jury, since the deceased was an important dignitary. In the course of the deliberations, the Asantehene (king of Ashanti) used the occasion to convey his concern about the subchief's negligence. His words, spoken undertone but overheard by many, were relayed simultaneously to the wider audience of eighty or more people, by one of his *akyeame*.

Note the shift in perspective between the two texts, and also the unique accompaniment of the king's words with confirmative phrases by the *akyeame* present. As the king spoke, his *akyeame* stood around him listening attentively and interspersing the speech with ratifiers (*sio*). At the end of a sentence or two, he would pause for one *okyeame* to relay his message to the audience present.

The king's words have been poetically arranged here to coincide with the occurrence of the responses from his *akyeame*:

Discourse 1

KING: I am concerned about this funeral *sio*
Because the gentleman who has returned to his soul's origins *sio*
Served in this palace for thirty nine-years *sio*
OKYEAME: Otumfuor, the Almighty, says he is concerned about these events, because the gentleman who has returned to his soul's origins, served in this palace for thirty-nine years.
KING: The role he has played in this palace is known to us all – *sio*
OKYEAME: He says the role he has played in this palace is known to all.

KING: We would have done him no greater honour – *sio*
Than to observe his wake – *sio*
To bid him farewell *sio*
OKYEAME: He says we would have done him no greater honour, than to observe his wake, to bid him farewell.
KING: That is why I said all elders should together *sio*
Attend to create a good impression
OKYEAME: He says that is why he said all elders should together attend, to create a good impression.
KING: You all know *sio*
I do not haphazardly *sio*
Observe the wake of my *akyeame sio*
OKYEAME: He says, for his *akyeame*'s wake, you know he does not haphazardly observe it.
KING: It's due to the importance of this *sio*
And the need to thank him *sio*
That we all went *sio*
OKYEAME: He says it is due to the importance of this, and the need to thank him, that we all went.
KING: Elders, my pardon, *sio*
Learn a good lesson from this, you all *sio*
If any tragedy occurs, we must all go and sympathise *sio*
For no one knows what tragedy the future brings *sio*
OKYEAME: He says he begs you all, elders; learn a lesson from this, you all. If any tragedy occurs, we must all go and sympathise. For no one knows what tragedy the future may bring forth.

Except for a few lexical changes and clause transpositions, the *okyeame*'s relay is a complete replica of the chief's message, with all its stylistic contours. There is, of course a shift in the orientation of the discourse, the chief's authorial voice maintaining a first-person pronoun to depict his power and control over the interaction situation, and the interpretation rendering these in the third person, to create a distance between the primary and secondary situations. This way, the force of the chief's illocution is stepped down.

Analytic relay

While a great many of the royal speeches were given near-verbatim renditions by the *okyeame*, there were certain segments of the situation that exemplify analytic reporting, editing the chief's words.

The subchief's failure to attend the important wake was not the end of the matter. He further displayed insubordination before the elders, which drew sharp words from the chief. Despite the chief's concern about the culprit's unruliness, he showed his mercy by pardoning him. In his words:

Discourse 2
KING: Tell X . . . he is pardoned
He should not do that again.

These words, which the chief said undertone, were further relayed by another *okyeame* with a proverb embellishment. The *okyeame* passed his relay through a chief, in whose jurisdiction the culprit belonged:

OKYEAME: Nana X, Otumfuor bids that it reach your ears. The misdemeanour by the elder should have drawn a severe penalty, to deter others. Apologies, apologies, apologies, *oburu*; if you walk in step with your colleagues, and they transform into beasts, do likewise; it may be a ploy to eat you up. Otumfuor says you are forgiven.

In this relay, the *okyeame* transforms the chief's brief words of pardon into an elaborate caution. Even though he routes the chief's official words of pardon through another chief, he exploits the situation to display his proverbial wit. The proverb he uses is not part of the chief's original diction, and momentarily appears out of context. Yet it telescopes sentiments that had been expressed in the initial segments of the interaction. Indeed, *akyeame* are at liberty to incorporate in their relay all relevant pieces of information they consider would enhance the logical appeal of their message.

The defendant, during the time of the wake, was at an informal meeting with other elders. Those elders had wisely left the meeting and attended the wake, knowing its political significance. The defendant should have followed suit, but had imprudently stayed put. The consequence he faces, according to the *okyeame*, is comparable to that of an imbecile who failed to join his colleagues' magical transformation and became their victim. Prudence requires that you adapt yourself, where necessary, to avoid alienation, the orator cautions.

The *okyeame* here overtly attributes his entire message to the chief: 'these are not my own words, but the chief's', he implies in humility. Equally important is the orator's over-indulgence in apologies prior to his words of wisdom. He profusely apologises to unratified participants in his message, as a way of reducing the discourtesy of appearing to teach wisdom to elders: 'Elders, the impending proverb caution is not directed at you, but at the imprudent defendant', he implies. His apology is reinforced with a polite term of address, *oburu*, directed at the chief.

Answering

The above pattern of formal speech interaction, in which intermediaries are used to ratify or interpret messages underscores the search for concord in the art of persuasion – the aim of the performer to solicit the support of his audience. Using an intermediary to repeat or confirm word or argument lends a measure of objectivity to opinion expressed, implying that the speaker's viewpoint is not a subjective one, but a shared experience.

A significant exemplification of the above viewpoint may be found in the phenomenon of 'answering' in certain performance traditions. Indeed, answering is a reflex of the basic rhetorical strategy discussed above and constitutes, in parts of Africa, an integral part of performance in oratory and other verbal genres including story-telling, libation prayer, epic performance, and folk-preaching and blues-singing in black America.

Besides established modes of expressing audience approval of performance, one tradition of story-telling in Africa has the institution of intermediary as a required component in the structure of performance. Prior to a performance, an intermediary of his choice is appointed by the narrator. The performer thus directs the narration first to the intermediary who passes it on to a wider audience, through phrasal interjections of approval. This pattern of performance has been reported in part of West Africa, where the institution of royal spokesman has been widely reported (see Finnegan 1967; Galli, 1983; Agovi 1973). In some parts, the designation for this functionary is the same as *okyeame* or its equivalent.

Pentecostal sermons and certain traditions of story-telling among black Americans constitute one widely studied example of antiphonal responses in performance, carried over from the practice of answering in narrative art.

In a recent study of oral literary practice among the Gullah of the sea islands in South Carolina – free descendants of slaves from Barbados and West Africa – Jones Jackson notes the widespread practice of not addressing a narration directly to an audience, but through an intermediary (Jones Jackson 1987: 44).

Verbal genres in which speech mediation is a built-in device, whether oratory, story-telling epic performance or Pentecostal preaching, tend to diffuse the hazards of performance, since the interaction is intrinsically conditioned to achieve token success.

In the royal domain, where political power needs to be constantly enacted to mystify royal ego, the most cherished modes of communication are those contrived to pose minimum threat to royal face. The circuit-travelled formal talk, the deployment of professional orators, as well as the communicative devices marshalled in the enactment, are all part of the consolidation of political and rhetorical power.

· CHAPTER 16 ·

Praise splits the subject of speech: constructions of kingship in the Manden and Borgu

Paulo Fernando de Moraes Farias

To focus on 'praise' practices, and to seize the configurations of subjects of speech posited by praise genres, is to zero in on what Amselle has described as the intra-ethnic and inter-ethnic 'politics of the concept of person' and of concepts of group identity (1990: 201–4).[1] Kingship and its mode of construction have been traditionally central to this politics, and continue to facilitate insights into the management of the act of praise.

'Praise' does not always mean praise in the conventional sense of the word (see Barber 1991: 13). Sumanguru's praises in the *Sunjata* epic celebrate what may be described as Sumanguru's violence and cruelty – his dressing himself in human skin. What praise discourses postulate is their capacity to seize upon the 'truth' of the praisee's being, and to activate it and generate acknowledgement of it by the praisee's private self and by the public at large. To achieve this, praise operates on 'the individual' not as if on an entity primarily defined by its boundedness, but rather as if on one whose singularity is constituted precisely by its participation in what lies beyond its boundaries. In this perspective, the 'person' is a swirling forcefield which is widely responsive to other force fields (Hampaté Ba 1973: 181, 191; Beattie 1980: 316–7; Barber 1991: 36–7, 75). It brings together what we call persona and what we call self, and office and office-holder, ethnic/professional identity and personal identity, in constellations that may not always fit the descriptive models mobilised by modern scholarship.[2]

The praisees are never passive recipients of praise, not even when they would wish to be so – i.e. when the praise act awakes disturbing agitations within them against their will (Kendall 1982: 202; Camara 1976: 182, 246). Rather, the praisees actively participate in the praise performance, even if they do this silently. Praise is a negotiation in which the community gives to the individual (to set in motion what s/he already possesses), but also places unavoidable demands on him/her.

If praise is celebration, nevertheless it is also an exercise in intrusion into the depths of one's being. It is hence a source of mixed feelings. In the Manding-speaking world, parallel traditions extol the truthfulness of praise specialists or, on the contrary, decry their 'mendacity'.[3] Thus, at one level, an emblematic figure of *jeli*, 'griot', commemorated in connection with the rulers of Segu in the second half of the eighteenth century and early nineteenth century, is remembered as Tinyɛtigiba – from *ba*, 'grand', and *tinyɛ-tigi*, 'he who possesses the truth' (Bazin 1979: 457). An even more emblematic figure, Sunjata's *jeli* Bala Fasɛkɛ, is depicted as one who felt compelled to proclaim the truth and oppose lies: following Sumanguru's defeat, after Sunjata's army had been searching for Bala Fasɛkɛ for a long time without success, it sufficed to shout an obviously untrue statement loudly for his voice to be heard in the distance in protest, allowing him to be located at last (Diabété 1970b: 75; Moser 1974: 313–14). In this light (and this is central to the argument of the present chapter), praise draws on knowledge born from participation in the self of the other, and this participation permits praise to be a veridical discourse that talks about what is 'really there', or what has the right and ability to be there. It is in principle categorically different from the language of lies, disguise and exaggeration.

However, at another level, praise is talked about in a rather different way. Zahan (1963: 141) maintains that Banmana speakers are generally agreed that the *jeliw* are socially necessary 'liars', because their role is to generate enthusiasm, courage and valour, and all these are qualities of character based on one's illusion to be greater than one really is. Nakamura (1988: 331–2, 343) states that the Markajalan among whom he did his research often describe the *jeliw* as but 'rapacious people', who will say no matter what for gain. And he himself argues – along Zahan's lines – that 'embellishment' and lying inhere in *jeli* praise. Needless to say, the resentment against the 'rapacity' and 'sycophancy' of those who practise what is disparagingly referred to as *griotisme*, or *griotage*, is in part a result of rapid social change, which has led *jeliw* to abandon their traditional patrons in search of new ones (Diawara 1994). But, as we will see from the stories of Sumanguru and Sunjata, resentment of griot intrusiveness has probably existed for as long as enjoyment of praise has also existed.

This ambivalent relationship between praiser and praisee has been perceptively discussed, in a number of West African contexts, in its political, textual, 'cosmological', sociological, and psychological aspects.[4] It will be useful to take now a closer look into the relationship, in its capacity as an operation whose logic alternatively postulates the amalgamation and the splitting of subjects of speech, and also postulates permutations of the positions of addresser and addressee, human voice and instrumental music.

In the context of kingship, at one extreme of praise's range of manifestations (in the *Sunjata* epic of the Manden), 'praise' addresser and addressee are described as being originally the same human being, but as becoming later two separate yet simultaneously present subjects. Both the voicing of praise and the response to it are depicted as taking place, at first, wholly within grammar's first person, albeit with the help of an 'inanimate' (though 'magical' or 'genie-produced') musical instrument. The subject and object of language, the praiser and the praisee, are one. There is no silent praisee. At the other extreme of the range (in the kingship festival of Nìkì, in Borgu), praise postulates an 'absent' or 'inanimate' *addresser* – in a manner reminiscent of Jakobson's suggestion that an absent or inanimate *addressee* is postulated by the magic or incantatory function of language (1963: I, 216–17). Yet that 'absent' or 'inanimate' addresser (embodied in a musical instrument) is in a powerful sense the essential part of the live king who is present at the festival.

All this suggests that, within the Manding-speaking and other African cultural worlds, practices of praise and kingship move on the edge of horizons of thought where clashing perceptions of being and communication are opposed to one another, and are temporarily reconciled *ad hoc*. When we talk about 'praise' and 'kingship' we are referring to dynamic conceptions of being, and to the manipulation of its ebbs and flows. In this dynamic sense, praise empowers (and even forces) people to be what they 'are', or – in a very literal sense – what they have it in them to be.

THE EVIDENCE

In this essay I compare two regions which are geographically far apart in West Africa, and two different orders of evidence: kingship rituals from Borgu (more precisely from the Gaani festival of Nìkì, in the north of the Republic of Bénin) recorded on video in October 1990, and classical narratives concerning the origins of praise told in the core of Mande culture (in the Republic of Mali and the Republic of Guinea-Conakry), and in other Mandekan-speaking areas. The link between the two regions and orders of evidence are the *gɛsɛrɛbà* (sg. *gɛsɛrɛ*), a category of Borgu traditionists with roots in the Manding-speaking cultures of the western Sahel and upper Niger valley. These oral specialists are the counterpart of the *geseru* (sg. *gesere*) of the Soninke heartlands in north-western Mali, southern Mauritania, and eastern Senegal. The *gɛsɛrɛbà* migrated into Béninois Borgu via Soŋoy (Songhay) centuries ago. They perform in Wakpaarɛm, a language derived from Soninke, but often bear patronymic-group names borrowed from Mandekan-speaking areas: thus they call themselves Tarawɛrɛ (pronounced Tarawere, Tarawele, or Traoré in Mali), Fãfana (Fofana in Mali), etc. They preserve at least one of the best-known aetiological tales about praise from the Mande, and their traditional specialism is to praise the kings of Nìki, the title-holders ('princes') belonging to the various segments of the royal dynasty, and other members of the Wasangari social estate, which includes most of the chiefly lineages of Béninois Borgu. The *gɛsɛrɛbà* play a crucial role in the annual Gaani festival.

PRAISE AS 'INTRUSION': THE *SUNJATA* EPIC

Let us first examine the striking image of the origin of praise offered in Mande epic narratives (see Bulman 1990: 337–45). In the Mandekan-speaking cultures, that which is subsumed under the label 'praise' by contemporary scholarly literature in fact belongs to a number of interlocking oral genres. There may be no single agreed word for what we call 'epic'. Rather, performances of the matter of Sunjata and Sumanguru are referred to as *fɔli*, 'the action of telling a tale and/or playing a tune', *kumaw* or *komaw* (sg. *kuma* or *koma*), 'word', *kuma kɔrɔ*, 'discourse of old', *kokɔrɔ*, 'olden-day matters', *maana*, 'meaning', 'sense', (from the Arabic *maᶜnan*), *fasaw* or *faasaw* (sg. *fasa* or *faasa*), 'praise chanting', etc. Some genres find niches within other genres. Thus within the epic one encounters *kan fiŋ*, 'black discourses' (i.e. archaic sayings), *nzana*, 'proverbs', and also *fasaw* or *faasaw* – in the sense of relatively short 'praise' songs sung to well-known tunes such as the 'Janjon', the 'Kala jata', ('Lion with the bow'), sometimes referred to as *Sunjata Fasa*, and the 'Boloba' ('Big arm'). Other names for overlapping genres that fall under the label 'praise' are *matɔ*, 'praise centred on one's personal *tɔgɔ* or *tɔ*, "name/renown"', *majamu*, 'praise centred on one's *jamu* or patronymic-group name', and *balimali* or *balemani*, 'a panegyric which is recited, not sung, but which may be incorporated in *fasa* songs'.[5] The etymology *fa siya*, 'father's progeny', 'paternal genealogy' is often proposed for the word *fasa* (see Diabété 1970a: 43). But the homophonous word *fasa*, 'muscle', 'tendon', plays a central role in stories about the origins of praise, and the meaning of 'something meant to foster muscle-like vigour and tonicity' seems to be attached to the name of the *fasa* praises (Zahan 1963: 133).

Tales about the origins of praise are narrated in the *Sunjata* epic and are centred on the performance of *fasa* songs/panegyrics, but other tales about the same topic are told independently of the epic.

Sunjata Keyta's great rival, Sumanguru Kante the ruler of Soso, was a *numu* (a label often reductively translated as 'blacksmith'), i.e. a transformer of both 'the physical and the supernatural' (McNaughton 1988: 151). He either obtained from a supernatural helper or produced with his own skills a 'magical' *bala* or xylophone, which he played while singing his own praises.[6] Several tellings of this story explicitly state that this was the first *bala* to have appeared on earth (Innes 1974: 200–1; Johnson 1986: 148). According to most versions, Sumanguru kept the instrument locked away from all other human beings, in his secret chamber. It is not at all stated, nor implied, that his self-praising was a fatuous game of self-indulgence and self-delusion. Rather, it appears as part of the secrets of Sumanguru's actual power and invulnerability. In other words, it is probably to be seen as part of his *daliluw* or 'means to success' (on this notion see Bird and Kendall 1980: 16; McNaughton 1988: 42–3). To praise himself was to call his being forth as an inner response, and to make his power actual. And so it was until the day somebody else intruded into Sumanguru's inner chamber of secrets (or got hold of the *bala* in some other way) in Sumanguru's absence, and played the magical instrument (Konaré Ba 1983: 60–3). In nearly all versions of the epic that contain this episode, the intruder (described as Sunjata's *jeli* or griot) is called Jakuma Dɔka, 'Dɔka the Cat' or dialectal variants of this name, or alternatively this is said to be his father's name.

But though there had been yet nobody to take up the griot role by replacing Sumanguru's voice with his own, self praise already required an alter ego for the praisee – in the circumstances an 'inanimate' one. The *bala* was Sumanguru's alter ego. He and the musical instrument are shown being both addressed as *Soso kɛmɔgɔ* or *Soso kɛmɔkɔ*, 'the Grand Man, or Patriarch, of Soso', and Sumanguru himself referred to the *bala* in this way. In other words, both of them are categorised as *mɔgɔ/mɔkɔ*, 'human being', and as 'male' (*kɛ*) (Ly-Tall et al. n.d.: 50, 204–7; Cissé and Kamissoko 1988: 128–9). So intimate was the link between Sumanguru and his xylophone that, in spite of the distance between them on that occasion, he immediately knew somebody else was playing it. He rushed back to his palace to kill the intruder. But the musician Dɔka the Cat escaped death by singing Sumanguru's 'praise' (without having been taught it). Though enraged by this appropriation of what was solely his own, suddenly Sumanguru discovers something new:

A ko Jakuma Doka jaga mɔgɔ fasa ka di mɔgɔ gwɛdɛ da i yɛdɛ di!
He said: 'ah, Doka the Cat, a person's *fasa* is sweeter in another person's mouth than in one's own!' (Ly-Tall et al. n.d.: 204–7)

(In some variants of this tale, statements similar to this are made by Dɔka the Cat himself, who thus underlines his own indispensability, and his power to change the praisee's emotions by moving them from rage to pleasure – see Diabété 1970b: 57–8). Sumanguru then decides to keep Dɔka the Cat by his side at all costs, cuts his Achilles' tendons (*fasa*) to prevent his departure, and renames him Bala Fasɛkɛ (or Faseke) Kuyatɛ (or Kwaatɛ).[7] If Sumanguru and the xylophone until then had been addressed by the same title, now the musical instrument and its new player were both called Bala. A process of transference and assimilation taking place between these three entities is implied in the tale. The instrumental alter ego remains the same, whether the praising voice attached to it is Sumanguru's or Bala Fasɛkɛ's. But hasn't Bala Fasɛkɛ then become Sumanguru's alter ego too? Consider the following: the Kuyatɛ, whose acknowledged ancestor is Bala Fasɛkɛ, are traditionally the griots of the Keyta *Masarenw* (royalty) descended from Sunjata, and in addition have a joking relationship (*sanankuɲa*) with them (Innes 1974: 60–1; Camara 1976: 37–9). This link with the Keyta is a fundamental datum of Kuyatɛ identity. But, at the same time, there are Kuyatɛ panegyrics virtually identical to those of the Kante, Sumanguru's patronymic group (see Cissé and Kamissoko 1991: 106–7, 114–15; 1988: 232–3). This is probably not the result of indiscriminate borrowing. Rather, it is a continued affirmation of Bala Fasɛkɛ's sharing of Sumanguru's identity.

At one level, what the tale of Sumanguru's encounter with Dɔka the Cat/Bala Fasɛkɛ portrays is the 'perversion' or inversion of another tale, told in the dialects of Mandekan both within and without the Sunjata epic, and also told in Soninke as the story of origin of the Daraame oral specialists of the Soninke heartlands (on these 'people of the mouth' see Diawara 1990: 40–4). It is also told within other linguistic communities in contact with Mandekan speakers and Soninke speakers.[8] In the Mandekan versions outside the *Sunjata* epic, it is the story of the partaking of the flesh and blood of an anonymous, prototypical, patron and praisee (in other words a *hɔrɔn*, i.e. a free man who is not a member of the *ɲamakalaw* or 'casted' groups), by an equally anonymous, prototypical, *jeli* (hence naturally a *ɲamakala*). However, at the beginning of the story there is very little difference in status between the two characters. They do not belong to different social categories (see Bulman 1990: 334–5). Rather, they are brothers. As they travel together, the junior brother suffers from hunger to the point (in some versions) of coming close to death. Since no game nor any other food is available, the senior brother secretly cuts a piece of his own calf, or of his thigh, roasts it, and feeds it to the junior brother. Later the junior brother discovers what had happened, is filled with gratitude and admiration and becomes the senior brother's praiser or *jeli*.

A game of oral and 'muscular' metaphors of exchange is played out in this story. The senior brother sacrifices muscle (*fasa*) in order to satisfy the junior brother's hungry mouth and belly, i.e. in order to preserve his vigour. In compensation, the junior brother uses his mouth to sing the other's praise (*fasa*), i.e. to invest the other with vigour and 'muscle' (*fasa*) by making language into 'flesh'.

A very similar tale is part of the *gɛsɛrɛ* tradition of Béninois Borgu, of which I speak again later. The Tarawɛrɛ *gɛsɛrɛbà*, 'oral specialists', and the Wasangari royal and chiefly estate, are described as respectively descended from two brothers who journeyed together into Borgu. As they travelled, the junior brother began to chant a refrain indicating that he was hungry. The senior brother then cut a piece of flesh from his own thigh, roasted it and fed it to the junior brother. Later the junior brother again felt hungry and chanted, and was fed again in the same way by the senior brother. This establishes the paradigm of the relationship between patron (the Wasangari senior brother, who takes responsibility for feeding the other) and griot (the Tarawɛrɛ *gɛsɛrɛ* junior brother, who inaugurates the use of chanting as the means to proclaim his need to be fed by the other).[9]

By contrast, Sumanguru both cuts Bala Fasɛkɛ's tendons and demands praise from him. The logic of exchange that presides over the story of the two travelling brothers is entirely disrupted. The whole burden of the relationship falls on Bala Fasɛkɛ's side. Sumanguru imposes a loss of *fasa* (tendon matter, vigour) on the *jeli* and not only fails to compensate him for that, but instead extracts *fasa* (praise-induced vigour) from the victim: a case of the debtor insisting on being paid by the creditor. This outrageous behaviour is one among other illustrations offered by the epic as to Sumanguru's lack of commitment to proper social arrangements. This is set against the image of orderly social exchanges between specialised groups characterising the rule of

Sunjata, who does not have to sing his own praises, nor cripple a griot to keep him by his side. Actually, in some versions of the epic it is Sunjata who, as in the tale of the two brothers, from his own flesh feeds Bala Fasɛkɛ (see Bulman 1990: 334).

However, in yet other renderings of the epic it is Sunjata who obtains the primordial xylophone from a genie and plays it by himself, but later gives it to Bala Fasɛkɛ (who, according to some tellings, is caught playing the *bala* without permission thus incurring Sunjata's anger). Having discovered the pleasure of hearing the *bala* played by another hand, Sunjata cuts the *jeli*'s Achilles' tendons to force him to stay around and 'make the xylophone talk' (Innes 1974: 213–14; Bulman 1990: 337–8). Or, alternatively, after Sumanguru's defeat it is Sunjata who – as he listens again to Bala Fasɛkɛ – confirms Sumanguru's insight by saying 'it is sweet to be sung by another' (Diabété 1970b: 77).

Bala Fasɛkɛ Kuyatɛ not only is the acknowledged ancestor of all the Kuyatɛ or Kwaatɛ *jeliw*, but he is also described as the ancestor or prototype of all *jeliw* (Innes 1974: 281). Non-Kuyatɛ griots may also refer to him as 'father' (see Johnson 1986: 149). The tune he played on the magical xylophone is said to be the first praise hymn (*fasa*) known in the Manden – sometimes this is said to have been the 'Janjon', sometimes the 'Boloba', etc. (cf. Cissé and Kamissoko 1988: 164–5; Johnson 1986: 149–50, 210). Thus, whether linked to Sumanguru or to Sunjata, the *bala* episode operates as a story of the origin of praise singing, and as an ontology of the *fasa* genre.

The professional hereditary praiser is shown as having become indispensable once he has transgressed into the praisee's inner world and has incorporated this world in his own. He discovers that which the praisee kept for himself alone, and opens up and colonises that which until then had been only virtual space: the space between addressee and addresser combined into one in the self-praising singer/player. Alternatively, in the story of the two travelling brothers, griots become griots by assimilating to their bodies, and communing with, some of the physical substance of their patrons. Significantly, this establishes between the *jeli*-to-be and the patron-to-be an even closer flesh-and-blood link than that which they already had as brothers.

Hence praise is postulated to occur within a close dyadic relationship between subjects of speech who share their singularity. First (in the myth) the relationship is between the hero as addresser and the hero as addressee (something quite different from any paralysing narcissistic self-absorption). Then (in the myth and in historical time) it is between the intimate partners who are kings and their griots. The enraged Sumanguru (or Sunjata) instantly recognise themselves, i.e. their own message to themselves, in Bala Fasɛkɛ's praise. They do not suspect him of insincere flattery, even though they knew he was singing to save his life. Bala Fasɛkɛ gives to Sumanguru/Sunjata what they know to be theirs beyond doubt. Even when coming from another, 'praise' is instantly one's own. In Bazin's words: 'the royal actor, no matter how self-possessed [*certain de soi*] he may be, is separated from his 'truth', which somebody else – his alter ego placed as a mirror – holds and makes acknowledged' (1979: 457). The colonisation of the praiser/praisee space by the oral specialist signifies the opening up of state politics. Praise is no longer a private exercise in Sumanguru's secret chamber or in Sunjata's compound. Rather, it now affirms itself as a public exercise. While its first aim is still the inner and outer deployment and enjoyment of the praise addressee's own powers, now (in the historical eras that have the Sunjata imperial era as their paradigm) the construction of the king is an investment and a complicity mobilising the whole community through the *jeliw* (see Bazin 1979: 458–9). It is this that makes kingship viable. And it is also this that makes the imperial *Sunjata* epic a deliberate celebration as much of griotship as of kingship.

In all this the king as addresser of his own praise is removed from the open scene. But we will see that at the royal Gaani festival of Nìkì ('Nikki' on most maps), in northern Bénin, praise chanting is still best understood as something that happens in the space between an addresser and an addressee who in a very fundamental sense are the same. Yet the addresser and the addressee are separately embodied, and the space between them requires mediation by griots.

THE *GESEREBÀ* OF BÉNINOIS BORGU

Borgu is a region displaying considerable linguistic diversity. The majority language is Bààtↄ̀núm (a Gur or Voltaic language). Other important languages are Bo'o or Boko (a variety of Bo'o – Busa, a Manding language), Fulfulde, and Dèndí – a variety of Soŋoy (Songhay) established in the country by a pre-colonial diaspora of long-distance traders (Heine 1970: 161).[10]

Since the early colonial period, Borgu has been divided by an international border, which formerly ran betwen the French and the British colonial empires, and which now runs between the Republic of Bénin and the Federal Republic of Nigeria.

The *gɛsɛrɛ* category is one of several 'griot' categories reported from the Béninois part of Borgu, but they are ranked above all other local griots. The *gɛsɛrɛbà* (sg. *gɛsɛrɛ*) are Muslim and play a central role in the management of tradition in Béninois Borgu. They are praise chanters and specialists of the past, traditionally attached only to kings, princes and chiefs (the Wasangari social estate). The *gɛsɛrɛbà* are associated with the string instrument known as *mɔrɔku* or *mɔrɔgu*, but often they chant without musical accompaniment.

Gɛsɛrɛ formal praise performances divide and complicate the process of emission and reception of praise. These formal performances are in a Soninke-derived language (Wakpaarɛm), which is unintelligible to all other sectors of the local population. A translation into Bàatɔ̀núm has to be intercalated by auxiliary *gɛsɛrɛ* performers, or by non-*gɛsɛrɛ* performers schooled in the role of interpreters.[11] This is a limit-case of the type of communication in which a performance has to be relayed by another performance, and in which intermediaries are inserted between addressees and addressers.[12]

Moreover we will see that the conventional distinction between addressee, mediator, and addresser, becomes problematic in unexpected ways in the context of the Gaani royal festival of Nìkì (the main traditional political capital of Béninois Borgu). This is a useful reminder that little has been done so far, at the theoretical level, to clarify what exactly distinguishes formal praise from other uses of language.

It should be noted that the survival of the special performance language works to the benefit of the Wasangari patrons. Wakpaarɛm (which nevertheless is not understood by the Wasangari) has been made into a distinctive attribute of theirs, as much as of the *gɛsɛrɛbà*.

THE ROYAL GAANI FESTIVAL OF NÌKÌ

The Gaani is the principal festival of Borgu's traditional polities.[13] The festival lends its name to the third lunation of the royal calendar, which corresponds to the third lunation (*Rabīʿ al-ʾawwal*) of the Islamic calendar.

In 1990 at Nìkì, over two days (1 and 2 of October), all ceremonies were centred on kingship. They constituted a ritual arena for the enactment of the relations between the *Sìnà Boko*, 'king', and the various categories of his subjects. On the first day this included visits by the king, in procession, first to the *Imām* – who recites Arabic prayers on the occasion – and later to a number of shrines. The *Imām* figured again, in a similarly important role, towards the end of the second day's ceremonies. But clearly the festival is not focused on Islamic worship, though its first day coincides with the date of commemoration of the birth of prophet Muhammad (12th of *Rabīᶜ al-ᵓawwal*).

By being attached to the Muslim calendar, which moves over the seasonal year, the Gaani severs any links it may have historically had with seasonal rites. In other words, it has been freed from other functions and has been concentrated entirely on kingship *qua* kingship (cf. Drucker-Brown 1984: 79). It is a striking example of the usefulness of the Muslim calendar for non-Muslim rulers.[14]

In the afternoon of the first day, after the return of the royal procession to the palace, princely title-holders and other high potentates conspicuously figured in the celebrations in front of the royal compound. It was an occasion for the demonstration of their horsemanship, magnificent attire and munificence towards drummers and trumpeters.

During the *Kaayesi* – the celebrations in the morning of the second day of the festival, also conducted in front of the palace – yet other office-holders, and groups representing different social categories, came to salute the *Sìnà Boko*.

On both occasions the king was reclining on cushions, surrounded by members of his court, inside a round thatched hut erected on a raised platform. This hut, called *sɛ̂kɔ*, is of great symbolic significance. It is a special enclosure and gatehouse, which allows communication between two different orders of space while clearly delimiting the two. It is built against the external wall of the royal compound and has two doors. One door communicates with the palace's internal area, the other opens up onto the public square before the palace. This second door has a hatch that can be applied to its outer side. It remains shut up to the moment when the *Sìnà Boko* comes into the *sɛ̂kɔ*, and is shut again as he departs.

The king enters and leaves the *sɛ̂kɔ* only through the first door. During the ceremonies I recorded on video, neither he nor anybody else ever crossed the door leading into the public square. It is through this second door that the king sees, and is seen by, the crowd in the square and those who approach the *sɛ̂kɔ* to greet him, or to perform other ritual acts.

During the *Kaayesi* ceremonies, some of the greeters prostrated themselves once, others thrice, yet others crawled, at some distance from the platform that supports the *sɛ̂kɔ* and extends before it. By contrast, four office-holders – the *Yarari Sìnà Kararugii*, the *Sùn̄ɔ̀ Sinrari*, the *Sùn̄ɔ̀ Tooto* and the *Sìnà Sako* – successively came onto the raised platform, and close to the door of the *sɛ̃̀kɔ*. They put on acts of ritual disrespect or, worse, menacing behaviour towards the ruler (cf. Drucker-Brown 1984: 73; and Agovi in this volume). But they never crossed the doorway. When the *Imām* and his retinue came to pray for the king, they sat right at the door but did not cross the threshold either – though the *Imām* and two of his deputies came closer to the king that any other greeter, by leaning across the sill to touch hands with the *Sìnà Boko*.

When the *sɛ̃̀kɔ* was opened on this second day of the Gaani, the king's official messenger, the *Sɔnkɔrɔ*, sat on the ground in the square, at some distance from the *sɛ̃̀kɔ* and facing away from it. Throughout the ensuing *Kaayesi* ceremonies, the king sent gifts (token sums of money) to those who had completed their ritual greetings to him and had then withdrawn to the periphery of the square, across from the *sɛ̃̀kɔ* . He did so by handing over the gifts to the *Sɔnkɔrɔ*, who kept going to the *sɛ̃̀kɔ* and collecting them in a metal bowl passed through the door, and shuttling incessantly across the square. (However, in the *Imām*'s case, the king's gift was deposited on a bowl collected directly by the receiving party, without interposition of the *Sɔnkɔrɔ*).

But the space on the other side of the square from the *sɛ̃̀kɔ* was not simply opposed to, and distant from, the locus of royalty. Far from it. It is there that are permanently planted the crutch-like supports on which rest the kingship drums, when they are brought out (see Orou Yorouba 1982: 39, photograph).[15]

These kingship drums were played during the first day of the Gaani attended by us. In Béninois Borgu, only Nìkì has such drums. They are two wooden drums shaped like kettledrums. They replace the metal kettledrums lost in the 1830s at the great battle of Ìlọrin.[16]

These drums are often said to be the highest embodiment of kingship, and are described as 'sacred' (Bagodo 1978: 85, 184–6). They were also described to us as invested with the powers of all earlier kings. Reportedly, they are (or were) honoured with sacrifices – which in olden days may have included human sacrifices (Dunglas n.d.).

The king himself, when his procession returned to the palace on the first day of the festival, rode towards the kingship drums to salute them from a little distance, and to be saluted by them. This is customary at the Gaani, and it is also what new kings do after their installation is completed, but before they cross the entrance to the palace for the first time (Lombard 1953).

The *kãkãki* or *kãkãgi* (Hausa *kakaki*) trumpets are also played from the side of the square which is across from the palace, near the kingship drums. They are played on both the first and the second days of the Gaani, to salute the king and the princes, high chiefs and other personages – including some before whom the kingship drums remain silent. Other Béninois Borgu traditional rulers also have *kãkãki*, but – in principle – the king of Nìkì has a larger number of them than any other chief. They are an important element of the music of kingship, but secondary in relation to the kingship drums.

Owing to the positioning of the musical instruments, a second (but not secondary, and arguably more salient) focus of kingship is created. It is centred on the kingship drums and faces the anthropomorphic focus (the incumbent king in the *sɛ̃kɔ*) across the square. In the Gaani we attended, the princely title-holders, and other high dignitaries, as is customary, directed their salutes to the kingship drums (rather than to the *sɛ̃kɔ* where the incumbent king was sitting in state), and were saluted by the drums in return (see also Dunglas n.d.; Lombard 1965: 209, 327; Orou Yorouba 1982: 28).

The intermediate space between the two foci of kingship is marked out, from both sides, as the public stage for the performance of rites of allegiance and challenge. It is traversed in one direction by the often reiterated sound of the drums of kingship (on the first day), and of the trumpets (which second the drums on the first day, and which continue to play on the second day). It is traversed in the opposite direction by the gifts repeatedly sent out by the *Sìnà Boko* (the incumbent king) on the second day of the festival.

The second-day celebrations (*Kaayesi*) had the participation of *Wōrū Tokura* Bukari, the elderly head of the *gɛsɛrɛbà*, who is said to rank above the *tufarukpe* (the player of the kingship drums) himself (Lombard 1965: 207). Sitting by the side of *Wōrū Tokura* was the *Yã̀ãkpe*, who belongs to the category of drummers, not vocalists or string players. The title of *Yã̀ãkpe* is not hereditary in Nìkì. It is given to the drummer selected by each new king to be a personal griot to the ruler (Lombard 1965: 206–10; Sacca 1987: 49, 65). The *Yã̀ãkpe* must always be on call to the king, and must always accompany him on horseback. He enjoys the licence to tell unpalatable truths to the king, acting as a jester (Dunglas n.d.).

Placing himself near the *kãkãki* players and the site from which the drums of kingship are played, *Wōrū Tokura* chanted at length in Wakpaarɛm (at times handing over this task to a somewhat younger deputy). He chanted in praise of *tunkara* 'kingship' and the *tunka* 'king', with much reiteration and variation of formulas about the relations between clients and good, and bad, patrons. He received gifts from the king and others.

As *Wōrū Tokura* chanted, the *Yããkpe* intercalated into the chant a declamatory, not chanted, translation into Bààtɔ̀núm, punctuated by the playing of his under-arm tension drum, the *sãkpã*. And in the background the playing of the *kãkãki* also punctuated the double vocal performance.[17] At times *Wōrū Tokura* made a show of dissatisfaction with the Bààtɔ̀núm translation, and pointedly repeated his lines for retranslation, or slowed down the translator.

The point is that *Wōrū Tokura* did not sit on the *sẽkɔ* platform (as other dignitaries did) as a member of the court of the incumbent king. Nor did he address anybody on behalf of the incumbent king. Rather, he sat across the square in the area from which comes the music of kingship, and added his voice to the sound of the trumpets. It was also from across the square that, on the first day, kingship in the drums had addressed the living king, i.e. addressed its living self. (It had also addressed the princes of royal extraction, some of them strong candidates to the succession, come to salute the drums.)

There is here something at play that is not a dialogue. Rather, it is a relationship between the actual and its ground of being, between the reigning king and the kingship that to him is, somehow, both self and other. The incumbent ruler is a vessel for kingship as are the drums, but he himself ritually salutes them in the way that that which is self salutes that which is other. On this tense horizon of African thought, kingship in the drums is physically separate from the living king, but is also his own being, from the moment his installation is completed and his body becomes kingship's living body.

This relationship, constructed in music, language and the visual dynamics of the festival, cannot be fully understood as a postulated continuity between the present king and his royal ancestors and predecessors, a bridge between the present and the past. Rather, its vitality resides in present time. And the space it bridges is not simply the interval between different, and successive, individual kings, but also – and more crucially – the gap between two ever-contemporary manifestations of the being of kingship.

CONCLUSIONS: PRAISE SPLITS THE KING

Far from taking a marginal position in the Nìkì polity, into which they came as outsiders, the *gɛsɛrɛbà* have successfully exploited the possibilities offered to them by the local rules governing marriage exchanges, and by the local representations of kingship. They have placed themselves at the very centre of the traditional panoply of power in the region, and have created a niche for their leaders at the very hub of the Gaani festival.[18]

Like the *kākāki* trumpets imported from Hausaland, Wakpaarɛm – the foreign performance language of the *gɛsɛrɛbà* – became available to be ritually added to the beat of the drums of kingship during the Gaani. But because the *gɛsɛrɛ* register is a language register, it makes a central aspect of the festival clearer than it would have been solely from the playing of the drums and trumpets.

The Gaani represents kingship as something that at the same time is the king but is also beyond him and addresses him from outside. This addresser/addressee conundrum is thought through in a way which is not necessarily borrowed ready-made from the Manding-speaking lands, but which becomes easier to grasp by contrast with the Mandenka myth of Bala Fasɛkɛ discussed in the first part of the chapter.

Wōrū Tokura performs in the Gaani in his capacity as the hereditary chief of the *gɛsɛrɛbà* of Nìkì. In the context of the festival, he situates himself on the side of 'impersonal' kingship. The griot/patron side of his relationship with the incumbent king seems to be temporarily suspended.[19] Because his performance is verbal instead of instrumental, his alien idiom requires and solicits interpretation. The interpreter, the *Yããkpe*, is associated with personal kingship: he is not an hereditary office-holder, and he is closely linked to the incumbent king. Together with the *Sɔnkɔrɔ*, the *sɛ̃kɔ* and the width of the square, the *Yããkpe* is part of the interposed apparatus that segregates the king and constitutes boundaries for him, but which also creates channels of communication for the ruler. The voice of the *gɛsɛrɛ* – on this occasion a surrogate for the impersonal voice of the drums – is processed through another voice that has a personal attachment to the living *Sìnà Boko*. The interplay between the personal and the impersonal in kingship is thus forcefully underlined, more so than in the purely instrumental performances of the drums and trumpets.

Clearly, this is different from the positing of an absent/inanimate addressee when language is used in incantatory mode (Jakobson 1963: I, 216–17). In the Gaani, the drumming, trumpeting, and chanting performances are addressed in the first place to the incumbent king (though they also signify him/his kingship). A main addressee is clearly present and animate. It is the addresser who is refractory to easy definitions.

In the same way the sounding of the drums of kingship, the trumpeting, and the chanting and its translation, deploy themselves as if originating in an absent or inanimate addresser, temporarily summoned and animated by the players and by *Wōrū Tokura*. The three categories of performance become links in the chain that extends between kingship and kingship, and the unintelligibility of Wakpaarɛm just adds another degree of distance to the division generated within the oneness of kingship by the festival. The addresser is kingship *qua* kingship, but as such it remains the ground of being of the incumbent king *qua* king throughout the Gaani.

If so, addresser and addressee never cease to be in some sense the same, yet require intermediaries. Through these mediators who link him to what he is, the living ruler elicits, from an outside which is also an inside, that which is already in him. The borders between self and other, person and persona, are vertiginously shuffled up.

Thus in the Gaani of Nìkì, we return to a situation in which, as in the initial stages of the story of Bala Fasɛkɛ in the *Sunjata* epic, kingship is postulated as both the addresser and the addressee of praise. There is, however, an important difference. In the Gaani, addresser and addressee have separate physical embodiments. They stand physically apart as they do not at the beginning of the Bala Fasɛkɛ tale, and the addresser is embodied in the kingship drums.

There are sound pragmatic reasons for this in Nìkì's traditional political context. The local dynasty is divided into competing segments. In theory, kingship rotates among them in an orderly manner. But, in practice, this norm is far from being always respected. Hence strong rivalry and political intrigue obtain between dynastic segments and between individual princes. Not surprisingly, resentments fester against each newly elected ruler (Lombard 1965: 321–2; Orou Yorouba 1982: 37, 80; Sacca 1987: 48, 56–7).

In the Gaani, the simultaneous embodiment of kingship in two different sites potentially defuses such tensions. As we have noted earlier, the princes salute kingship in the drums rather than kingship in the king himself. But in so far as the king is kingship manifest, his power is concretely nurtured by the reverence ostentatiously addressed not to him but to the kingship drums. However, it comes to mind that, in situations of acute conflict between king and princely title-holders, the tensions within Nìkì representations of kingship are ideally suited to licensing rebellion against the incumbent ruler.

NOTES

This chapter draws on oral evidence gathered from the following Borgu informants: (a) Maamaa Sābī Adam, known as Bààbu Adam, a senior gɛsɛrɛ of the Bàà Maro lineage, interviewed in his compound in the Gàá ward of Kpàràkú ('Parakou' on most maps) in April 1988 and January 1990; (b) Wōrū Tokura, the head of the gɛsɛrɛbà of Nìkì ('Nikki'), interviewed at the Nìkì–Wɔɔre ward in April 1988 and January 1990; and (c) Bààbà Damagii, a senior traditional office-holder interviewed at the Sìnà Gūrù ward of Kpàràkú in April 1988.

All these interviews were jointly conducted by Mr O. B. Bagodo (lecturer at the National University of Bénin) and myself, in some cases together with Dr Solomon Oyèéwọlé Babáyẹmí (then of the Institute of African Studies, University of Ìbàdàn, now Ọba Akínrìnọ́lá I, the Olúfì of Gbọ̀ngán in Ọ̀ṣun State, Nigeria), who participated in interviews (b) 1988 and (c); and with Mr O. Banni-Guénné (Secretary-General of Bénin's National Commission for the Bo'o Language), who participated in interviews (a) 1990, (b) 1990. I also draw extensively in this essay from my video recording of the Gaani festival of Nìkì, made on 1 and 2 October 1990 with the valuable assistance of Mr O. B. Bagodo. I thank the above-named colleagues and informants for their kind help.

1 See also Bazin (1985: 119–20).
2 For discussions of the relationship between the overlapping components of the personal, see among others Mauss (1985), Middleton (1973), La Fontaine (1985), Lienhardt (1985), Hollis (1985).
3 In this chapter I use the term 'Manding' in a very wide sense, as a name for the family of languages which includes Soninke and 'Mandekan' in addition to others. By 'Mandekan' ('the Mande language') I mean the group of closely related idioms which includes, among others, Juula (Dyuula), Banmana (Bambara) and Maninka (the idiom of the inhabitants of the Manden or Mande, who call themselves Mandenka or Maninka, but who are also widely known as Malinke). These idioms may be regarded as dialects of Mandekan (see Bird 1970). The Mande or Manden, which is regarded as the motherland or classical nucleus of the Mandekan-speaking cultures, stretches from the outskirts of Bamako (the capital of the Republic of Mali) in the north-east to Korosa (in the Republic of Guinea-Conakry) in the south-west (Moraes Farias 1993: 14).
4 See for instance Bazin (1979), Barber (1991), Cissé (1973: 157–8), Olivier de Sardan (1973), Smith (1973), Bird and Kendall (1980), Kendall (1982).
5 On these genres, their taxonomy and interrelations, and their variable descriptions, see Austen (1992), Bazin (1979: 445), Belcher (1985: 283–94, 311–12), Bird (1992), Camara (1976: 243-8), Cissé and Diabété (1970: 81–2), Cissé and Kamissoko (1988: 32, 389–92), Diabété (1970a: 43), Diawara (1994), Innes (1974: 20–4), Jansen (1993), Johnson (1986: 47–8), Moser (1974: 35–6), Traoré (1992), Wilks (1992), Zahan (1963: 133–41).
6 See Niane (1960: 74–8), Johnson (1986: 148–51, 210–11), Cissé and

Diabété (1970a: 81), Cissé and Kamissoko (1988: 162–5), Diabété (1970b: 57).

7 The new name includes the xylophone name (*bala*) and other elements. *Kuyatɛ* is interpreted as the abbreviation of a Maninka phrase meaning 'there is a matter/secret between us', *ku ye an tyɛ* (Diabété 1970b: 95; Johnson 1986: 211). Bulman (1990: 333) lists the different etymologies put forward for *fasɛkɛ* or *faseke*, and for the variants of this name, ranging from a word meaning 'witness' (*seere*) to expressions meaning 'you will settle/sit here' (*i be sigi la le*), 'do your praise' (*i fasa kɛ*), and 'cut tendon' (*fasa sege*).

8 See Zemp (1966: 632–3), Smith (1973: 477), and Camara (1976: 100–1, 147–8).

9 However, the prohibition on marriage between the descendants of the two brothers, which is classical in the versions of this myth reported from the Mandekan-speaking lands, is on the contrary entirely absent in the Borgu version, which has no rules of griot endogamy to account for because oral specialists are not a 'casted' group in Borgu.

10 In addition, a little studied idiom said to be a dialect of the Yorùbá language is spoken among the Mokɔle (called Feribu, sg. Feri, in Bàɑ̀tɔ̀núm), who are established to the north-east, east and south-east of Kâni. They maintain that their name is derived from the Yorùbá *mo kọ ilé*, 'I reject home', and that this phrase encapsulates their ancestors' decision to emigrate from old Ọ̀yọ́ (cf. Lombard 1965: 79, 87). Gur languages other than Bàɑ̀tɔ̀núm are also represented in the region, and Hausa speakers are found in towns and villages along commercial routes.

11 Interview: B. Adam.

12 Elsewhere in this volume Kwesi Yankah, using Akan evidence, discusses other types of this little-studied mode of performance. He concentrates on circuits of formal talk, i.e. on situations in which verbal messages are sent out from both ends of the chain of communication. This is different from what happens in *gesɛrɛ* praise chanting.

13 See Lombard (1965: 330–40), Bagodo (1978: 86), Orou Yorouba (1982), CEAP-Borgou (1986), Bio Bigou (1990).

14 Most kings of Nìkì have been non-Muslim.

15 I deliberately write 'kingship drums' instead of simply 'royal drums', because the first expression seems better to signify the role attributed to these drums. Anything associated with the king is obviously 'royal', but will not necessarily become an embodiment of kingship as such.

16 In the old days the kingship drums were carried into battle. Now they are only played at the Gaani, and at two crucial *moments de passage*: after the election (and later after completion of the installation) of a king, and at his death (Zinkpé 1952; Lombard 1953; Orou Yorouba 1982: 26; Sacca 1987: 45, 51; Bio Bigou 1990). During the interregna rivalries between contenders for the succession flash up most conspicuously. The playing of the kingship drums at the death of the king, and at the installation of his successor, affirms not only the permanence of kingship over time, but also its integrity over and above contemporary fractionalisms. In the past,

intra-dynastic rivalries led each new king to build a new palace, or renew the palace occupied by the last king from the same dynastic branch. There are at least three ruined palace sites still recognisable in Nìkì (Bramoulle 1950; Sacca 1987: 36,64; CEAP-Borgou 1986: map). But, since the colonial days, economic pressures have rendered the custom unworkable. Nevertheless, Nìkì still has two standing royal palaces instead of one. The first is at Nìkì-Gūrù and is now regarded by most people as the permanent location of the court. The other is at Nìkì-Dããri, and it is owned by the Yari-Laafiaru (or Yari-Daafiaru) dynastic branch. Significantly, the Gaani royal procession visits the Nìkì-Dããri palace before returning to Nìkì-Gūrù – we saw this being done in October 1990 under the late king Sero Taasu, who did not belong to the Yari-Daafiaru branch. This was yet another way of affirming the integrity of kingship over intra-dynastic differences.

17 It is always the *Yããkpe* who interprets the voice of the head of the *gesɛrɛbà* of Nìkì during the Gaani (interview: B. Adam, see also Orou Yorouba 1982: 23, Bio Bigou 1990).

18 However, the precise extent to which the *gesɛrɛ* Manding cultural heritage has helped to shape the contents of the Gaani remains unclear. We are far from claiming that the characteristics of the festival are wholly imported from outside Borgu.

19 It is clear that in other contexts he behaves as a normal griot and resorts to the king for help with feeding his family, etc. (Interview: W. *Tokura*) When younger W. *Tokura* accompanied the king on horseback during the Gaani procession (Orou Yorouba 1982: 21–40).

CHAPTER 17

Beyond the communal warmth: the poet as loner in Ewe oral tradition

Kofi Anyidoho

Song texts by major Ewe oral poets reveal the poets as loners, frequently celebrated and even envied but marginalised individuals, expressing their opinions from beyond the mainstream of their communities though eternally engaged with issues central to communal life. This persistent theme of the poet's ultimate loneliness points to a context of ambiguities and paradoxes in which society celebrates poetry but tends to ignore or even threaten the poet, a context in which the poet often laments the gift of song as a social handicap but then boasts about the power of song to transpose society's achievements and failures into monuments that may outlast material and social prestige. A close critique of the politics of song in Ewe oral tradition suggests that, at least in certain cases, the dominance of images of loneliness may be an essentially artistic, symbolic projection that need not reflect actual circumstances of the poet's life and social standing:

> I am on the world's extreme corner,
> I am not sitting in the row with the eminent
> But those who are lucky
> Sit in the middle and forget
> I am on the world's extreme corner
> I can only go beyond and forget.
> (Awoonor 1990: 49–50)[1]

These lines originally from Akpalu Vinoko and incorporated into the poem 'Songs of sorrow' by Kofi Awoonor, underscore the Ewe poet's view of himself as a loner, an often celebrated, even envied, but marginalised individual. Drawing partly on published texts and on material I have collected from on-going fieldwork, I hope to demonstrate that this theme of the poet's ultimate loneliness is, indeed, persistent in Ewe oral tradition, and that it carries implications and consequences worth examining in some detail. Much of the essay is a critique of this recurrent claim of the poet's loneliness and isolation from the communal circle. In particular, I examine certain possible explanations for this sense of isolation, dwelling at some length on a number of special demands on the poet as a professional verbal artist that confer privileges as well as exact severe obligations. The poet as a critical assessor of human relations is often engaged in a fluctuating situation of conflict and reconciliation with various individuals and social groups whom the poet sees as possessors of certain forms of power or influence from which the poet often feels isolated, if not alienated. What precisely is the nature of the poet's power over society? What are the kinds of power that the poet combats in song?

My central point of reference is the Akpalu and other song traditions, with special attention to the lives of the poets, on the one hand, and on the other, to those songs in which the poets reflect upon the implications of their career as artists. The material available to me suggests that in certain instances at least, the dominance of images of loneliness and powerlessness may indeed be essentially an artistic, symbolic representation and nothing more. The case of Akpalu, for instance, is especially instructive, in the light of his own persistent claims and the general view already established in available literature that he must have been the loneliest and the saddest of men.

OF SOLITUDE: THE POET AS A SOUL APART

In a summing-up chapter on studies of the artist in African tradition, Roy Sieber observes that 'In several of the papers the artist is characterized by a distinctive status, or social distance from the rest of the group' (1973: 430). He wonders whether such 'status is based on his actions or on his role, i.e. is it achieved or ascribed' (pp. 430–1). In Ewe oral tradition we may begin to understand the nature of the poet's 'distinctive status' and his relative isolation from the social group by first turning our attention to the fundamental belief, shared by both poet and society, about the origins of artistic creativity, or 'the gift of songs'.

There is hardly any Ewe poet who does not acknowledge Sé or the Creator God as the source of the gift of songs. Akpalu tells us: 'I was made by a Great God / I was made together with other poets / . . . The song of the drum / I do not sing it merely' (Awoonor 1974: 42). Dunyo puts it even more forcefully and with certain significant elaborations:

It is in the hands of destiny
our life is in the hands of the Creator . . .
He gave me nothing
not even good looks;
so the rich ones howl in the lanes
proclaiming their wealth . . .
Dunyo says I know not what to do
My Creator gave me songs.
I will not refuse them
I receive them with both hands.
(Awoonor 1974: 56)

The first and significant point here is the concept of the gift of songs as a sacred obligation. Such an understanding is crucial to the sense of total devotion with which most Ewe poets pursue their calling. We may in this case compare them to traditional priests, who, like poets, must carry on their sacred obligation, in spite of a life of suffering and self-denial that such obligations may impose. This comparison with priests will prove useful later in our consideration of a major complication of the poet's life and career. But first we must take note of the evidence of the poets themselves – their insistence that given a choice they would gladly do without the gift of song. They often claim that despite their own desire to lead a 'normal' life, song possesses them as a deity demanding full worship.

The singer Tayibor of Atiavi, in one song, sees her gift in the image of a very demanding deity known as Agbosu. In another song she travels to far away Kpoga in the Republic of Togo for the master-diviners there to seek out the proper origins and true identity of her god of song. They inform her it is an old ancestral deity, and that it is her turn to serve as chief priestess who will pass it on to posterity. Another major singer, Domegbe of Wheta, complains of how he 'never aspired to take to song' but now finds that 'Song is dragging him to trial before the town' and causing 'fear to sink into his flesh' (Anyidoho 1980: 58). And the singer Atsubota of Alakple typically begins her performances with a formal song of invocation which is at the same time a protest:

This song is disturbing me
This Agoha is harassing me
It was Akpalu who once said
Agoha is not an easy thing to sing.[2]

Another song of invocation by Atsubota may lead us into an even better understanding of the apparent resistance that these poets express towards the gift of song:

> Song is breaking loose on me
> I'm lost in thought, I'm scared ...
> Let Atsubota know song is breaking loose [on her]
> The songsters are scattered, I'm scared
> I have no one behind me, and I must be *heno*[3]
> I'm all alone, and I must be *heno*
> I have no headkerchief, and I must be *heno*
> I have no cloth on me, and I must be *heno*.

The last lines of this song point out at least one reason why the poet is so worried and unwilling to take up song. It would appear that the *heno*'s career deprives her of the opportunity to acquire wealth. The point is taken up by Tayibor in a song in which she regrets how, unlike her peers, *Sé* endows her with nothing but song:

> Agoha is not wealth,
> I'll sing it, it turns to cloth for me to wear.
> I keep singing it, hunger also keeps killing me.
> My people, please cook some food for me to eat.

Both Akpalu and Domegbe suggest that though they tried in their lives to acquire some wealth by engaging in various occupations, not one attempt yielded any gains (Nayo, n.d.: 25; Anyidoho 1980: 56). Both singers introduce us to the Ewe concept of *aya*, a kind of pre-destined poverty and misery (Anyidoho 1980). The argument seems to be that because the deity of songs insists on full attention from the devotee, it ensures that the *heno* prospers at nothing else, especially in the acquisition of material wealth, lest the *heno* loses concentration or, worse, abandons the god of songs in the search for worldly pleasures.

It is against this background that we must consider the following observation:

I was struck by the discovery that each poet within the tradition is a distinct individual, propelled by a deep sense of loneliness and an overwhelming ennui that are the burdens of all true poets. (Awoonor, 1974: 2)

Awoonor further suggests that Akpalu in particular 'is a good example of the poet as a man apart, plagued by a powerful sense of solitude'. I demonstrate later that, to some extent at least, Akpalu's claims of solitude and of poverty and low social status may not accord entirely with the facts of his life, though such claims do make sense within the framework of his poetic career.

It is important that we move the poets out of the domain of the sacred and situate them within the framework of a secular social dynamic. Once we do this a somewhat different understanding begins to emerge about their claims of isolation from the community. The gift of songs may indeed have a divine origin as the poets tell us, but in its manifestations, the gift engages both poet and the immediate society in an interactive process that calls for more than religious interpretation or evaluation. This is where we may talk of the politics of the power of song. It has already been suggested that, at one level, the poet's sense of isolation can be defined with reference to social, political and, especially, economic status. In this regard, we find that the poet's isolation, whether real or fictive, becomes a moral justification for keeping a critical searchlight on the rest of society. For whatever reasons, such a searchlight is often, though not exclusively, directed at the activities or behaviour of those who have access to certain forms of power.

POWER BEYOND POWER

My song came from the Creator's house
simmering in my head.
Please, I say gently.
There is something beyond
whose leg is larger than the hippo.
I will be mute; let someone abuse me
then I will tell it to him.
                              (Awoonor 1974: 57)

In the above words we find that the poet Komi Ekpe not only accepts his gift of song, but actually boasts of it as a source of power over those who seek to discredit him. And yet it is this same poet, earlier in the same song, who complains that his creator has cheated him by endowing him with no worthy gift, 'not even good looks'. It has been suggested that society's views of and attitude towards the poet are often ambivalent (Merriam 1973: 266–72). We must now add that the poets are themselves even more ambivalent about their gift of songs. Regret often alternates with joy, lamentation with celebration, curses with boasts or self-congratulation. Such ambivalence tends to make it difficult to achieve a satisfactory classification of song texts into clear-cut categories, say, laments or praise songs or songs of abuse. Komi Ekpe laments his fate in one song as 'the orphan left in the village lanes'; in the very next song he swears an oath to be true to the voice of his god of songs:

> When he wants to say it,
> they say do not say it.
> But I say I will say it
> and die upon my saying it.
> Komi Ekpe will persist
> and die in song.
> (Awoonor 1974: 94–5)

In the final analysis it is perhaps in this moral courage to stand by the truth that we may find one of the most important sources of the poet's often-acknowledged threat to powerful individuals and groups in society. It is important to note in this regard that the poets of Ewe tradition with whom we are concerned here rarely, if ever, play the role of court poets. Another important factor that makes it easier for these poets to maintain their independence of judgement is the fact that in Ewe tradition it is rare to find poets who try to make a living by their songs. The poets referred to here are professional artists only in the sense of the seriousness with which they devote themselves to their careers as artists. For their living, they each turn to any of the occupations open to members of their community – farming, trading, fishing, etc. And if we find so much lament among them over song as a career of poverty, it is precisely because by devoting so much time to song without any direct and reliable economic gains from it, they are found to have little time and energy left for their normal economic activities. This problem of divided but unequal attention to art as art and to 'gainful employment' may be largely responsible for the situation described by Awoonor as follows:

But there is also a traditional suspicion that it is men who are very lazy, who shun work and are stunningly handsome that make good poets. They are thus, unless crowned with great success like Akpalu, not considered as very serious-minded people who can be relied upon in moments of great crises and action. Most poet-cantors are therefore plagued by ennui and a deep feeling that they are not in the mainstream of the human family. They make neither great farmers nor great fishermen; and in a society where leaders are men of measurable success, poet-cantors, even though they may be respected, are never among the aristocracy of leaders. (Awoonor 1974: 19)

Perhaps it is just as well that the poets are not found among the aristocracy of leaders. In such a position of secular power and privilege, they may have the greatest difficulty keeping up their loyalty to the voice of their god of songs, to truth beyond political or personal convenience. Paradoxically, their distance from 'the corridors of power' confers on them that other power of the critical assessor. Thus in one song Komi Ekpe can look back upon the wealthy ones with a sense of personal sorrow, perhaps envy:

> You are lucky,
> Fate planted your grinding stone under a tree
> No earthly harm ever touches you.
>   (Awoonor 1974: 89)

But he can in the same breath say of himself: 'Komi Ekpe has become the leper-animal, / He fears no living man.' Precisely because the poet has perhaps tasted all the sorrows of life, he has nothing left to dread. This makes it possible for the poet to look society full in the face and claim the right to speak the truth, however unpleasant. And society is obliged to listen, even if it is with embarrassment or in anger. After all, as Atsubota tells us 'When Ear is there / You do not whisper into Nose.'

THE POET'S ARROW AND ITS TARGETS

What are the powers the poets do combat with in their songs? Perhaps it should come as no surprise that one of the most frequent victims of the poet's anger is none other than the god of songs or even the Creator God himself. Komi Ekpe expresses his displeasure with the Creator in words of shocking frankness:

> The Creator sent me along this way;
> I am all alone. He is not very wise.
> I joined a cult whose shrines I cannot build. . .
> If I say something please understand it.
> I was about to sing so I called my Creator in abuse.
> Slowly, I shall go home.
> I shall question him closely
> For he knows not that I shiver
> from companion's cold.
> My enemies, I beg you,
> Do not eat salt till your heart hurts
> I will die soon. And this town will be empty
> for you to crawl over one another.
> Questioners, what ancient laws did I break?
>   (Awoonor 1974: 86)

It is significant that Komi Ekpe names the drum he founded as 'Questioners'. His poetic bow and arrow are loaded with heavy questions, gods and humans as equal targets. Indeed, 'If Ear is there /

You do not whisper into Nose'. Who is better deserving of giving ear to his complaints about life's sorrows than the owner of life himself? The poet Domegbe may not have the vitriolic tongue of Ekpe, but his own accusation against the Creator is no less direct:

> I say she tricked me off into the world
> Domegbe says his Sé tricked him off into the world.
> She gave me a basket to go to the stream.
> I should return with water and receive fortune.
> No basket holds water
> And life's good things are lost to me.
>
> (Anyidoho 1980: 62)

One of the most problematic areas of the poets' social relations as reflected in their songs has to do with the family – the immediate family, the extended family and the human family. And here also, the general attitude is one of ambivalence. The poets often acknowledge and indeed praise and celebrate the reassuring warmth of the family circle. And yet, almost as often, we encounter bitter criticism and denunciation of family members. Perhaps it is too much to expect all members of the family always to be sympathetic and helpful. In a song credited to Dzogbede of Exi, we are told that a family is like cow meat; you must bite into it to determine its true taste: some parts delicious, but know that some parts are bitter. Atsubota suggests that 'The death you die, it comes from a relative / The life you possess, it comes from a relative.' All the poets understand that because your relatives are the closest to you, your prosperity or misery depends on them more than on anyone else. Consequently, some of their bitterest words are reserved for kinsfolk who default on their obligation to share their warmth with the rest of the family, including the poets, of course.

The poets' own propensity towards unfavourable assessment of human behaviour is in itself an eternal threat to family harmony. Relatives expect the poets to spare them the sharp arrows of exposure to public ridicule and censure. But the poets are often unable to keep to themselves their knowledge of messy family secrets. Against expectations of family loyalty, one poet may protest: 'I am not a sheep when hurt / Groans in its stomach to death' (Awoonor 1980: 51). And in giving voice to ill-treatment from relatives, the poets are further alienated from the family circle. No matter what injury the poet may have suffered, it should be very hard for the relative not to react with further hostility to such denunciation as we find in one of Tayibor's most popular songs:

Some bird has snatched the Eagle
A bird with name unknown has caught Eagle
And dropped it among vultures
I have gone astray
The human being is a source of fear for me.
   I insist it serves you right
   My mother's people, it serves you right.
   I thought we were kith and kin
   Your parents are dead
   The survivors with too much foolishness
   Keep messing the family up.
   Just tell me where I came from.

Reaction of relatives to such contempt and insult can sometimes be extreme. Probably the best-known case in Ewe tradition is that of Akpalu, who was reportedly taken by relatives to the highest court of arbitration in Anlo, charged with character assassination, and challenged to give up song unless he could stop his insults (Sheshie 1973: 7–9). The court was unable to impose any injunction, but the fact that the poet was dragged to court by those he thought should have offered him protection left great bitterness in him towards his family. His songs are filled with many hard words for unspecified relatives. And the very name Akpalu, which he is said to have adopted early in life as a result of personal misery within an uncle's household, remains a major poetic symbol for his sense of isolation from the warmth of the family circle. In its full recitation, the name paints a picture of the poet as one for whom only improperly cooked food is reserved. And in order to get even such food, his relatives must yell at him 'over the fence' to come into the homestead. Clearly the poet locates himself outside the family circle, beyond the protective fence, abandoned to the cold and misery that come from lack of human warmth.[4]

The impression may have been created that the works of these poets reflect nothing but bitterness towards the family and a sense of alienation from it. This is far from the case. Indeed, for many of these poets perhaps their greatest joy in life is the support they can at least sometimes count on from relatives. Of the poets I have worked with none sings more often of the joy of family warmth than Atsubota. Almost all the poets make a particular point about identifying the most dependable of all relatives, and that is *dadavi*, a 'mother's child', apparently considered as the closest of family members. Some of the most moving laments in Ewe tradition are songs dedicated to the memory of close relatives, especially 'mother's children'. One of the groups I have been working with, the Haikotu Drum of Wheta

(Anyidoho 1983a) has in its corpus a favourite song of the type they call *nuxlõmeha*, a song of consolation and advice, in this case composed by their lead poet Do Kligu, following the death of Adato, another poet and member of the group. It is meant as a song that expresses the group's condolences to Adato's surviving brother, Agbadua. In this song the poet captures not only the pain of death but also the irreplaceable nature of the loss of 'a mother's child' to death:

> Adato should have been alive
> To be a brother to Agbadua
> So they can live as one mother's children
> One of them had any worries
> He would confide his sorrow in the other
> But see what death has come to do! . . .
> > Adato became an egg
> > That fell upon the rocks for his parents
> > There is no way to pick it up . . .
> > I would sing and die upon my song.

We can also cite the wealthy and the politically powerful as frequent targets of attack from the poets. Many of these attacks end with a reminder that wealth and power may be great, but they have no influence over death. And in death all are made equal. Akpalu reminds the mighty and the proud that their pride is good but only for termites. Atsubota is content to keep worshipping her god of songs though she remains poor, for, after all:

> The death of an owner of wealth is no different
> We are all going to the same place
> No one died and was buried in the sky.

Even with poets who operate mainly within the dirge tradition associated with Akpalu, one sometimes encounters very pointed political satire in their songs. Akpalu has a song that dates back to the Second World War in which he wondered about the wisdom of world leaders who seemed to take special pleasure in inflicting misery and death on the human family. In the face of acute shortages of the most basic needs, the poet asked for no more than a box of matches, so that ordinary people could light a fire to cook their meagre meals. This image of the box of matches that enables people to cook the meal of life, strikes a sharp and ironic contrast with the guns and bombs of war and their capacity to bring death to the human family. One of the most pointed satirical commentaries on political leadership at the local level may be seen in another well-known Tayibo song:

I made one song for the Anlos
They are all whimpering in their rooms
Just sing it out, sing it out
And ask for explanation
You lying crooks

I say I saw it and I bear witness
My people I saw it and I bear witness
My grandfather Amamu himself
Was a royal spokesman in days of old
He was still alive when I was born
Kponyo is my chief witness in Adina.

This one gets up and claims he is King
This child too gets up and claims he is King
Those snoring grandfathers of yours
always sprawled in depths of their rooms
Never once would they come to the King's court
Here are their children pushing fingers into my face.

In sharp contrast to such political satire, we find many songs in which the target group is identified as *dzoduametowo*, 'those who deal in evil medicine'. This is one group the poets must handle with great care. These are people who stand for death. They would use their knowledge of the occult to bring death to an often innocent person. So that openly to take them to task in song is to invite death. The point is made by Do Kligu in one *Haikotu* song when he compares these evil men to a piece of bone stuck between your teeth; you remove it with the greatest care, lest the toothpick too breaks and gets stuck between the teeth. This is where an important complication arises for the poet's dedication to truth and social justice. Must one keep mute over evil, for fear of personal harm?

As suggested earlier, the comparison between the poet and the priest is more than merely fortuitous. In a sense, the poet is a priest who must exorcise or at least expose evil wherever it appears in society. Like the true exorcist the poet can only take on *dzoduametowo* at great personal risk. There are hardly any of these evil ones who are not afraid of public exposure. Given the poets' readiness to expose anyone who threatens society, it is understandable that one finds such deep mutual suspicion between the two groups. As Tayibo suggests in one song, the *dzoduameto* is most anxious to get rid of the poet:

The day *Sé* appointed for me
That day is nowhere near
See how *Dzotowo* are rushing me off.

In order to get rid of the poet, they would even try poison, as the singer suggests in the first part of the above song: she is offered a drink she suspects very much and so she prays for the drink to turn into water for her. The poets may not go out of their way to provoke the evil ones. But if the evil ones press their case too hard, the poets may be provoked into sharp retort: death will come anyhow, so why be afraid of those who threaten death?:

> Dunyo says the workers of evil medicine boasted
> that the poet shall accompany them to the land beyond
> That is no matter.
> Death and song are the same mother's children.
> He is not afraid of death.
>
> (Awoonor 1974: 64)

And Dunyo the poet assures the evil ones: 'I have taken no one's grave.'

THE DELIGHT OF TEARS

At this point we must pause and reconsider the ground so far covered in our assessment of the basic preoccupations of poets in Ewe oral tradition. The impression so far created seems to suggest that Ewe poets are not much given to the pleasures of life. I must hasten to correct such an impression. My focus so far has been largely determined by the basic theme marked out for consideration here – the theme of power, marginality and oral literature. My emphasis on poets from the dirge tradition may have served somewhat to over-dramatise the point about the poet's sense of isolation. Yet we may observe that even in their role as dirge singers, the poets are ultimately dedicating their songs to a sense of joy in the knowledge that beyond death, beyond human misery and beyond all vagaries of life, there is hope for everyone in the larger community of departed souls. And in any case, as miserable as this life may often become, it has pleasures all its own, pleasures such as the communal support offered by the living to those bereaved. What we have here is poetry's special power to give us joy and solace, to provide some security against feelings of isolation, powerlessness and helplessness. It is in this sense that the poets may speak of their dirges as songs of joy. One of Akpalu's most widely performed songs is one in which he celebrates his funeral drum as a drum of joy: he performs it and is mobbed by the people of Anlo. It may be 'a debtor-drum', but it is worth playing; it makes 'the poor forget their sorrows'. The point is picked up and elaborated upon in the following song by Agevodu of Togo:

> This drum's song I keep singing it
> So the children of sorrow can take heart
> Agevodu says I am sorrow's child
> For lack of a better place I'm here in Kodzogbe
> Stranded among the hawks and crows
> This drum's song I keep singing it
> So the children of sorrow can take heart.[5]

Outside the tradition of the lament or funeral song, poets are more likely to celebrate joy of life rather than express the sorrow of death. Indeed, a number of the poets cited here – especially Amega Dunyo, Komi Ekpe and Do Kligu – are acknowledged masters of the hilarious and provocative *halo*, or songs of abuse (Awoonor 1974: 86–7; 1975: 121–5; Anyidoho 1983b: 233–8). There are vast areas of Ewe oral literature, such as the contemporary popular forms like *bobobo* which are dominated by a mood of relative happiness about life's many pleasures. We may find however that even in these forms, the poets would often balance their profane expressions of joy against contemplative and philosophically enriching song texts. The voice may be proverbial, such as in the *bobobo* song that advises eternal vigilance against life's secret traps: 'A trap has caught Monkey / Creatures that walk the earth beware.' Another one assures us that no human is so worthless as not to be of any profit to relatives: 'I am a certain tree standing by the highway / I do not bear any fruit / Yet I provide some shade for my relatives.' A song from the Milé Novisi Akpese group from Ho compares the poet to the lake in the wilderness: the day it dries, the hunters go into mourning. So let it keep flowing on, so the hunters may always have a drink of cool water. A fourth and final example from popular song tradition is the following:

> I've killed buffalo, I've killed wild cow
> And a dead crab has bitten me
> Bitten me so real bad
> And crab is no great creature, just ordinary crab.
> I'll pluck its claw and throw it into the Volta
> So it flows far far away.

The poet here reminds us that no one should feel so helpless as to surrender to even the slightest threat to life. Perhaps this poet is coming to us from a personal experience of misfortune. More than likely, however, the poet may be sharing with us the lessons of someone else's, perhaps a fictive person's, hope beyond misfortune.

One of my instructors in my field research, Thomas Kumassah of Anyako, himself a poet, describes the poet as one who carries other people's burdens. He made the point in connection with his claim that Akpalu the poet is not quite the same as the man Akpalu he knew. He insisted that Akpalu indeed had known misery in his youth, but in his later years Akpalu's personal circumstances were much happier than he so often portrays them in his songs. For instance, the poet complains he is so poor he can hardly eat. Kumassah assures us that Akpalu the man was not as destitute as he or others have suggested (Sheshie 1973: 7-13). Kumassah himself as a young man once lived with Akpalu and worked for him. Akpalu for many years owned a boat and a net, and did reasonable business with fishing. Again, Akpalu the poet claims in song after song that he has no 'mother's child', and as if that is not enough he has lost his only child to death. We discover that Akpalu indeed lost one child, but there was at least one other who survived well beyond the dates of the composition of these songs, and may still be alive. At least there must have been one who lived long enough to give him a grand-daughter. This grand-daughter was still alive in 1988 when I visited Akpalu's homestead in Anyako. And the homestead was no worse than many other home-steads I found in Anyako. At least, it had not been taken over by termites, as Akpalu the poet was so certain would be the fate of his homestead.

It seems clear then that we must maintain a distinction between the poets and their art. There is no necessary and inevitable correspondence between the poetic self and the individual or social self, though the two must obviously interconnect. Many of our earlier evaluations of Akpalu, for instance, failed to make this separation and now stand faulted by new facts about Akpalu the man. But such separation would not make his songs any less relevant. If anything at all, it may help us to understand a fundamental problem in our assessment of the life and career of the poets in the oral tradition. It would appear that society has learnt to separate artist from art. Hence it is possible for society to place such a high premium on the art and leave the artists to their own devices in confronting life. Perhaps this sounds unpleasant, even ungrateful. The paradox is real and perplexing. But we must wonder whether the poets may not, after all, be teaching us one fundamental lesson of life. In order fully to savour the pleasures of life, we need to taste a good sampling of many of its sorrows. And if our personal circumstances are such that we are shielded from the worst of life's sorrows, we can at least benefit from other people's experience. That may be the most valuable lesson of all. We do not have to die ourselves in order to learn all there is to know about life and death. Ewe oral tradition, like that of the Bala, has learnt to take the work of poets seriously, even if the poets are not always properly compensated:

Without musicians [poets] a village is incomplete. People want to be happy, and music making [poetry] is associated with happiness. Without musicians [poets] a proper funeral cannot take place ... Musicians [Poets] perform a variety of functions in village life which no one else can replace; life without them cannot be normal and it is not to be contemplated seriously. (Merriam 1973: 270).

The man Domegbe in many of his songs offers us some of the most remarkable images of the poet as a loner. But Domegbe as poet is well aware that though he is no centrepiece of the communal circle, it is his song that keeps the circle alive:

> I am the ailing frog
> But I shall play the drum for Kings to come and dance . . .

> > I say I'll sing and it'll be a proverbial act
> > The drum's song, I'll sing and it'll be a proverbial act.
> > The old leopard skin is exposed to the rains
> > But the spots are always there
> > The tree has shed all leaves;
> > It will once again be green
> > The children shall come to find great joy with me.

If the claim that life cannot be normal without the poet-musician sounds somewhat exaggerated, perhaps we only need to contemplate a world without the sound of music, a world without poetry's peculiar ability to give rhythmic intensity to our joys, its ability to lift our spirits above our many sorrows. Such a world, if indeed it is possible, must be the end of desire and dream, and the beginning of fear and endless fear. The Ewe poets' ultimate gift to their community is their unfailing ability to move even kings into dance, though they themselves may be as handicapped as the ailing frog. It is also their ability, through the creative power of the human voice, to paint back on to a drying tree those green leaves and flowers that carry the promise of future fruits. Ewe traditional thought defines life in the image of *Kodzogbe*, a desert of poverty and misery. The poets in their songs create that essential oasis without which all travellers on life's road are doomed to endless hallucination and to eventual death by dehydration. But it is also the lot of the poet, it would appear, to suffer the lonely life of the pilgrim who must keep vigil over life's fortunes and misfortunes.[6]

NOTES

1 See Awoonor's own critique of the poem 'Songs of Sorrow' in Awonoor (1975: 202–8).
2 Unless otherwise indicated, illustrative texts are my own translations from unpublished field recordings.
3 *Heno* is an Ewe word for composer of songs, that is, a poet-musician.
4 For a full account of Akpalu's sorrows as a youth in an uncle's home, see the introduction to Sheshie (1973).
5 Song text from an unpublished collection made in the field by Dallas Galvin and Jeremy Harding. Translation by Kofi Anyidoho.
6 I am grateful to the faculty and staff and students of the Africana Studies and Research Center, Cornell University, for their comradeship during my stay with them as a 1990–1 Faculty Visiting Fellow under the Rockefeller Foundation-sponsored programme in African Cultural Studies. Fieldwork on which this paper is based was partly sponsored by the Research and Conferences Committee, University of Ghana.

Bibliography

Abdulkadir, Dandatti. 1975. 'The role of an oral singer in Hausa/Fulani society: a case study of Mamman Shata', unpublished Ph.D dissertation, University of Indiana.

Abokor, Axmed Ali. 1990. *Somali Pastoral Work Songs: The Poetic Voice of the Politically Powerless*, Uppsala: EPOS, Research Programme on Environmental Policy and Society, Department of Social and Economic Geography, University of Uppsala.

Abrahams, Roger. 1972. 'Personal power and social restraint in the definition of folklore', in A. Paredes and R. Bauman (eds.) *Toward New Perspectives in Folklore*, Austin: University of Texas Press.

Abu-Lughod, Lila. 1986. *Veiled Sentiments: Honour and Poetry in a Bedouin Society*, Berkeley: University of California Press.

Afigbo, A. E. 1972. *The Warrant Chiefs: Indirect Rule in South-Eastern Nigeria, 1891–1929*, Lagos: Longman Nigeria.

Agovi, J. K. 1973. 'Preliminary observations on the modern short story and the African folktale tradition', *Research Review* 9: 123–9.

Agovi, K. E. 1979. 'Kundum: festival drama among the Ahanta-Nzema of South-West Ghana', unpublished Ph.D thesis, Institute of African Studies, University of Ghana, Legon.

  1995. 'Theatre, law and order in pre-colonial Africa', in *Theatre and Politics in Africa*, UCLA: Department of Film and Theatre.

Ahmad, A. 1987. 'Jameson's rhetoric of Otherness and the "National Allegory"', *Social Text* 17: 3–25.

  1992. *In Theory: Classes, Nations, Literatures*, London: Verso.

Ahmad, Sa'idu Babura. 1986. 'Narrator as interpreter: stability and variation in Hausa tales', unpublished Ph.D dissertation, University of London.

Akegwure, P. O. 1978. 'The hero in Isoko heroic narratives', BA Honours essay, Department of English, University of Ibadan.

Alagoa, E. J. 1976. 'The Niger delta states and their neighbours to 1800', in J. F. Ajayi and Michael Crowder (eds.) *The History of West Africa*, vol. I, pp. 331–72, London: Longman.

Allen, J. van. 1987. '"Aba riots" or Igbo "women's war"?: ideology, stratification and the invisibility of women', in Nancy J. Hafkin and

Edna G. Bay (eds.) *Women in Africa: Studies in Social and Economic Change*, pp. 59–85, California: Stanford University Press.

Ames, David W. 1973. 'A sociocultural view of Hausa musical activity', in Warren L. D'Azevedo (ed.) *The Traditional Artist in African Societies*, pp. 128–61, Bloomington and London: Indiana University Press.

Amselle, Jean-Loup. 1990. *Logiques métisses: anthropologie de l'identité en Afrique et ailleurs*, Paris: Editions Payot.

Anderson, Benedict. 1983. *Imagined Communities: Reflections on the Origin and Spread of Nationalism* (revised edn 1991), London: Verso.

Anene-Boyle, F. A. 1979. 'The hero in Ukwuani heroic narrative', BA Honours essay, Department of English, University of Ibadan.

Anyidoho, Kofi. 1980. 'Henoa Domegbe and his songs of sorrow', *The Greenfield Review* 8 (1/2): 54–64.

  1983a. 'The Haikotu Song and Dance Club of Wheta: a communal celebration of individual talent', in Kofi Anyidoho et al. (eds.) *Cross Rhythms: Occasional Papers in African Folklore*, pp. 179–92, Bloomington: Trickster Press.

  1983b. 'Oral Poetics and the tradition of verbal art in Africa', unpublished Ph.D thesis, University of Texas at Austin.

Asante, M. K. and Asante, K. W. (eds.) 1985. *African Culture: The Rhythms of Unity*, Connecticut and London: Greenwood Press.

Austen, Ralph A. 1992. 'The historical transformation of genres: Sunjata as panegyric, epic(s) and novel', paper contributed to the Conference on the Sunjata Epic, 13–15 November, Evanston: Institute for Advanced Study and Research in the African Humanities, Northwestern University.

Austin, J. L. 1962. *How To Do Things With Words*, Oxford University Press.

Awoonor, Kofi. 1974. *Guardians of the Sacred Word: Ewe Poetry*, New York: Nok Publishers.

  1975. *The Beast of the Earth*, New York: Doubleday Anchor Press.

  1980. 'Twenty songs of Vinoko Akpalu', *The Greenfield Review* 8 (1/2): 47–54.

Bagodo, Obarè Bouroubin. 1978. 'Le Royaume Borgou Wasangari de Nikki', unpublished mémoire de maîtrise, Cotonou: National University of Benin, Faculty of Letters, Arts and Humanities.

Bailey, F. G. 1983. *The Tactical Uses of Passion*, Ithaca: Cornell University Press.

Bakhtin, M. M. 1966. *Rabelais and his World*, Cambridge, Mass.: Massachusetts Institute of Technology Press.

  1981. *The Dialogic Imagination*, ed. Michael Holquist, trans. Caryl Emerson and Michael Holquist, Austin: University of Texas Press.

  1986. *Speech Genres and Other Late Essays*, Austin: University of Texas Press.

Bamony, P. 1984. 'Equilibre social et pouvoir chez les Lyela de la Haute Volta', *Anthropos* 79: 433–40.

Barber, Karin. 1986 'Radical conservatism in Yoruba popular plays', in E. Breitinger and R. Sander (eds.) *Drama and Theatre in Africa* (Bayreuth African Studies Series 7), pp. 5–32, University of Bayreuth.

  1991. *I Could Speak until Tomorrow: Oriki, Women, and the Past in a*

Yoruba Town (International African Library 7), Edinburgh University Press for the International African Institute.

Basden, G. T. 1921. *Among the Ibos of Nigeria*, London: Seeley Service.

Bauman, R. 1977. *Verbal Art as Performance*, Rowley: Newbury House.

1986. *Story, Performance and Event: Contextual Studies of Oral Narrative*, Cambridge University Press.

Bauman, R. and Briggs, C. L. 1990. 'Poetics and performance as critical perspectives on language and social life', *Annual Review of Anthropology* 19: 59–88.

Bauman, R. and Sherzer, J. (eds.) 1989. *Explorations in the Ethnography of Speaking* (2nd edn), Cambridge University Press.

Bayili, E. 1983. 'Les populations Nord-Nuna (Haute Volta) des origines à 1920', dissertation, University of Paris I.

Bazin, Jean. 1979, 'La Production d'un récit historique', *Cahiers d'études africaines* 73–6 (XIX1–4): 435–83.

1985, 'A chacun son Bambara', in Jean-Loup Amselle and Elikia M'Bokolo (eds.) *Au Cœur de l'ethnie: ethnies, tribalisme et état en Afrique*, pp. 87–127, Paris: Editions La Découverte.

Beattie, John. 1980. 'Representations of the self in traditional Africa', *Africa* 50 (3): 313–20.

Beinart, William. 1987. 'Amafelandawonye (the Die-hards): popular protest and women's movements in Herschel district in the 1920s', in William Beinart and Colin Bundy (eds.) *Hidden Struggles in Rural South Africa: Politics and Popular Movements in the Transkei and Eastern Cape 1890–1930*, pp. 222–69, Johannesburg: Ravan.

Belcher, Stephen Patterson IV. 1985. 'Stability and change: praise-poetry narrative traditions in the epics of Mali', unpublished Ph.D dissertation, Brown University.

Bell, R. T. 1976. *Sociolinguistics*, London: Batsford.

Bello, Gidado. 1976. 'Yabo, zuga da zambo a wakokin sarauta' (Praise, exhortation and ridicule in songs of the aristocracy), *Harsunan Nijeriya* 6: 21–34.

Ben-Amos, D. (ed.) 1976. *Folklore Genres*, Austin: University of Texas Press.

Ben-Amos, D. and Goldstein, K. S. (eds.) 1975. *Folklore: Performance and Communication*, The Hague: Mouton.

Besmer, F. E. 1971. 'Hausa court music in Kano, Nigeria', unpublished Ph.D dissertation, Columbia University.

Bio Bigou, L. B. 1990. *La Gani à Nikki*, Parakou: PARECAR.

Bird, Charles S. 1970. 'The development of Mandekan (Manding): a study of the role of extra-linguistic factors in linguistic change', in David Dalby (ed.) *Language and History in Africa*, pp. 146–59, London: Cass.

1992. 'The production and reproduction of Sunjata', paper contributed to the Conference on the Sunjata Epic, 13–15 November, Evanston: Institute for Advanced Study and Research in the African Humanities, Northwestern University.

Bird, Charles S. and Kendall, Martha B. 1980. 'The Mande hero: text and context', in Ivan Karp and Charles S. Bird (eds.) *Explorations in African*

Systems of Thought, pp. 13–26, Bloomington: Indiana University Press.

Birniwa, Haruna Abdullahi. 1987. 'Conservatism and dissent: a comparative study of NPC/NPN and NEPU/PRP political verse from ca. 1946 to 1983', unpublished Ph.D dissertation, University of Sokoto.

Bloch, M. (ed.) 1975. *Political Language and Oratory in Traditional Society*, London: Academic Press.

Bokwe, John Knox. 1914. *Ntsikana: The Story of an African Convert* (2nd edn), Lovedale Press.

Bonner, P. L. 1979. 'The 1920 black mineworkers' strike: a preliminary account', in Belinda Bozzoli (ed.) *Labour, Townships and Protest: Studies in the Social History of the Witwatersrand*, pp. 273–97, Johannesburg: Ravan.

Bosman, W. 1967. *A New and Accurate Description of the Coast of Guinea* (reprint), London: Cass.

Boyd, Jean. 1989. *The Caliph's Sister: Nana Asma'u (1793–1865) Teacher, Poet and Islamic Leader*, London: Cass.

Bradbury, R. E. 1967. *The Benin Kingdom and the Edo-Speaking Peoples of South-Western Nigeria*, London: International African Institute.

Bramoulle, A. 1950. 'Les Redevances coutumières dans le cadre de la chefferie supérieure de Nikki' (unpublished MS), Cotonou: Library of the Benin Centre for Scientific and Technical Research, uncatalogued.

Brenneis, Donald L. and Meyers, Fred (eds.) 1984. *Dangerous Words: Language and Politics in the Pacific*, New York University Press.

Bryant, A. T. 1929. *Olden Times in Zululand and Natal*, London: Longman Green.

Bulman, Stephen P. D. 1990. 'Interpreting Sunjata', unpublished Ph.D dissertation, Centre of West African Studies, University of Birmingham.

Burton, Richard. 1966a. *First Footsteps in East Africa* (reprint of 1856 edn with introduction and additional chapters by Gordon Waterfield), London: Routledge and Kegan Paul.

  1966b. *A Mission to Gelele, King of Dahomey* (first published 1864), New York: Frederick A. Praeger.

Calame-Griaule, G. and Görög-Karady, V. 1972. 'La Calebasse et le fouet: le thème des objets magiques en Afrique Occidentale', *Cahiers d'Etudes Africaines* 12: 12–75.

Callinicos, Luli. 1981. *Gold and Workers 1886-1924: A People's History of South Africa*, vol. I, Johannesburg: Ravan.

  1987. *Working Life 1886-1940: Factories, Townships, and Popular Culture on the Rand: A People's History of South Africa*, vol. II, Johannesburg: Ravan.

Camara, Sory. 1976. *Les Gens de la parole: essai sur la condition et le rôle des griots dans la société malinké*, Paris: Mouton.

  1978. 'Paroles de nuit ou l'univers imaginaire des relations familiales chez les Mandenka', unpublished dissertation, Paris: René Descartes University.

CEAP-Borgou. 1986. *Table ronde sur les origines de la Gaani, fête traditionnelle des Baatombu (Baribas)*, Parakou: Comité d'Etat d'administration de la province du Borgou.

Chama Cha Mapinduzi (CCM). 1988. *Programu ya Chama 1987–2002*, Dar es Salaam: Government Printers.

Charry, Eric. 1992. 'Music thought, history, and practice among the Mande of West Africa', unpublished Ph.D dissertation, University of Princeton.

Chimhundu, H. 1980. '*Shumo, Tsumo* and Socialization', *Zambezia* 8 (1): 37–51.

1987. 'Language, literature and sex sterotypes', paper presented at the Eighth PWPA Annual Conference, Siavonga, Zambia, 3–6 July.

1995. 'An assessment of the achievement of Zimbabwean writers in African languages', unpublished mimeograph.

Chubb, L. T. 1961. *Ibo Land Tenure*, Ibadan University Press.

Chukwuma, Helen. 1990. 'Place setting and historicity in Igbo oral tales', unpublished mimeograph.

Cissé, Diango and Massa Makan Diabété. 1970. *La Dispersion des mandeka*, Bamako: Editions populaires.

Cissé, Youssouf [Tata]. 1973. 'Signes graphiques, représentations, concepts et tests relatifs à la personne chez les Malinké et les Bambara du Mali', in *La Notion de personne en Afrique noire* (International Colloquia of the National Centre for Scientific Research 544), pp. 131–79, Paris: CNRS.

Cissé, Youssouf Tata and Wa Kamissoko. 1988. *La Grande geste du Mali*, vol. I, Paris: Karthala and ARSAN.

1991. *La Grande geste du Mali*, vol. II: *Soundjata, la gloire du Mali*, Paris: Karthala and ARSAN.

Clanchy, M. T. 1979. *From Memory to Written Record: England 1066–1307*, London: Edward Arnold.

Cope, Trevor. 1968. *Izibongo: Zulu Praise Poems*, Oxford University Press.

Coplan, David B. 1985. *In Township Tonight! South Africa's Black Music and Theatre*, Johannesburg: Ravan Press.

Crocker, J. C. 1977. 'The social functions of rhetorical forms', in J. D. Sapir and J. C. Crocker (eds.) *The Social Use of Metaphor: Essays on the Anthropology of Rhetoric*, pp. 33–66. Philadelphia: University of Pennsylvania Press.

Daba, Habib Ahmed. 1978. 'Hausa oral poetry: a case study of Dan Maraya Jos', unpublished MA dissertation, University of Khartoum.

1981. 'The case of Dan Maraya Jos: a Hausa poet', in U. N. Abalogu, G. Ashiwaju and R. Amadi-Tshiwala (eds.) *Oral Poetry in Nigeria*, pp. 209–29, Lagos: Nigeria Magazine.

Derive, J. 1978. 'Le chant de Kurubi à Kong', *Annales de l'université d'Abidjan* (series J, II, Oral Traditions): 85–114.

1980. 'La maison éclatée : quelques devinettes dioula de Kong', in G. Dumestre (ed.) *Recueil de littérature manding*, pp. 182–214, Paris: ACCT.

1984. 'Une Paillardise rituelle: chants de captifs dioula', *Cahiers de littérature orale* 15: 103–34.

1987a. 'Parole et pouvoir chez les Dioula de Kong', *Journal des Africanistes* 57 (1/2): 19–30.

1987b. *Le Fonctionnement sociologique de la littérature orale: l'exemple des Dioula de Kong (Côte d'ivoire)*, (Archives and documents, Human Sciences Collection), Paris: Institute of Ethnology.

1990. 'Gestion de la variabilité des récits historiques dans une communauté dioula', in V. Görög-Karady (ed.) *D'un conte à l'autre*, pp. 291–301, Paris: CNRS.

Derive, M. J. 1978. 'Chants de chasseurs dioula', *Annales de l'université d'Abidjan* (series J, II, Oral Traditions): 67–94.

1980. 'Bamori et Kowulen: chant de chasseurs de la région d'Odienné', in G. Dumestre (ed.) *Recueil de littérature manding*, pp. 74–107, Paris: ACCT.

Derive, M. J. and Diabaté, V. T. (eds.) 1977. *Table ronde sur les origines de Kong, Annales de l'université d'Abidjan* (series J, I, Oral Traditions).

Derive, M. J., Derive, J. and Barro, B. 1980. *Contes Dioula*, Abidjan: CEDA.

Diabaté [Diabété], Massa Makan. 1970a. *Janjon et autres chants populaires du Mali*, Paris: Présence Africaine.

1970b. *Kala Jata*, Bamako: Editions populaires.

1975. *L'Aigle et l'épervier, ou la geste de Sunjata*, Paris: Pierre Jean Oswald.

Diawara, Mamadou. 1990. *La Graine de la parole*, Stuttgart: Franz Steiner Verlag for the Frobenius-Institut.

1994. 'Production and reproduction: the Mande oral popular culture revisited by the electronic media', paper contributed to the Conference on Media, Popular Culture, and the Public in Africa, 29 April–May, Evanston: Institute for Advanced Study and Research in the African Humanities, Northwestern University.

Dinslage, S. 1986. *Kinder der Lyela: Kindheit und Jugend im kulturellen Wandel bei den Lyela in Burkina Faso*, Hohenschäftlarn: Renner.

Dorson, Richard. 1972. *Folklore: Selected Essays*, University of Chicago Press.

Drucker-Brown, Susan. 1984. 'Calendar and ritual: the Mamprusi case', *Systèmes de pensée en Afrique noire* 7: 57–85.

Dubb, A. A. 1966. 'Red and school: a quantitative approach', *Africa*, 36: 292–302.

Dubow, S. 1986. 'Holding "a just balance between white and black": The Native Affairs Department in South Africa c. 1920–33', *Journal of Southern African Studies*, 12 (2): 217–39.

1989. *Racial Segregation and the Origins of Apartheid in South Africa, 1919–36*, Basingstoke: Macmillan.

Dunglas, E. n.d. [c. 1947, drawing on information gathered in 1941–42] 'Le Royaume bariba de Nikki: étude historique' (unpublished MS), Cotonou: Library of the Benin Centre for Scientific and Technical Research, uncatalogued.

Duperray, A. M. 1984. 'Le gourounsi et les gourounsi', in E. Haberland (ed.) *Les Gourounsi de la Haute Volta* (Studien zur Kulturkunde 72), Wiesbaden: Steiner.

Durán, Lucy. 1989. 'Djelimousso: women of Mali', *Folk Roots* 75: 34–9.

1993. 'Savannah sex wars', *The Wire* 114: 42–4.

1994. 'Jaliya: the art of the Manding jalis', in *The Rough Guide to World Music*.

Duval, M. 1985. *Un totalitarisme sans état: essai d'anthropologie politique à partir d'un village burkinabé*, Paris: L'Harmattan.

Ebeogu, Afam. 1989. 'Of progress and distortions: a pattern in the panegyric ethos in Igbo life and culture', *Lore and Language* 8 (1): 81–94.

Egharevba, Jacob. 1968. *A Short History of Benin*, Ibadan University Press.

Egudu, R. N. 1973. *The Calabash of Wisdom and Other Igbo Stories*, New York and Lagos: Nok Publishers.

Ejiofor, Lambert U. 1981. *Dynamics of Igbo Democracy*, Ibadan University Press for The University of Nigeria Press, Nsukka.

Fabian, J. 1986. *Language and Colonial Power: The Appropriation of Swahili in the Former Belgian Congo 1880–1938*, Cambridge University Press.

  1990. 'Presence and representation: the Other and anthropological writing', *Critical Inquiry* 16: 753–71.

Fanon, F. 1967. *Black Skin White Masks*, New York: Grove Press.

Fardon, Richard (ed.) 1985. *Power and Knowledge: Anthropological and Sociological Approaches*, Edinburgh: Scottish Academic Press.

February, Vernon. 1988. *And Bid Him Sing: Essays in Literature and Cultural Domination*, London and New York: Kegan Paul.

Finnegan, R. 1967. *Limba Stories and Story-telling*, Oxford: Clarendon Press.

  1970. *Oral Literature in Africa*, Oxford University Press.

  1977. *Oral Poetry, its Nature, Significance and Social Context*, Cambridge University Press.

  1988. *Literacy and Orality: Studies in the Technology of Communication*, Oxford: Basil Blackwell.

  1992. *Oral Traditions and the Verbal Arts: A Guide To Research Practices*, London: Routledge.

Furniss, Graham. 1977. 'Some aspects of modern Hausa poetry: themes, style and values with special reference to the "Hikima" poetry circle in Kano', unpublished Ph.D dissertation, University of London.

  1988a. 'The language of praise and vilification: two poems by Muhammadu Audi of Gwandu about Abubakar, emir of Nupe', in Graham Furniss and Philip J. Jaggar (eds.) *Studies in Hausa Language and Linguistics*, pp. 181–201, London: Kegan Paul International in association with the International African Institute.

  1988b. 'Money, marriage and the young as issues in modern Hausa poetry', *African Languages and Cultures* 1 (1): 45–60.

  1989. 'Typification and evaluation: a dynamic process in rhetoric', in Karin Barber and P. F. de M. Farias (eds.) *Discourse and Its Disguises: the Interpretation of African Oral Texts* (CWAS Interdisciplinary African Studies Series 1), pp. 24–33, Birmingham: CWAS.

  1991. 'Burlesque in Hausa: "And my text for today is food"', said Mr Matches', in Paul Baxter and Richard Fardon (eds.) *Voice, Genre, Text: Anthropological Essays in Africa and Beyond*, Special Issue of the *Bulletin of the John Rylands University Library of Manchester* 73 (3): 37–62.

Gaidzanwa, R. B. 1985. *Images of Women in Zimbabwean Literature*,

Harare: College Press.

1987. 'Reading between the lines: race, class and gender in Zimbabwean literature', seminar paper, Department of Sociology, University of Zimbabwe.

Gaitskell, Deborah. 1982. '"Wailing for purity": prayer unions, African mothers and adolescent daughters, 1912–1940', in Shula Marks and Richard Rathbone (eds.) *Industrialisation and Social Change in South Africa: African Class Formation, Culture, and Consciousness, 1870-1930*, pp. 338–57, London: Longman.

Galli, Silvano. 1983. 'Story-telling among the Anyi Bona', in Kofi Anyidoho et al. (eds.) *Cross Rhythms*, pp. 13–42, Bloomington: Trickster Press.

Geertz, C. 1980. *Negara: The Theatre State in Nineteenth-century Bali*, Princeton University Press.

1983. *Local Knowledge: Further Essays in Interpretive Anthropology*, New York: Basic Books.

Gidley, C. G. B. 1967. 'Yan kamanci – the craft of the Hausa comedians', *African Language Studies* 8: 52–81.

1974. '*Karin magana* and *azanci* as features of Hausa sayings', *African Language Studies* 15: 81–96.

1975. 'Roko: a Hausa praise crier's account of his craft', *African Language Studies* 16, 93–115.

Giray-Saul, E. 1989. 'Jula oral narratives in Bobo–Dioulasso: continuity, recreation and transcultural communication (Burkina Faso)', unpublished Ph.D dissertation, University of Indiana.

Goffman, Erving. 1974. *Frame Analysis: An Essay in the Organization of Experience*, New York: Harper Colophon.

Gombe, J. 1981. 'A study of the language used in certain purposeful gatherings in Shona culture', unpublished MPhil. dissertation, University of Zimbabwe.

Goody, J. 1986. *The Logic of Writing and the Organization of Society*, Cambridge University Press.

Görög, V., Platiel, S., Rey-Hulman, D. and Seydou, C. 1980. *Histoires d'Enfants Terribles (Afrique Noire)*, Paris: Maisonneuve and Larose.

Görög-Karady, V. 1976. *Contes Bambara du Mali*, Paris: Publications Orientalistes de France.

Görög-Karady, V. and Gérard Meyer. 1988. *Images féminines dans les contes africains (Aire culturelle manding)*, Paris: Conseil International de la Langue Francaise (CILF).

Green, Margaret M. 1948. *Igbo Village Affairs, Chiefly with Reference to the Village of Umueke Agbaja* (reprint 1964), London: Cass.

Grillo, R. 1989. 'Anthropology, language, politics', in R. Grillo (ed.) *Social Anthropology and the Politics of Language*, pp. 1–24, London: Routledge.

Gunner, E. 1984. 'Ukubonga nezibongo, Zulu praising and praises', unpublished Ph.D dissertation, University of London.

1986. 'A dying tradition? African oral literature in a contemporary context', *Social Dynamics* 12 (1): 31–8.

Gunner, L. and M. Gwala. 1991. *Musho! Zulu Popular Praises*, East Lansing: Michigan State University Press.

Gyekye, K. 1975. 'Philosophical relevance of Akan proverbs', *Second Order: An African Journal of Philosophy* 4 (2): 45–53.

1978. 'An African concept of philosophy (wisdom)', *Studia Africana: An International Journal of Africana Studies* 1 (2).

Haasbroek, J. (ed.) 1988. *Uyavaya Hwenduri dzeChinyakare*, Gwelo: Mambo Press.

Haasbroek, J., Majaya, E., et al. 1978. *Nduri dzoRudo*, Gwelo: Mambo Press.

Hampaté Ba, Amadou. 1973. 'La Notion de personne en Afrique noire', in *La Notion de personne en Afrique noire* (International Colloquia of the National Centre of Scientific Research 544), pp. 181–92, Paris: CNRS.

Hamutyinei, M. A. and Plangger, A. B. 1974. *Tsumo-Shumo: Shona Proverbial Lore and Wisdom*, Gwelo: Mambo Press.

Hanks, W. F. 1989a. 'Texts and textuality', *Annual Review of Anthropology* 18: 95–127.

1989b. 'Metalanguage and the pragmatics of deixis', unpublished MS.

Haring, Lee. 1994. 'Introduction: the search for grounds in African oral tradition', *Oral Tradition* 9 (1): 3–22.

Heine, B. 1970. *Status and Use of African Lingua Francas*, Munich: Weltforum Verlag.

Henderson, R. N. 1972. *The King in Everyman: Evolutionary Trends in the Onitsha Ibo-Speaking Society and Culture*, New Haven: Yale University Press.

Herman, Edward S. and Chomsky, Noam. 1990. *Manufacturing Consent: The Political Economy of the Mass Media*, New York: Pantheon Books.

Hiskett, M. 1977. *An Anthology of Hausa Political Verse: Hausa Texts Edited and Annotated*, London: Department of Africa, SOAS.

Hobsbawm, E. and Ranger, T. (eds.) 1983. *The Invention of Tradition*, Cambridge University Press.

Hodgson, Janet. 1980. *Ntsikana's Great Hymn: A Xhosa Expression of Christianity in the Early 19th Century Eastern Cape*, Centre for African Studies, University of Cape Town.

Hodza, Aaron C. 1984. *Ugo Hwamadzinza AvaShona*, Harare: Longman.

Hodza, Aaron C. and Fortune, George. 1979. *Shona Praise Poetry*, Oxford University Press.

Hofmeyr, I. 1994. *We Spend our Years as a Tale that is Told: Oral Historical Narrative in a South African Chiefdom*, Johannesburg and London: Wits University Press, Heinemann and James Currey.

Hollis, Martin. 1985. 'Of masks and men', in Michael Carrithers, Steven Collins, and Steven Lukes (eds.) *The Category of the Person: Anthropology, Philosophy, History*, pp. 217–33, Cambridge University Press.

Holt, Basil. 1954. *Joseph Williams and the Pioneer Mission to the South-eastern Bantu*, Lovedale Press.

Honko, L. 1976. 'Genre theory revisited', *Studia Fennica* 20: 20–5.

1989. 'Folkloristic theories of genre', *Studia Fennica* 33: 13–28.

Hussein, E. 1975. 'On the development of theatre in East Africa', unpublished Ph.D dissertation, Humboldt University.

Hymes, Dell. 1975. 'Breakthrough into performance', in D. Ben-Amos and K. S. Goldstein (eds.) *Folklore: Performance and Communication*, The Hague: Mouton.

Ifemesia, Chieka, n.d., (c. 1979/80). *Traditional Humane Living Among the Igbo: A Historical Perspective*, Enugu: Fourth Dimension Publishers.

Innes, Gordon. 1974, *Sunjata: Three Mandinka Versions*, London: University of London, SOAS.

Iroaganachi, John. 1973. *Oka Mgba na Akuko Ifo Ndi Ozo*, Lagos: Longman.

Iwe, Anya. 1963. *Akuko Ifo Ufodu Kwesiri Ka Umu Mmadu Mara* (facsimile reprint, University Publishing Company, Onitsha, 1976), Aba: African Literature Bureau.

Iworisha, Magdalen E. O. 1978. 'The form and function of Oguta folktales', BA long essay, Department of English, University of Nigeria, Nsukka.

Izevbaye, D. S. 1971. 'Politics in Nigerian poetry', *Présence Africaine* 78: 143–67.

Jakobson, Roman. 1960. 'Linguistics and poetics', in Thomas Sebeok (ed.) *Style in Language*, pp. 350–77, Cambridge, Mass.: Massachusetts Institute of Technology Press.

1963. *Essais de linguistique générale*, 2 vols., Paris: Editions de Minuit.

Jameson, Fredric. 1981. *The Political Unconscious: Narrative as a Socially Symbolic Act*, London: Methuen.

Jansen, Jan. 1993. 'The Sunjata epic and the Jabaté griots of Kela: a preliminary ethnography' (unpublished MS).

Jason, H. 1986. 'Genre in folk literature: reflections on some questions and problems', *Fabula* 27: 167–94.

Jobson, Richard. 1968. *The Golden Trade* (1st edn 1623), London: Pall Mall.

Johnson, J. W. 1974. *Heellooy Heelleellooy: The Development of the Heello in Modern Somali Poetry*, Bloomington, Indiana: Research Center for the Language Sciences.

Johnson, J. W. (transl.) 1986. *The Epic of SonJara, a West African Tradition. Text by FaDigi Sisòkò. Analytical Study and Translation*, Bloomington: Indiana University Press.

Jones Jackson, Patricia. 1987. *When Root Die: Endangered Traditions on the Sea Island*, Athens: University of Georgia Press.

Jordan, A. C. 1973. *Towards an African Literature: The Emergence of Literary Form in Xhosa*, Berkeley: University of California Press.

Kahari, G. P. 1986. *Aspects of the Shona Novel*, Gwelo: Mambo Press.

Kamlongera, C. 1989. *Theatre for Development in Africa with Case Studies from Malawi and Zambia*, Bonn: ZED.

Kendall, Martha B. 1982. 'Getting to know you', in David Parkin (ed.) *Semantic Anthropology*, (ASA monograph 22), pp. 197–209, London and New York: Academic Press.

King, Anthony V. 1969. 'Music at the court of Katsina: gangaa and kaakaakii', unpublished Ph.D dissertation, University of London.

1981. 'Form and functions in Hausa professional songs', in U. N. Abalogu,

G. Ashiwaju and R. Amadi-Tshiwala (eds.) *Oral Poetry in Nigeria*, pp. 118–35, Lagos: Nigeria Magazine.

Knight, Roderic. 1984a. 'Music in Africa: the Manding contexts', in Gérard Behague (ed.) *Performance Practice, Ethnomusicological Perspectives*, pp. 53–89, London: Greenwood.

1984b. 'The style of Mandinka music: a study in extracting theory from practice', in J. H. Kwabena Nketia and Jacqueline Cogdell DjeDje (eds.) *Selected Reports in Ethnomusicology*, vol. V: *Studies in African Music*, pp. 3–66, Los Angeles: UCLA.

Köhler, O. 1975. 'Geschichte und Probleme der Gliederung der Sprachen Afrikas', in H. Baumann (ed.) *Die Völker Afrikas und ihre traditionellen Kulturen*, vol. I, pp. 141–373, Wiesbaden: Steiner.

Konaré Ba, Adam. 1983. *Sunjata, le fondateur de l'empire du Mali*, Dakar, Abidjan, and Lomé: Les Nouvelles Editions africaines.

Kriel, A. 1971. *An African Horizon*, University of Cape Town Press.

Kropp-Dakubu, M. E. (ed.) 1988. *The Languages of Ghana*, London: Kegan Paul International for the International African Institute.

Kunene, M. 1979. *Emperor Shaka the Great*, London: Heinemann.

La Fontaine, J. S. 1985. 'Person and individual: some anthropological reflections', in Michael Carrithers, Steven Collins and Steven Lukes (eds.) *The Category of the Person: Anthropology, Philosophy, History*, pp. 123–40, Cambridge University Press.

La Hausse, Paul. 1988. *Brewers, Beerhalls and Boycotts: A History of Liquor in South Africa*, Johannesburg: Ravan.

Lacey, M. 1980. *Working for Boroko: The Origins of a Coercive Labour System in South Africa*, Johannesburg: Ravan.

Leith-Ross, Sylvia. 1939. *African Women: A Study of the Ibo of Nigeria*, London: Routledge and Kegan Paul.

Levinson, Nan. 1990. '"Five filters": a review of Edward S. Herman and Noam Chomsky's *Manufacturing Consent: The Political Economy of the Mass Media*' *American Book Review* (Boulder, Colo.), 12 (1): 20.

Levinson, Stephen. 1983. *Pragmatics*, Cambridge University Press.

Lienhardt, Godfrey. 1985. 'Self: public, private: some African representations', in Michael Carrithers, Steven Collins, and Steven Lukes (eds.) *The Category of the Person: Anthropology, Philosophy, History*, pp. 141–55, Cambridge University Press.

Lihamba, A. 1985. 'Theatre and politics after the Arusha Declaration', unpublished Ph.D thesis, University of Leeds.

Limon, J. E. and Young, E. J. 1986. 'Frontiers, settlements, and development in folklore studies', *Annual Review of Anthropology* 15: 437–60.

Literature Bureau. 1969. *Mabvumira Enhetembo*, Gwelo: Mambo Press.

Little, K. 1974. *African Women in Town*, Cambridge University Press.

1980. *The Sociology of Women's Image in African Literature*, London: Macmillan.

Lombard, J. 1953. 'L'Intronisation d'un roi bariba', *Notes africaines* 59: 45–7.

1965. *Structures de type 'féodal' en Afrique noire*, Paris and The Hague:

Mouton.

Ly-Tall, Madina, Seydou Camara and Bouna Diouara (eds. and transls.) n.d. [1987], *L'Histoire du Mandé d'après Jeli Kanku Madi Jabaté de Kéla*, Paris: Association SCOA for Scientific Research in Black Africa.

Mack, Beverly B. 1981. '"Waƙoƙin Mata": Hausa women's poetry in northern Nigeria', unpublished Ph.D dissertation, University of Wisconsin.

1986. 'Songs from silence: Hausa women's poetry', in Carole Boyce Davies and Anne Adams Graves (eds.) *Ngambika: Studies of Women in African Literature*, pp. 181–90, New Jersey: Africa World Press.

McNaughton, Patrick R. 1988. *The Mande Blacksmiths: Knowledge, Power, and Art in West Africa*, Bloomington and Indianapolis: Indiana University Press.

Mauss, Marcel. 1985. 'A category of the human mind: the notion of person; the notion of self' (first published 1938), in Michael Carrithers, Steven Collins, and Steven Lukes (eds.) *The Category of the Person: Anthropology, Philosophy, History*, pp. 1–25, Cambridge University Press.

Mbaeme, Eleazar Nnaemeka. 1983. 'The performance of Okuzu Oba Igbo folktales', BA long essay, Department of Linguistics and Nigerian Languages, University of Nigeria.

Mbughuni, L. 1974. *Tanzanian Cultural Policy*, Paris: UNESCO.

Meredith, H. 1967. *An Account of the Gold Coast of Africa* (reprint), London: Cass.

Merriam, Alan P. 1973. 'The Bala musician', in Warren L. D'Azevedo (ed.) *The Traditional Artist in African Societies*, pp. 266–72, Bloomington: Indiana University Press.

Meyer, Gérard. 1987. *Contes du pays Malinké (Gambie, Guinée, Mali, Sénégal)*, Paris: Karthala.

Middleton, John. 1973. 'The concept of the person among the Lugbara of Uganda', in *La Notion de personne en Afrique noire* (International Colloquia of the National Centre for Scientific Research 544), pp. 491–506, Paris: CNRS.

Mlama, P. 1983. 'Tanzanian traditional theatre as a pedagogical institution, the case of the Kaguru', unpublished Ph.D dissertation, University of Dar es Salaam.

1991. *Culture and Development: The Popular Theatre Approach in Africa*, Nordiska Afrikainstitut, Uppsala.

Mnyampala. 1971. *Ngonjera za ukuta*, Dar es Salaam: East African Literature Bureau.

Moraes Farias, P. F. de. 1993. 'The oral traditionist as critic and intellectual producer: an example from contemporary Mali', in T. Fálólá (ed.) *African Historiography: Essays in Honour of Jacob Adé Àjàyí*, pp. 14–38, London: Longman.

Moser, Rex E. 1974. 'Foregrounding in the Sunjata, the Mande epic', unpublished Ph.D dissertation, Indiana University.

Muhammad, D. 1977. 'Individual talent in the Hausa poetic tradition: a study of Akilu Aliyu and his art', unpublished Ph.D dissertation, University of

London.

1979. 'Interaction between the oral and the literate traditions of Hausa poetry', *Harsunan Nijeriya* 12: 85–90.

Nakamura, Yusuke. 1988/90. 'Mendicité et louange: le statut social des griots villageois (Cercle de San)', in Junzo Kawada (ed.) *Boucle du Niger: approches multidisciplinaires*, 2 vols., vol. I, pp. 325–51, Tokyo: Institute for Research in the Languages and Cultures of Asia and Africa.

Nayo, N. Z. n.d. 'Akpalu and his songs', *Papers in African Studies* 3: 24–34, Legon: Institute of African Studies, University of Ghana.

Nebie, M. 1984. 'Etude ethnolinguistique d'un corpus de Contes dioula', dissertation, University of Paris III.

Niane, D. T. 1960. *Soundjata*, Paris: Présence Africaine.

1984. *Sundiata: An Epic of Old Mali* (trans G. D. Pickett, 1st edn 1960), Essex: Longman Drumbeat.

Nketia, J. H. K. 1964. 'The artist in contemporary Africa: the challenge of tradition', *Okyeame* 2 (1): 57–62.

Nwaozuzu, Gabriella Ihuaru. 1985. 'Child image in Igbo folktales', MA project report, Department of Linguistics and Nigerian Languages, University of Nigeria.

Nwasogwa, Godwin Chukwunwike. 1983. 'Children's songs and games in Lejja', BA long essay, Department of Linguistics and Nigerian Languages, University of Nigeria.

Nwoga, Donatus I. 1983. *Nka na Nzere: Focus on the Igbo Worldview* (Ahiajoku Lecture), Owerri: Cultural Divison, Ministry of Information, Culture, Youth and Sports.

Nyembezi, C. L. S. 1989. *Zulu Proverbs* (1st edn 1954), Johannesburg: Witwatersrand University Press.

Nyerere, K. 1962. *Presidential Inaugural Speech*, Dar es Salaam: Government Press.

Ogbalu, F. Chidozie. 1966. *Mbediogu: About the Controversial Tortoise*, Onitsha: University Publishing Company.

1973a. *Nza na Obu*, Onitsha and London: University Publishing Company and Thomas Nelson.

1973b. *Igbo Mbu 4* (1981 reprint), Onitsha and London: University Publishing Company and Thomas Nelson.

1974. *School Certificate/GCE Igbo* (1980 reprint), Onitsha and London: University Publishing Company and Thomas Nelson.

Oguine, Priscilla Ngozi. 1974. 'Igbo folktales: a study of plot, characterization and performance techniques', BA long essay, Department of English, University of Nigeria.

Okanlawon, Tunde. 1990. 'Royalty in the oral literature of the Niger Delta', *International Folklore Review* (London), 7: 8–9.

Okeke, Uche. 1971. *Tales of Land of Death: Igbo Folktales*, New York: Zenith Books, Doubleday.

Okpewho, Isidore. 1987. '"Once upon a kingdom . . .": Benin in the oral traditions of Bendel State', in B Almqvist, S. O'Cathain and P. O'Healai (eds.) *The Heroic Process*, Dublin: Glendale Press.

Okwesa, Uzoechi Idu. 1979. 'Tortoise tales in Ossomala folklore', BA long essay, Department of English, University of Nigeria.

Olivier de Sardan, J. P. 1973. 'Personnalité et structures sociales (A propos des Songhays)', in *La Notion de personne en Afrique noire* (International Colloquia of the National Centre for Scientific Research 544), pp. 421–45, Paris: CNRS.

1982. *Concepts et conceptions songhay-zarma*, Paris: Nubia.

Onwuejeogwu, M. A. 1981. *An Igbo Civilization: Nri Culture and Hegemony*, London and Benin: Ethnographica and Ethiope Publishing Corporation.

Opland, Jeff. 1983. *Xhosa Oral Poetry: Aspects of a Black South African Tradition*, Cambridge University Press.

1989. 'The Bible in front, the musket behind: images of white oppression in Xhosa oral poetry', paper presented to the Fourth National Technological Literacy Conference, Washington, 3–5 February.

1989. 'The structure of Xhosa eulogy and the relation of eulogy to epic', in J. B. Hainsworth (ed.) *Traditions of Heroic and Epic Poetry*, vol. II, pp. 121–43, London: Modern Humanities Research Association.

Orou Yorouba, R. 1982. 'La Gani et ses implications socio-économiques', unpublished Masters dissertation, Cotonou: National University of Benin, Faculty of Letter, Arts and Humanities.

Paine, R. (ed.) 1981. *Politically Speaking: Cross-cultural Studies of Rhetoric*, Philadelphia: ISHI.

Paredes, A. and Bauman, R. (eds.) 1972. *Toward New Perspectives in Folklore*, Austin: University of Texas Press.

Park, Robert E. 1928. 'Human migration and the marginal man', *American Journal of Sociology* 33: 881–93.

Parkin, D. 1984. 'Political language', *Annual Review of Anthropology* 13: 345–65.

1985. 'Controlling the U-turn of knowledge', in Richard Fardon (ed.) *Power and Knowledge: Anthropological and Sociological Approaches*, pp. 49–60. Edinburgh: Scottish Academic Press.

Parry, B. 1987. 'Problems in current theories of colonial discourse', *Oxford Literary Review* 9 (1–2): 27–58.

Paulme, D. 1976. *La Mère dévorante: essai sur la morphologie des contes africains*, Paris: Gallimard.

Paulme, D. and C. Seydou. 1972. 'Le conte des "Alliés Animaux" dans l'Ouest africain', *Cahiers d'Etudes Africaines* 45: 76–108.

Pauw, B. A. 1975. *Christianity and Xhosa Tradition: Belief and Ritual among Xhosa-speaking Christians*, Cape Town: Oxford University Press.

Peires, J. B. 1981. *The House of Phalo: A History of the Xhosa People in the Days of their Independence*, Johannesburg: Ravan.

1989. *The Dead will Arise: Nongqawuse and the Great Cattle-killing Movement of 1856-7*, Johannesburg: Ravan.

Piersen, W. D. 1976. 'Puttin' down ole massa: African satire in the New World', *Research in African Literatures* 7 (2): 166–80.

Pilaszewicz, Stanislaw. 1984. 'The craft of the Hausa oral praise-poets', in *Folklore in Africa Today: Proceedings of the Workshop, Budapest, 1–4 November 1982*, pp. 269–76, Budapest: Department of Folklore, ELTE.
1985. 'Literature in the Hausa language', in B. W. Andrzejewski, S. Pilaszewicz and W. Tyloch (eds.) *Literatures in African Languages: Theoretical Issues and Sample Surveys*, pp. 190–254, Cambridge University Press.
Pongweni, Alec J. C. 1989. *Figurative Language in Shona Discourse: A Study of the Analogical Imagination*, Gwelo: Mambo Press.
Ponton, G. J. 1933. 'Les Gourounsi du groupe voltaïque', *Outre Mer, Revue Générale de Colonisation* 5: 80–126.
Prouteaux, M. 1985. 'Divertissements de Kong', *Bulletin du Comité d'études historiques et scientifiques de l'AOF*.
Qabula, A. T., Hlatshwayo, M. and Malanga, N. 1986. *Black Mamba Rising*, Durban: Workers Cultural Cooperative.
Ranc, Elisabeth. 1987. 'Le sense contre la puissance. Logiques de pouvoir et de dynamique sociale: le mariage malinké', unpublished dissertation, Paris: Ecole des Hautes Etudes en Sciences Sociales.
Rattray, R. S. 1924. *Ashante*, Oxford: Clarendon Press.
Renwick, Roger de V. 1980. *English Folk Poetry: Structure and Meaning*, London: Batsford.
Rubusana, W. B. (ed.) 1911. *ZemkKinkomo magwalandini* (1st edn 1906), Frome and London: Butler and Tanner.
Ryan, M. L. 1981. 'Introduction: on the why, what and how of generic taxonomy', *Poetics* 10: 109–26.
Sacca, F. D. 1987. 'La Dévolution du pouvoir en pays baatonu', unpublished Masters dissertation, Cotonou: National University of Benin, Faculty of Legal, Economic and Political Science.
Samatar, Said S. 1982. *Oral Poetry and Somali Nationalism: The Case of Sayyid Mahammad 'Abdille Hasan*, Cambridge University Press.
Samuelson, R. C. 1929. *Long, Long Ago*, Durban: Knox.
Sangaré, A. 1986. 'Dioula de Kong (Côte d'Ivoire): phonologie, grammaire, lexique et textes', dissertation, University of Grenoble II.
Sansom, B. 1970. 'Leadership and authority in a Pedi chiefdom', unpublished Ph.D dissertation, University of Manchester.
Sapir, J. D. 1977. 'The anatomy of metaphor', in J. D. Sapir and J. C. Crocker (eds.) *The Social Use of Metaphor: Essays on the Anthropology of Rhetoric*, pp. 3–32, Philadelphia: University of Pennsylvania Press.
Sapir, J. D. and Crocker, J. C. (eds.) 1977. *The Social Use of Metaphor: Essays on the Anthropology of Rhetoric*, Philadelphia: University of Pennsylvania Press.
Saule, Ncedile. 1989. 'A consideration of S. E. K. Mqhayi's contributions to *Umteteli Wabantu* under the pseudonym "Nzululwazi"', unpublished MA dissertation, University of South Africa.
Saussure, Ferdinand de. 1977. *Course in General Linguistics*, New York: McGraw Hill.

Scheub, H. 1985. 'A review of African oral traditions and literature', *African Studies Review* 28 (2–3): 1–72.

Schott, R. 1984. 'Contrôle social et sanctions chez les Lyela du Burkina Faso', *Droit et Cultures* 8: 87–103.

Schuh, Russell G. 1988. 'Préalable to a theory of Hausa poetic meter', in Graham Furniss and Philip J. Jaggar (eds.) *Studies in Hausa Language and Linguistics*, pp. 218–35, London: Kegan Paul International in association with the International African Institute.

1988/9. 'The meter of Imfiraji', *Harsunan Nijeriya* 14: 60–70.

1989. 'Toward a metrical analysis of Hausa verse prosody: MUTADAARIK', in Isabelle Haïk and Laurice Tuller (eds.) *Current Approaches to African Linguistics* 6 (Publications in African Languages and Linguistics 9), pp. 161–75, Dordrecht: Foris.

Searle, J. 1969. *Speech Acts*, Cambridge University Press.

1979. *Expression and Meaning*, Cambridge University Press.

Shaw, Thurstan. 1970. *Igbo-Ukwu* (2 vols.), London: Faber and Faber.

Sheshie, L. Klutse M 1973. *Akpalu Fe Hawo*, Accra: Bureau of Ghana Languages.

Simmel, Georg. 1971. 'The stranger', in Donald N. Levine (ed.) *Georg Simmel, On Individuality and Social Forms: Selected Writings*, pp. 143–49, University of Chicago Press.

Skinner, A. Neil. 1980. *Anthology of Hausa Literature in Translation*, Zaria: Northern Nigerian Publishing Company.

Skota, T. D. Mweli. 1965. *The African Who's Who* (3rd edn), Johannesburg: Central News Agency.

Smith, M. G. 1957. 'The social functions and meaning of Hausa praise singing', *Africa* 27: 26–45.

1978. *The Affairs of Daura*, Los Angeles and London: University of California Press.

Smith, P. 1973. 'Principes de la personne et catégories sociales', in *La Notion de personne en Afrique noire* (International Colloquia of the National Centre for Scientific Research 544), pp. 467–90, Paris: CNRS.

Sprott, E. M. 1958. *Human Groups*, Harmondsworth: Penguin.

Steinbrich, S. 1987. *Frauen der Lyela: Die wirtschaftliche und soziale Lage der Frauen von Sanje (Burkina Faso)*, Hohenschäftlarn: Renner.

Street, B. V. 1984. *Literacy in Theory and Practice*, Cambridge University Press.

Suru, U. L. 1980. 'A critical study of specimens of Hausa political verse relating to the 1979 general election in Nigeria', unpublished MA dissertation, University of London, SOAS.

Talbot, P. A. 1926. *The Peoples of Southern Nigeria*, London: Frank Cass.

TANU. 1976. *Tamko la mkutano mkuu wa TANU juu ya Utamaduni wa Taifa*, Dodoma: TANU.

Tarr, Delbert Howard, Jr. 1979. 'Indirection and ambiguity as a mode of communication in West Africa: a descriptive survey', unpublished dissertation, University of Minnesota.

Tauxier, L. 1917. *Le Noir du Yatenga*, Paris: Larose.

Thiongo, Ngugi wa. 1986. *Decolonising the Mind: The Politics of Language in African Literature*, London: James Currey.

Thomas, Northcote W. 1913/14. *Anthropological Report on Ibo-Speaking Peoples of Nigeria*, Parts I–VI (fascimile reprint 1969), New York: Negro University Press.

Thompson, Stith. 1946. *The Folktale*, Bloomington: Indiana University Press.

Traoré, Karim. 1992. '*Jeli* et *Sɛrɛ* ou la dialectique du discours au Manden', paper contributed to the Conference on the Sunjata Epic, 13–15 November, Evanston: Institute for Advanced Study and Research in the African Humanities, Northwestern University.

Ugochukwu, C. N., Meniru, T. and Oguine, P. 1977. *Omalinze: A Book of Igbo Folktales* (retranscribed and ed. by E. Nolue Emenanjo), Ibadan: Oxford University Press.

Umeasiegbu, Rems Nna. 1969. *The Way We Lived: Ibo Customs and Stories*, London, Ibadan and Nairobi: Heinemann.

Volosinov, V. N. 1973. *Marxism and the Philosophy of Language*, Cambridge, Mass.: Harvard University Press.

Wilks, Ivor. 1992. 'The history of the Sunjata epic: a review of the evidence', paper contributed to the Conference on the Sunjata Epic, 13–15 November, Evanston: Institute for Advanced Study and Research in the African Humanities, Northwestern University.

Willan, Brian, 1984. *Sol Plaatje: South African Nationalist 1876–1932*, Johannesburg: Ravan.

Yahaya, Ibrahim Yaro. 1979. 'Hausa folklore as an educational tool', *Harsunan Nijeriya* 9: 91–7.

1981. 'The Hausa poet', in U. N. Abalogu, G. Ashiwaju and R. Amadi-Tshiwala (eds.) *Oral Poetry in Nigeria*, pp. 139–56, Lagos: Nigeria Magazine.

Yankah, Kwesi. 1985. 'Risks in artistic performance', *Journal of Folklore Research* 22 (2/3): 133–53.

1991. 'Oratory in Akan society', *Discourse and Society* 2 (1): 47–64.

Zahan, Dominique. 1963. *La Dialectique du verbe chez les Bambara*, Paris and The Hague: Mouton.

Zemp, H. 1966. 'La Légende des griots malinké', *Cahiers d'études africaines* 24 (VI-4): 611–52.

Zinkpé, T. 1952. 'Le Borgou en deuil', *France–Dahomey* 45, 4 June, p. 3.

Zinyemba, R. M. 1986. *Zimbabwean Drama: A Study of Shona and English Plays*, Gwelo: Mambo Press.

Zurmi, Idi. 1981. 'Form and style in Hausa oral praise songs', in U. N. Abalogu, G. Ashiwaju and R. Amadi-Tshiwala (eds.) *Oral Poetry in Nigeria*, pp. 96–117, Lagos: Nigeria Magazine.

Index